MW01674597

Introduction to Public Administration

Introduction to Public Administration

Idris Bean

CLANRYE
INTERNATIONAL
www.clanryeinternational.com

Clanrye International,
750 Third Avenue, 9th Floor,
New York, NY 10017, USA

Copyright © 2021 Clanrye International

This book contains information obtained from authentic and highly regarded sources. All chapters are published with permission under the Creative Commons Attribution Share Alike License or equivalent. A wide variety of references are listed. Permissions and sources are indicated; for detailed attributions, please refer to the permissions page. Reasonable efforts have been made to publish reliable data and information, but the authors, editors and publisher cannot assume any responsibility for the validity of all materials or the consequences of their use.

Trademark Notice: Registered trademark of products or corporate names are used only for explanation and identification without intent to infringe.

ISBN: 978-1-64726-078-1

Cataloging-in-Publication Data

Introduction to public administration / Idris Bean.
p. cm.
Includes bibliographical references and index.
ISBN: 978-1-64726-078-1
1. Public administration. 2. Political science. 3. Public officers. I. Bean, Idris.
JF1351 I58 2021
351--dc23

For information on all Clanrye International publications visit our website at www.clanryeinternational.com

CLANRYE INTERNATIONAL

Table of Contents

Preface

This book aims to help a broader range of students by exploring a wide variety of significant topics related to this discipline. It will help students in achieving a higher level of understanding of the subject and excel in their respective fields. This book would not have been possible without the unwavered support of my senior professors who took out the time to provide me feedback and help me with the process. I would also like to thank my family for their patience and support.

Public administration primarily studies the implementation of government policies. Some of the fundamental branches of public administration are organization theory, ethics, policy analysis, public budgeting and human resource management. Organization theory studies the structure of governmental entities. Ethics in public administration serves as a normative approach to decision making. Policy analysis functions as an empirical approach to decision making. The allocation of scarce resources among unlimited demands is conducted within public budgeting. There are numerous decision making models which are studied within this field such as Niskanen's budget-maximizing and Dunleavy's bureau-shaping model. This book is a valuable compilation of topics, ranging from the basic to the most complex theories and principles in the field of public administration. It aims to shed light on some of the unexplored aspects of this field. This textbook will serve as a valuable source of reference for those interested in this field.

A brief overview of the book contents is provided below:

Chapter - What is Public Administration?

The academic discipline that studies the implementation of government policy is referred to as public administration. This is an introductory chapter which will introduce briefly all the significant aspects of public administration such as its principles, management models within it and public administration theory.

Chapter - Fundamental Aspects of Public Administration

Some of fundamental components of public administration are administrative law, administrative discretion, public interest, decentralization, advocacy evaluation, public service, civil service and bureaucracy. This chapter has been carefully written to provide an easy understanding of these key components of public administration.

Chapter - Public Policies

The principled guide to action taken by the administrative executive branches of the state in relation to a class of issues in accordance to the law and institutional customs is termed as public policy. Some of the major domains within public policy are agricultural policy, commercial policy, cultural policy, domestic policy, foreign policy, etc. This chapter closely examines these key types of public policies to provide an extensive understanding of the subject.

Chapter - Sub-fields of Public Administration

Public administration can be divided into diverse sub-fields such as public-sector ethics, policy analysis, public budgeting, organizational theory and human resource management. The topics elaborated in this chapter will help in gaining a better perspective about these sub-fields of public administration.

Chapter - Decision-making Models

The cognitive process which results in the selection of a belief or a course of action among various alternative possibilities is referred to as decision making. Some of the important decision-making models are Simon's rational decision-making process and rationalist model. This chapter discusses in detail these types of decision-making models.

Chapter - Understanding E-Governance

The use of information and communication technologies, particularly the internet, for delivering government services is referred to as e-Governance. Some of the major components of e-Governance are e-Rulemaking, e-Participation and e-Services. These diverse components of e-Governance have been thoroughly discussed in this chapter.

Chapter - Personnel and Financial Administration

The domain of public administration which is concerned with people at work and with their relationships within an organization is known as personnel administration. Financial administration refers to the management of financial tasks of an organization. It includes writing financial reports, controlling budget, etc. The topics elaborated in this chapter will help in gaining a better perspective about personnel and financial administration.

Idris Bean

1

What is Public Administration?

The academic discipline that studies the implementation of government policy is referred to as public administration. This is an introductory chapter which will introduce briefly all the significant aspects of public administration such as its principles, management models within it and public administration theory.

Public administration is like any other administration which is carried out in public interest. Before we dwell deeper into understanding public administration it would be beneficial to try and see how different authors have tried to define what administration is.

Marx defines administration as - Administration is determined action taken in pursuit of a conscious purpose. It is the systematic ordering of affairs and the calculated use of resources aimed at making those happen which one wants to happen.

Frederic k Lane defines administration as organizing and maintaining human and fiscal resources to attain a group's goals.

A complete definition for public administration however is difficult to arrive at due to the sheer number of tasks that fall under it. Some academicians argue that all the government related work falls into this category while other choose to argue that only the executive aspect of government functioning comprises of public administration.

We can also see how different authors have defined public administration:

According to L D White, Public administration consists of all those operations having for their purpose the fulfillment or enforcement of public policy. On the other hand as per Woodrow Wilson public administration is a detailed and systematic application of law. One can also say that public administration is nothing but the policies, practices, rules and regulation etc, in action.

Now, can public administration be divorced from social and political systems; certainly not and therefore emerged another definition provided by F A Nigro who argues that public administration is essentially a cooperative group effort in public setting. Secondly, it covers all the three branches of government machinery, the executive, the legislative and the judicial. He further added that since public administration plays a crucial role in formulation of policies therefore it is a part of the political process as well (for e.g. Bills and Acts). Negro also said that public administration is different from private administration in numerous ways and that it interacts with various private groups and individuals in providing services to the community.

Also, on the nature of public administration there have been two popular views, one being the

Integral view and the other one is the Managerial view. The Integral view is all encompassing and consists of sum total of all managerial, clerical, technical and manual activities and employees form all levels. This view was endorsed by L D White and Dimock. It may differ from one agency to another depending on their sphere of work.

On the other hand the Managerial view, as the name suggests says that the public administration involves only the managerial activities. This view was supported by Simon, Smithburg, Thompson and Luther Gulick.

After having said that; the word administration itself is highly contextual, and may vary in meaning and definition from one organization to another.

So if you want to understand it from the context and setting of an organization, it can be roughly explained that; the top leadership or the Board decides the vision, mission, short and long term goals and the business unit heads then draw out action plans and create or reform processes, allot responsibilities, direct planning, get people on board and start working towards achieving those set goals as per defined guidelines. So, the Board can be the Government and the Business Unit Heads and their teams can be the public administrators who are the implementers and actually the people who run the show.

Public administration is the single most important aspect of bureaucracies across the world; be it a democratic, socialist or a capitalist state, more so in a socialist state, as all aspects of the citizen life are influenced and decided by the government.

There has been considerable shift in the way the public administration was carried out in ancient and medieval times when the initiatives were nothing more than sporadic administrative functions like maintaining law and order and collecting revenues with little or no welfare activities. The people who carried out those activities were selected by the monarchs and were no better than their personal servants.

With changing times, the objective of public administration also underwent a change and by the nineteenth century; an organized approach to public servants and public administration was adopted. This approach was based on an exhaustive legal framework replacing the patriarchal and hereditary function with bureaucracy.

The advent of this new approach to public administration happened due to many reasons. The foremost being the Industrial revolution. With Industrial Revolution, the Government forayed into trade and commerce; which was followed by Imperialism, Nationalism and Internationalism which added on to the widening avenues of Government duties and responsibilities.

The times today are again vastly different from what existed a century ago and once again the scope of public administration has also undergone a shift, it's difficult to decide whether it is paradigm or not. However, the increasing awareness amongst people especially in the developing countries [for e.g. The Right to Information Act or RTI act in India] and an acquired knowledge of rights, privileges and laws amongst the people of developed countries[for e.g. the debates on The Health Care and Education Reconciliation Act of 2010] have thrown new challenges for the public administrators and policy makers.

The demand for unified national services, the conflicting interests between the various economic sections of the society and with global migration and subsequently globalization; the protection of the interests of the multi-ethnic groups of the society have kept the public administrators occupied.

Administration matters so much because it is not enough to make policies and laws on paper. The interpretation and translation of those policies and laws into actions and carrying them out is the difficult part. The public administrators therefore have to play an important role in running the government as machinery. Bureaucracy has often been sneered and ridiculed at but if the administrative work is stopped, nothing really would be happening.

In almost all the countries the number of people employed in public administration work is appalling like in USA the figure roughly stands at 2036000 civilians excluding the employees of Congress and Federal courts, in England the figure runs into several thousands and in India the civil services exam itself draws lakhs and lakhs of applicants while the selection percentage is meager for e.g the 2006 numbers for selection in the UPSC was 383983 applicants and 474 actually recommended for posts.

The various important roles that public administration plays, the most important one are implementing laws and policies and acting as their adjudicators. It is therefore important that the reader approaches the study of public administration with an open mind and without prejudices to appreciate the full nature, role, importance and relevance of the bureaucracy.

PRINCIPLES OF PUBLIC ADMINISTRATION

Throughout the 20th century the study and practice of public administration has been essentially pragmatic and normative rather than theoretical and value free. This may explain why public administration, unlike some social sciences, developed without much concern about an encompassing theory. Not until the mid-20th century and the dissemination of the German sociologist Max Weber's theory of bureaucracy was there much interest in a theory of public administration. Most recent bureaucratic theory, however, has been addressed to the private sector, and there has been little effort to relate organizational to political theory.

A prominent principle of public administration has been economy and efficiency, that is, the provision of public services at the minimum cost. This has usually been the stated objective of administrative reform. Despite growing concern about other kinds of values, such as responsiveness to public needs, justice and equal treatment, and citizen involvement in government decisions, efficiency continues to be a major goal.

In its concern with efficiency and improvement, public administration has focused frequently on questions of formal organization. It is generally held that administrative ills can be at least partly corrected by reorganization. Many organizational principles originated with the military, a few from private business. They include, for example:

1. Organizing departments, ministries, and agencies on the basis of common or closely related purposes,
2. Grouping like activities in single units,

3. Equating responsibility with authority,
4. Ensuring unity of command (only one supervisor for each group of employees),
5. Limiting the number of subordinates reporting to a single supervisor,
6. Differentiating line (operating or end-purpose) activities from staff (advisory, consultative, or support) activities,
7. Employing the principle of management by exception (only the unusual problem or case is brought to the top), and
8. Having a clear-cut chain of command downward and of responsibility upward.

Some critics have maintained that these and other principles of public administration are useful only as rough criteria for given organizational situations. They believe that organizational problems differ and that the applicability of rules to various situations also differs. Nonetheless, and despite much more sophisticated analyses of organizational behaviour in recent decades, such principles as those enumerated above continue to carry force.

Public administration has also laid stress upon personnel. In most countries administrative reform has involved civil service reform. Historically, the direction has been toward "meritocracy"—the best individual for each job, competitive examinations for entry, and selection and promotion on the basis of merit. Attention has increasingly been given to factors other than intellectual merit, including personal attitudes, incentives, personality, personal relationships, and collective bargaining.

In addition, the budget has developed as a principal tool in planning future programs, deciding priorities, managing current programs, linking executive with legislature, and developing control and accountability. The contest for control over budgets, particularly in the Western world, began centuries ago and at times was the main relationship between monarchs and their subjects. The modern executive budget system in which the executive recommends, the legislature appropriates, and the executive oversees expenditures originated in 19th-century Britain. In the United States during the 20th century, the budget became the principal vehicle for legislative surveillance of administration, executive control of departments, and departmental control of subordinate programs. It has been assuming a similar role in many of the developing countries of the world.

Recent Interpretations

The classical approach to public administration described above probably reached its fullest development in the United States during the 1930s, although since that time, through educational and training programs, technical assistance, and the work of international organizations, it has also become standard doctrine in many countries. However, some of its elements have been resisted by governments with British or continental-legal perspectives, and even during the 1930s it was being challenged from several quarters. Since that time study of the subject has greatly developed. It has also become somewhat confused as a result of certain inconsistencies in approach.

The orthodox doctrine rested on the premise that administration was simply the implementation of public policies determined by others. According to this view, administrators should seek maximum efficiency but should be otherwise neutral about values and goals. During the Great Depression of the 1930s, and even more so during World War II, however, it became increasingly evident that many new policies originated within the administration, that policy and value judgments were implicit in most significant administrative decisions, that many administrative officials worked on nothing except policy, and that, insofar as public policies were controversial, such work inevitably involved administrators in politics. The supposed independence of administration from policy and politics was seen to be illusory. Since the 1930s there has thus been increasing concern with policy formation and the development of techniques to improve policy decisions. Although the concept of a value-free, neutral administration is regarded by many as no longer tenable, no fully satisfactory substitute has been offered. How to ensure that responsible and responsive policy decisions are made by career administrators, and how to coordinate their work with the policies of politically elected or appointive officials, remain key preoccupations, especially in democratic states.

It was with governmental efforts to combat the Depression that new informational devices were introduced, including national income accounting and the scrutiny of gross national product as a major index of economic health. The applied techniques of fiscal and monetary policy have become established specializations of public administration. Economists occupy key posts in the administrations of most nations, and many other administrators must have at least elementary knowledge of the economic implications of government operations. France, Sweden and other Scandinavian nations, Great Britain, and the United States were among the leaders in developing economic planning techniques. Such planning has become a dominating concern of public administration in many of the developing countries.

Responses to Incrementalism

As economic and social intervention by governments has increased, the limitations of "incrementalism" as a public administration practice have become increasingly apparent. Incrementalism is the tendency of government to tinker with policies rather than to question the value of continuing them. A number of techniques have been introduced to make decisions more rational. One such technique, widely applied, is cost–benefit analysis. This involves identifying, quantifying, and comparing the costs and benefits of alternativeproposals. Another, less successful, technique was the Planning, Programming, and Budgeting System (PPBS), introduced into the U.S. Department of Defense in 1961 and extended to the federal budget in 1965. According to PPBS, the objectives of government programs were to be identified, and then alternative means of achieving these objectives were to be compared according to their costs and benefits. In practice, PPBS made little difference in federal budgeting, partly because the objectives of governmental programs were difficult to specify and partly because comprehensive evaluation took too long. PPBS was abandoned in 1971, and similar attempts, such as Management by Objectives and Zero-Base Budgeting, both introduced in the 1970s, were equally short-lived and ineffective. Comparable schemes in western Europe, such as the method called "rationalization of budgetary choice" introduced into France in the late 1960s and the so-called Programme Analysis and Review in Great Britain in the 1970s, were likewise unsuccessful.

Quantitative economic measurement is useful up to a certain point, but the value of human life, of freedom from sickness and pain, of safety on the streets, of clean air, and of opportunity for achievement are hardly measurable in monetary terms. Public administration has thus increasingly concerned itself with developing better social indicators, quantitative and qualitative—that is, better indexes of the effects of public programs and new techniques of social analysis.

Another development has been an increasing emphasis on human relations. This originated in the 1930s when what became known as the Hawthorne research, involving the workers and management of an industrial plant near Chicago, brought out the importance to productivity of social or informal organization, good communications, individual and group behaviour, and attitudes (as distinct from aptitudes).

Awareness of the importance of human relations influenced the conduct of public administration. Many shibboleths of administration (hierarchy, directive leadership, set duties, treatment of employees as impersonal "units" of production, and monetary incentives) were challenged.

By the late 1930s the human relations approach had developed into a concept known as "organization development." Its primary goal was to change the attitudes, values, and structures of organizations so that they could meet new demands. Trained consultants, usually from outside the organization, undertook intensive interviewing of senior and junior staff, and sensitivity training and confrontation meetings were also held. Unlike the rationalistic PPBS approach, organization development stressed the identification of personal with organizational goals, the "self-actualization" of workers and managers, effective interpersonal communication, and broad participation in decision making. Its direct use within governmental agencies has been limited and has not always been successful, but it has had considerable indirect influence upon administrators.

Another modern movement in public administration has been the greater participation of citizens in government. It was stimulated during the 1950s and '60s by a growing feeling that governments were not responding to the needs of their citizens, particularly minority groups and the poor. A variety of experiments to involve citizens or their representatives in making governmental decisions were begun in the 1960s. These involved the delegation of decision making from central to local offices and, at the local level, the sharing of authority with citizen groups.

Public Policy Approach

From the early 1970s increasing analysis of the way government policies affected the public resulted in a concept called the "public policy approach" to administration. This examines to what extent each stage in devising and executing a policy affects the overall shape and impact of the policy. According to the concept, the way a problem is conceived in the first place influences the range of remedies considered. The nature of the decision-making process may determine whether a course of action is merely incremental or truly radical. Indeed, it has been argued that the nature of the decision-making process shapes the outcome of the decision itself, particularly when the process is dominated by a powerful interest group. Moreover, the willingness of the government to evaluate programs, and modify them if necessary, affects the outcome. Many supporters of the public policy approach regard the concept as an important tool for constructing a body of knowledge on which recommendations can be based.

Until World War II there was relatively little exchange among nations of ideas about public administration. As early as 1910, however, a professional organization, which eventually became the International Institute of Administrative Sciences (IIAS), had been established. At first its membership consisted principally of scholars and practitioners of administrative law in the countries of continental Europe. By the late 1980s the IIAS had a membership drawn from some 70 countries. Its triennial congresses have covered all aspects of the field.

Since World War II international interest in administrative systems has grown, precipitated by the necessity of cooperation during the war, by the formation of international organizations, by the occupation of conquered nations and the administration of economic recovery programs for Europe and the Far East, and by aid programs for developing countries. One by-product of aid programs was a renewed appreciation of how crucial effective administration is to national development. It has also become apparent how parochial and culture-bound styles of public administration have often remained within individual countries.

Another effect of this international communication and sharing of experiences has been the realization that development is not exclusive to the so-called underdeveloped countries. All countries have continued to develop, and public administration has increasingly been perceived as the administration of planned change in societies that themselves have undergone rapid change, not all of it planned. Government has no longer been merely the keeper of the peace and the provider of basic services: In the postindustrial era government has become a principal innovator, a determinant of social and economic priorities, and an entrepreneur on a major scale. On virtually every significant problem or challenge—from unemployment to clean air—people have looked to the government for solutions or assistance. The tasks of planning, organizing, coordinating, managing, and evaluating modern government have likewise become awesome in both dimension and importance.

Approaches to Public Administration

Public administration as a serious subject which required scientific attention was first promulgated by Woodrow Wilson and as we read in the Wilsonian vision of Public Administration he fiercely recommended that there should be more scrutiny and debate and studies carried out in this area to make it more efficient and robust.

However, it was only during the beginning of the twentieth century that American Universities introduced Public Administration as a subject of academic study influenced by L.D White's important book called Introduction to the Study of Public Administration. There were also attempts made by scholars to differentiate between politics and administration, hence comparative study of two to understand Public Administration better came into existence.

Sometime later the Principles approach to public administration was introduced. This approach was influenced by W. F. Willoughby's work called Principles of Public Administration in 1927. His work emphasized that scientific study and research of administration can help derive fundamental principles regarding the same. This approach was championed by other authors and scholars like Fayol, Mooney, Lyndall, Urwick etc. So, resorting to scientific method of exploring, researching, observing, recording, classifying etc was used to study Public Administration.

By this time, some important work had started happening in the areas of Human Relations by the likes of Elton Mayo, his Hawthorne experiment threw interesting light on social and psychological forces in work situations. So the importance of attitudes, feeling, sentiments and social relations, work group dynamics etc started influencing the vey formal structure and way of working; present and preferred by the public organizations.

After the Second World War, behavioral sciences were quite a hot debate in the academics with a lot of research and work carried out in the field. Herbert Simon's Administrative Behavior and Robert Dahl's, The Science of Public Administration: Three Problems; critically questioned the inadequacies and limitations of the orthodox public administration of the pre war days. Simon focused on the aspect of decision making in Public Administration and stressed on the need to develop a robust and relevant administrative theory based on precise and logical study of human behavior.

And recently with the advent of technology in every walk of life and a common consensus amongst authors and scholars that both public and private administration are similar in many manner, the management science approach to public management came into existence.

The newest approach is that of policy analysis approach since the Government is venturing into new areas and different activities with increased involvement in welfare programs, the process of making public policies and its analysis, the measurement of the output etc became the new areas of study for the scholars and subject matter experts.

Institutional Approach to Public Administration

The instructional approach to the study of public administration concerns itself with the institutions and organizations of the State. The core area of this method lies in detailed study of the structure, the functioning, rules, and regulations of the executives, legislatures and the departments of the Government. The scholars who practice this approach consider administration to be an apolitical and technical function which lies only in the aspect of policy implementation.

Now, there were many authors like L D White and Luther Gulick who concentrated their effort in describing what an institutional structure was and did little to build any theory actually. The reader may be intrigued as to why this special attention was paid to define institutions. The present day definition of institution encompassing all kinds of rules, regulations and organizations is argued as inaccurate by many authors like B Guy Peters and Jon Pierre. Institutionalization of an organization takes time.

An organization keeps getting complex by adding informal norms and practices which happens through its interaction with the external environment and they are in a sense independent of the individuals who make an organization at a given point of time. However, according to Selznick, any organization which is complex needs to be infused with value which is beyond the technical requirement of the tasks that are performed by that organization. This means that an organization has a distinctive sense of self and identity and its way and its beliefs become important for the society as well. It also starts representing the aspiration of the community and in turn influences the community with their own values and beliefs. A real institution becomes a symbol for the community in many ways, like the very building in which it is housed. It can be interestingly explained and seen all through the history that the revolting group often occupy the presidential palace or offices or the parliamentary buildings or pose a threat to the powerful and symbolic structures like the terrorist threat on the Pentagon during 9/11 and the 26/11 Taj Hotel attack in India.

The discussion becomes relevant with respect to the study of public administration because Government organizations are institutional in many ways and represent the needs and aspirations of the community. Therefore, studying and understanding their administration becomes important to make them more efficient and result oriented.

The traditional study of public administration emphasized on the knowledge of history and law but this institutional approach focuses on the organizational structure, goals and principles as primary. So, a lot of attention was given to the problems related to the functioning of an organization like delegation, coordination & control and bureaucratic structure.

The main drawback to this approach was that little or no attention was given to the external sociological and psychological factors. These factors affect the organization in ways which are not always subtle, but have strong ramifications on the health and well being of an organization.

With this new approach the older approach and theories to the study of public administration also underwent a few changes. There were serious questions raised on the politics- administration bifurcation. The premise that the basic principles of administration can be applied universally was also challenged with the emergence of diverse administrative environments. The administrative goals of economy and efficiency were supplemented with social and economic progress. And also, a lot of management principles came into the field of public administration.

ADMINISTRATIVE CULTURE

The profession and the academic discipline of Public Administration all over the world is going through a period of turmoil, both in practice and in theory. After a period of unprecedented growth from the end of World War II until the mid-1970s the industrialized world experienced increasing financial difficulties for which it blames, among other things, its large bureaucracies and the welfare state that had been created. This led to strong challenges, mostly from politicians and people in business. Consequently, the management practices used in the business sector were seen as great cure-alls for the ills facing public sector management anywhere. This resulted in the creation of a new Public Management movement, and the remedies proffered by the movement are lionized in and by the West as the panacea for public management problems facing the world.

In recent years, this subject has received worldwide attention, especially as people wonder if the concept and operation of administrative processes are universally common or if there is a difference between the administrative cultures of nations. Thus, the main purpose of this study is to raise the fundamental question: Do administrative cultures really differ? Gerald Caiden, in 1998, alerted us to this issue. However, he also said that despite the lure of Americanization, people are interested in retaining their distinctive identity and culture. This appears to be true. For example, French people are keen to preserve not only their culture and language but also their administrative system. Similarly, other European nations have their distinctive administrative cultures, though they do share some core administrative values. In this study, we are interested in developing a general framework for understanding administrative culture, as well as examining what approaches can be utilized to study and compare different administrative cultures.

The most important challenge to conventional views of administration is the process of globalization. Irrespective of the definition used for "globality," the context, the structure, the processes, and the effects of administration are decisively influenced by it. The circumstances of administration are increasingly defined by parameters outside the confines of the nation-state. So are goals, resources (human, material, and "semiotic"), communications, and performance. The same is the case with the impact of policy decisions, non-decisions, actions, and inactions upon the context of administration. For the latter encompasses interwoven domestic and extraterritorial dimensions. In an era of growing interdependence, but also of mutual vulnerability, domestic and international micro and macro security is interconnected. At the centre of this global-local interface, there is an emerging global consciousness. This study focuses on the debate regarding administrative culture, understood here in its broadest sense as the modal pattern of values, beliefs, attitudes, and predispositions that characterize and identify any given administrative system. In this inclusive definition we are covering both the private and public spheres of the managerial ethos, for societies in general possess certain specific ways of "getting things done," which transcend the official sphere. We recognize that the construction of an administrative mind-set presents significant difficulties. Yet, we also recognize that it is possible to configure clusters of cultural matrices that have important heuristic value in understanding the relationship among contexts, structures, behaviors, and effects. This modal outline, though tentative, may also endow the analyst with ways to hypothesize upon the sources and effects of such culture upon the larger social and political order.

Dwivedi and Nef have suggested eight general propositions that researchers may explore, in their specific ways, because we believe that administrative cultures, like all cultures, do differ:

1. The administrative culture of any part of the globe reflects the distinctiveness and complexity of the various regional, national, and local realities; their unique historical experiences; their forms of insertion (subordination or domination) into the system of regional and global relations; and their levels of development and fragmentation.

2. Such cultures are historical products, where past experiences, myths, and traditions have shaped modal psychological orientations.

3. Any administrative culture is also conditioned by existing structural and conjunctural circumstances and challenges. Even perceptions of the past are mediated by current experience.

4. The administrative culture is part of a larger attitudinal matrix, containing values, practices, and orientations toward the physical environment, the economy, the social system, the polity, and culture itself.

5. Administrative cultures, like all cultures, are dynamic and subject to change. Syncretism, continuities, and discontinuities are part and parcel of their fabric and texture.

6. An administrative culture is the result of a process of immersion, acculturation, and socialization, whose structural drivers are both implicit as well as induced and explicit.

7. Most attempts at administrative reform and "modernization" address, either directly or indirectly, the question of administrative culture. Any profound administrative reform entails significant attitudinal and value changes.

8. Administrative cultures are influenced by global and regional trends. In the lesser-developed regions of the world, they are particularly derivative, reflecting a center-periphery mode of international political economy.

In addition, a researcher should ask the following questions: What is culture and where does it come from? What are the sources of such culture, and to what extent have these sources influenced the prevailing norms and values of administration? How might administrative culture, and particularly its values, be studied in a reasonably objective way? What are organizational culture, corporate culture, and administrative culture? And, finally, what do we mean by the term "culture"?

Culture

Anthropologists tend to define culture in broad terms. According to Singer, the anthropological concept of culture covers all facets of humans in society: knowledge, behavior, beliefs, art, morals, law, customs, etc. Culture should also be seen not only as a material possession but also consisting of institutions, people, behaviors or emotions, a style of accomplishing things, and, specifically, how people perceive, relate, and interpret events both from within and without. Essentially, culture in this sense refers to the shared values and representations of the members of an organization, such as a governmental bureaucracy.

Despite some differences of emphasis, anthropologists agree that a culture is the way of life of a given society. However, this concept has some implications:

1. The concept is holistic because it involves the entire society;
2. It implies a certain coherence among the elements of a culture; and
3. It reveals the fundamental values of a society, including its attributes, patterns (both explicit and implicit), and acquired behavior transmitted by symbols.

The author suggests the following definition of culture: A way of life of a group of people or a society through which it views the world around it, attributes meanings, attaches significance to it, and organizes itself to accomplish, preserve, and eventually pass on its legacy to future generations. The study of culture attracts our attention to the world of symbols and meanings, the values and patterns of organizations, and their behavior, which constitute particular ways of seeing, interpreting, and judging the world. However, when it comes to the transmission of culture from one place to another, several actors participate (both consciously and unconsciously) in the process, such as the state apparatus, socioeconomic and political factors as well as religious institutions.

Administrative Culture

We should note that like most other concepts used in the social sciences, the term "administrative culture" does not always mean the same thing for all people. Different perspectives may be offered, and a variety of conclusions can be drawn by people (from different places or geographic regions) studying the administrative culture. But, the most important question that we should ask is why should anyone study administrative culture? Will such study lead to new perspectives on the administrative history of a nation? Is it because by studying it, we are able to study the learning experiences by which an administrative culture is passed on from generation to generation? May be because by studying it, one can explain how the administrative system of the nation operates the way it does.

Two main perspectives may assist us in understanding the administrative culture of a nation. First, the government administration in all nations happens to be larger and more complex than any single organization, being composed of many departments, agencies, corporations, and so on. Of course, there are some multinational corporations with larger administrations than some small countries, but for our purpose, we are talking about the state which is, in reality, "an organization of organizations". Second, policies and administrative decisions get implemented through the state apparatus, state financial and other resources are distributed, and the entire society is affected in many ways by the attending administrative culture. The behavior of the state apparatus depends on the kind of administrative culture that prevails in a country. Lack of transparency and professionalism, as we have seen in several countries, are symptoms of malaise prevailing in the administrative culture (as well as in the political culture) of certain nations. We should also note that no administrative culture is monolithic; instead, it is a part of the wider culture of a society including its constituent parts such as political, economic, social, religious, corporate, and civil society cultures. Nevertheless, it is the political culture that influences the administrative culture most because it brings its political values to modulate the behavior of state employees. Finally, the culture of the administration is sometimes supported, sometimes challenged, by two important subcultures: first, the culture of each department or agency of government, with its own mandate, interests, client groups, and major professional and occupational components; second, professional subcultures, such as those of accountants, lawyers, economists, engineers, diplomats, and scientists, that cut across organizational boundaries. A composite administrative culture then reflects the values of all its constituent parts.

Place of Value in Administration

A value can be defined as a principle or a quality from which may be inferred a norm or standard conducive to ordering or ranking, by preference, objects, activities, results, or people. Values may be either personal or collective. Obviously, culture deals with collective values, but an important source of conflict may come when individual members' personal values are at a variance with the collective values of an organization. Values are, generally, of two kinds: the desired and desirable. The "desired" value is observable (for example, an audit of an account can tell us if the funds have been spent appropriately). But what is "desirable" need not be grounded or evident in behavior. Hofstede notes two possible contradictions coming from this: the contradiction between behavior and what is desired (we act so as to achieve what we desire); between what is desired and what is desirable (this involves someone else's judgment about what we desire). However, when it comes to the place of values in public administration, the subject, in the past, was untouchable.

Values and Facts Dichotomy

In the past century, two major events occurred which shaped the future of public administration as a discipline and profession. First was the emphasis that Woodrow Wilson and Frank W. Goodnow placed on the separation of administration from politics as the single most essential reform in achieving efficiency and removing the objectionable and unethical practices of spoils and patronage besetting the democratic system of governing. For Woodrow Wilson, administration as a field was outside the sphere of politics because administrative questions were not political questions. After Wilson, other scholars in the United States, the United Kingdom, and Germany joined a steady stream of advocates who viewed the politics-administration dichotomy both as a self-evident truth and as a desirable goal. Public administration was perceived as a self-contained world of its own, with its own rules and methods. Politics, then, came to be viewed as the domain of values, whereas administration was considered the universe of fact, enshrined in a valuefree environment. Thus, the stage was set in the education and training courses of public administration for the exclusion of ethical issues and value questions.

The second event that further strengthened the deliberate neglect of ethics and values from public administration programs was the rise of European-led scienticism in the discipline with the two core elements: rational objectivity and quantification. The main purpose of these scientific elements was, and still is, to remove the biases and fallacies of human thought by searching for "hard data," which can be measured, quantified, and then presented in an objective and rational manner. In this context, academics and practitioners of public administration were considered applied scientists who were to stay dispassionately aloof from that subjective (and therefore irrational) realm of values and ethical issues. The European ideal of detached "scientific" administration (or administrative science) meant that policies were to be implemented without much thoughtful reflection.

The impact of scienticism supplemented by the American-led public service reforms was most visible in the form of several administrative reforms introduced as "performance budgeting," "Planning Programming Budgeting System" (PPBS), "Zero Based Budgeting" (ZBB), "Policy and Expenditure Management System" (PEMS), New Public Management (NPM), and now New Public Expectations (NPE). These efforts in the West were made in the name of increasing efficiency while relying on quantification. The more complex the governing process became, the stronger was the insistence on the use of scientific methodology. One specific result by the use of this methodology was that the system became too obsessed with quantification, thereby bringing such dysfunctions into the public service system as social inequity, institutionalized biases, and the minimization of the human element. Perhaps the greatest fallacy of this approach was to imply that public servants were akin to "robots," blindly implementing policies. Experts failed to realize that government managers were also supposed to exercise thoughtful action while implementing policies and programs. Development administration, as a subfield of public administration, could not escape from the above excessive emphasis on formal aspects of organization while the effectiveness of institutions suffered.

It would not be wrong to say that the entire twentieth century either relegated the question of values and ethics to the periphery, or dismissed it altogether. The dichotomy between politics and administration has continued and it still appears to dominate the formulation, implementation, and evaluation of public policy issues without due regard to ethical implications and moral reasoning. Finally, the dichotomy is basically false that the field of public administration (or its subfield, development administration), is value-neutral and ought to be performed in a dispassionate, scientific, and almost mechanical manner.

Efforts to separate politics and administration, accompanied by the simultaneous movement to make a science out of the art of administration, account for an early and persistent neglect of ethics and values not only in the teaching of public policy and administration courses, but also in the public service training programs. The baneful influence of these two major factors has contributed to the rise of amoralism in the public sector (more insidious in the developing nations) as well as to the weakening of such underlying ideals as: (a) government is a public trust and the public service is a profession for those who should know how to behave morally; (b) public servants should perform their duties impartially, efficiently, and ethically; and (c) serving the state is the highest calling, which is intricately connected to serving democratic ideals.

The above set of ethical ideals have come into conflict with the narrow outlook characteristic of organizations that are influenced by business practices, including some precepts advocated by the New Public Management Movement (factors such as: budget restraint, downsizing bureaucracy, accent on results at any cost, treating the public as customers, decentralization and devolution, contracting out, and accountability), and essentially market-driven rhetoric. The rationale was that with fewer bureaucratic structures there would be fewer bureaucratic problems. Once more, heavy emphasis was placed on quantification in the name of applying objective criteria for securing accountability with a blind faith on structures, processes, and procedures while showing a total disregard for the moral or ethical dimension (called a subjective matter by NPM people).

Studying Administrative Culture: Approaches

The author suggests three main approaches to studying the administrative culture of a nation: Deontological approach, Teleological approach, and Spiritual approach. It should be noted that these three approaches are based on some common values such as fundamental rights and freedoms, efficiency, accountability, fairness, etc. These values can be considered the core values of any nation. The three approaches are discussed briefly.

Deontological Approach

Deontology is the study of duty and ethical/moral obligations of human beings as well as of the organizations they represent. By using this approach in the study of administrative culture, one focuses on the ethics and morality of the administrator.

This approach is based on the search for the cardinal virtues of the nation as reflected in the nation's constitution and other legal treaties. It seeks to emphasize a person's duty regardless of the circumstances. Deontological judgments take place in the realm of the desirable, or ethics. Thinking about ends and means has always been at the heart of public administration as a discipline. It has long been recognized that there are two great paths to improving the performance of an administration: you can either try to improve the people by leadership, motivation, and training, or tinker with institutions and systems in order to create an atmosphere of desired accountability among officials. The deontological approach also seeks its sources in either religion or philosophy. This author has for some years been an exponent of an "administrative theology" based on a synthesis of world cultures, religions, and their leaders. Such an attempt follows upon the invitation of Dwight Waldo to survey religion to see "what instruments of navigation it can provide". Dwivedi sees a secular administrative theology as providing guidelines for administrative ethics and the idea of a vocation in the service of the public good. This is tricky ground, for the modern secular state has had difficulty disengaging itself from the embrace of established religion, which often has had the effect of placing the spiritual beliefs of some over those of others.

Morality and spirituality, which have been guiding forces in the history of human civilization, are often seen as closely associated with religion. But, the moment one raises the issue of religion in relation to governmental affairs, the forces of secularism feel threatened. The result is not only the weakening of morality in state affairs, but also the emergence of "amorality" or "ethical relativism" in the individual's conduct and behavior, and the rise of unethical activities in the public sphere all over the world. If justice, equality, equity, and freedom are to be maintained, proximate political and administrative acts must draw on some ethical foundations, such as public service as a vocation. It is a concept based on the ideal of service to the community. That ideal draws upon the concept of sacrifice—a concept that rises above individualism and materialism in order to create a shared feeling or spirit of public duty among government officials. Of course, the concept of sacrifice, in the context of modern times, does not mean that public servants must take a vow of poverty. Rather, it means adhering to the principle of serving others by setting a high standard of moral conduct and by considering a job a vocation, a calling, with conviction and duty. By considering public service a vocation, emphasis is placed on the service dimension of public service, an ideal to be acknowledged by public servants as higher than other economic and material considerations. Public service, then, approaches the status of a secular religion, similar to medical practice or nursing, rather than a mere occupation. Public servants ought to derive inner satisfaction from rendering service unto others rather than from material gains.

For them, the symbols and myths of public service are equally, if not more, valued than other employment related benefits. In this traditional or classical role, there are correct ways of doing things by adhering to what Hennessy calls "a genetic code of conduct," which includes the following values: probity, care for the evidence, respect for reason, willingness to speak the truth to Ministers, a readiness to carry out instructions to the contrary if overridden, an appreciation of the wider public interest, equity, and a constant concern for democratic ideals. To them, any movement toward greater symbiosis with their political masters, as is the case in many countries, is to be avoided.

Teleological Approach

The teleological approach is based on analyzing the success of a decision in producing a desired effect. While still in the realm of the desirable, this approach pays much more attention to intervening realities on the path to realizing goals or respecting values. The teleological approach also concerns the causal relationship between means and desired ends. Teleology is the doctrine of final causes. As an approach to the study of administrative culture, the doctrine would assert that processes and procedures in government administration ought to be determined by their ultimate purposes/ends. Thus, the emphasis is on the effects observed, results achieved, and ends met.

Spiritual Approach

When we refer to spirituality, we generally mean a kind of energy source that (a) is beyond ourselves and transcendent; (b) impels us to search for the purpose of life here and after, as well as why are we here on earth; (c) has an overarching influence on our sense of right and wrong; (d) empowers us to care for others; and (e) inspires us to act for the common good. Willa Bruce and John Novinson, in an article dealing with spirituality in public service, suggested that an effort ought to be made to operationalize the concept. A few years ago, the present author suggested a similar approach about the place of morality and spirituality in managing statecraft by stating "the moral dimension of governance represents a concern for an improvement in the quality of public service and the conduct of statecraft". Although spirituality is supposed to be an integral part of our religious traditions and beliefs, its secular dimension (which is yet to be particularly acknowledged by secular institutions) is crucial in governance, especially with respect to public service ethics and values. That energy source, mentioned earlier in this paragraph, can be converted into a moral force to be used for good governance. How can this be possible? Through understanding the relevance of spirituality in the management of statecraft, a common strategy for good governance can be developed. Such a strategy depends upon how public officials (a) perceive a common future for their society; (b) act both individually and collectively toward protecting the common good; and (c) realize that they as individuals have a moral obligation to support their society's goals since their acts will have repercussions on the future of their society. In addition, it is important to note that the demonstration of social conscience and caring behavior by public officials is intertwined with the general concept of a common good. It is an obligation that human beings owe not only to each other within a society but also to others living elsewhere. It is most important for public officials to know how they can better serve the common good. In a liberal democratic system of governance, there is the no higher public service value than the mission of demonstrating social conscience and caring behavior by doing one's respective duties toward the common good and good governance.

There is a general misconception in the field of public policy and administration that the development of public policy and its application is purely an objective and secular endeavor, where moral, subjective, and spiritual factors have no specific role to play at all. However, values and morality are not limited to personal matters only. A democratic society is founded on the principle of the dignity and worth of all people; and that moral principles emanate from basic religious values that hold human life both sacred and social. Furthermore, every constitution is generally the embodiment of moral values that guarantee us fundamental freedoms, justice, rule of law, and the like. These are the moral foundations upon which public policy and its management must be based. We live in a world of interdependence, in which morality and secularism share and balance each other in the protection and development of human values. There is no need to fence out morality and spirituality in the name of secularism, public service objectivity, and neutrality, lest the moral vision that has shaped and guided humanity thus far may well be compromised by immorality, expediency, and corruption.

By insisting on morality in public policy and governmental decision making, we may be able to strengthen the ethical and moral obligations of the people as well as of the organizations they represent. The focus must be on the ethics and morality of the administrator. What sense of duty should the public servant have, toward whom, and how can this sense be operationalized? The spiritual approach assumes there are correct ways of doing things, that there are standards and rules that should be adhered to. Public servants in this mold believe that administrative responsibility is primarily a moral question. They are moved by a higher cause, believing they have been entrusted with the stewardship of the state, and therefore owe special obligations, have specific expectations, and reside in a fiduciary world. Here, the spiritual approach or spiritual dimension acquires a holistic tone. Ultimately, our public servants exist for the public they are employed to serve. This approach needs to be revitalized in our public service. The commitment to a collective vision is one of the cardinal virtues of public servants; it is derived from the concept of public service as vocation. For, if the profession of public service is not a calling, then it is merely a job. In that case, loyalty to that job will depend largely on the material benefits and satisfaction that job provides. Under these circumstances, no one can expect public servants to exhibit the virtues of service to society, prudence in the use of taxpayers' money, and commitment to the common good and collective welfare of the people. We are also aware that morality can lead to mastery over our baser impulses such as greed, exploitation, abuse of power, and mistreatment of people. Spirituality requires self-discipline, humility, and, above all, the absence of arrogance in holding public office. Morality enables people to center their values on the notion that there is a cosmic ordinance and divine law that must be maintained.

Spirituality serves as a model, and as an operative strategy, for the transformation of human character by strengthening the genuine, substantive will to serve the common people. If our goal is to serve and protect the common good, then spirituality can provide the incentive for public officials to serve the public with dignity and respect. A comprehensive account of the use of power and authority by public officials would be incomplete without these approaches (deontological, teleological, and spiritual). By using these approaches to good governance, we may be able to create a holistic vision for human governance. In their absence, no number of laws, codes of conduct, external or internal control mechanisms, or threats of punishment can force public officials to behave ethically and morally. Indeed, all the nations that are deemed the most corrupt, according to Transparency International, do have various laws and mechanisms to control corruption, and yet it continues. Unless public officials are guided also by a sense of a vocation, service to others, and inner spirituality, we cannot expect good governance.

This sense of vocation holds that "government is a public trust and public service is a vocation for persons who should know how to behave morally. Behavior emanating from ideals associated with service as the highest calling includes possessing and exhibiting such virtues as honesty, impartiality, sincerity, and justice. Further, it is equally desirable that the conduct of public administrators should be beyond reproach; and that they should perform their duties loyally, efficiently, and economically".

The author believes that confidence and trust in democracy can be safeguarded only when the governing process exhibits a higher, credible, and ethical stand, based on the trinity of justice, equity, and morality. Only by bringing together the domains of moral and procedural accountability, can we wage a strong fight against corruption, mismanagement, and bad governance. For no nation or society, irrespective of its political and religious orientation, can survive in a spiritual or moral vacuum. Furthermore, the author believes that there must be articles of faith (drawn from societal values, cultural traditions, and moral ideals) that govern our lives and that these should be encouraged, reinforced, resurrected, and strengthened, because good governance is essentially a moral enterprise. From a holistic viewpoint, a comprehensive study of administrative culture cannot be complete unless these approaches are utilized. That is why a study of administrative culture should employ all three approaches, although the author realizes that one treads difficult ground by venturing into the realm of spirituality.

New Public Management and Administrative Culture

Although public service reformers keep hoping (or claim to know) that their new institution, method, or device will deliver change in government policy and programs in order to bring efficiency, accountability and transparency, there are some propositions that are so well established they seem axiomatic. The first is that the choice of objectives depends in part on the means available. That is, in public policy and administration, most choices are not moral absolutes, but depend on calculations of costs and benefits, not only to the public, but also to politicians and public servants. Second, administrative reforms have both intended and unintended consequences.

When applied to Public Management, this approach offers the following observations: There is symmetry, for the managerial revolution is part of the worldwide triumph of democratic capitalist values; the metaphorical language of management seems easily adapted to the public sector, as in "corporate culture," "corporate management," "management by results," etc.; there is much ambiguity in expressions like "value for money" or "excellence"; it requires the suspension of disbelief, corresponding to what Dunsire says of doctrine: "it makes plain, but in the manner of 'revealed truth' rather than the tentative hypothesizing of theory: it shows what must be done but as if it were from necessity rather than the mere instrumentalism of policy"; selectivity in argument is found in the recourse to examples, to "best practices" and to anecdotal evidence without considering contrary evidence; a doctrine based on private interest, it is said to meet the requirements of the public good.

The trouble with New Public Management, then, is that it is all technique. If politics is about the art of the possible, or what is acceptable in a society, and if it is also about the major value choices of that society—"authenticity" and "justice" values—then management has forgotten politics.

Public management also appears to neglect the importance of law in public administration. This can be seen at two levels. At the top, in introducing notions like corporate management, corporate culture, and even that of management itself, it tends to obscure how relations between senior officials and ministers are constitutional in nature. As we have seen, when Canadian officials answer questions from members of parliament, they do so in the name of their minister. Faced with the complexities of day-to-day administration and the conflicting values that the system has thrust upon them, they need some fundamental reference point to which they may turn in case of doubt. As John Rohr states, the constitution must serve as a source of regime values for administrators. That is why at lower levels of administration, the law is a guarantor of democratic government. In this respect, a public manager differs from a private one, because while the latter may regard the law as a constraint, something he must obey, the public manager must also uphold the rule of law. To us, the greatest charge against managerialism is its reductionism and its lack of imagination. It tries to reduce a complex phenomenon to a single model drawn from business. We argued above that the appropriate image for the public administrator is the steward, not the entrepreneur. What remains to be pointed out is another curious paradox of management. Astley and Van de Ven have observed that there are two versions of organization theory, one which is basically deterministic and the other which is proactive in its outlook. The deterministic school sees management as a kind of fine tuning; adapting organizations to changes occurring in the environment. The proactive outlook takes a strategic view of that environment. It is there to be acted upon.

The paradox of the New Public Management is that while its language is full of references to a proactive stance, where strategic planning, innovation, change, and growth are promoted, in its basic thrust the NPM is profoundly deterministic. Its message is that there really are no choices; that deficits, structural economic change, and world trade competition are forcing governments of all developed countries to adopt the same policies. This obscures the fact that these same governments do things very differently, with European countries accepting a more corporatist form of national bargaining with business and labor, while Britain, the United States, and Canada have more liberal societies, where individualism reigns supreme. It also masks the fact that there are other models of the new state different from the market model. In sum, if the New Public Management movement (which is essentially based on the teleological model of administrative analysis) is carried to the extreme, technique drives out the desirable. What is feasible informs what is desirable, but if feasibility is the only criterion for the desirable, then our vision has become too limited. It is here where the deontological and spiritual approaches become relevant. Against this context, these two approaches acquire a holistic tone. In the end, our public servants exist for the public they are employed to serve. It is this aspect that needs to be revitalized in our public services. Even with the current emphasis on downsizing public services, one should not abdicate its belief in serving the collective interests of its society. Rather, it should express more of a concern for the collective welfare of its people.

This commitment to a collective vision is one of the cardinal virtues of our public servants. Abandonment of the commitment for public service as a vocation that would follow from the adoption of market-based practices would be highly undesirable. Any predisposition to reject duty and commitment to vocation among public servants is not going to serve a country well. Of course, duty-based deontological approaches have disadvantages apart from the fact that not all agree on their contents. In public administration, difficulties often arise because two or more values are in conflict, such as the sense of patriotism and the obligation to do one's legal and constitutional duty.

Diversity in Theory

The trilogy of approaches employed in the study of administrative culture and administration should not be seen as contradictory; each is incomplete without the other. No amount of factual analysis can allow one to escape certain moral and spiritual judgements, fundamental choices about both the public service and public life of a country. On the other hand, the kind of all-embracing ethical and spiritual dimensions do provide us with a deeper perspective but not the whole picture. That is why all three approaches should be used to study administrative cultures. The three approaches discussed ought to be considered a package deal when one wishes to examine the administrative culture of any nation. Among these three, the deonotological approach has its basis both in philosophy and policy analysis.

The most relevant school of philosophy, utilitarianism, took as its slogan "the greatest good for the greatest number." However, such an approach offers little help in deciding when the rights of the larger number may be invoked to limit those of the few, nor does it give consideration to the means to achieve a desired end. On the other hand, the teleological approach is blamed for being all method and no result. Complementing the above two approaches is the spiritual approach that, while accentuating the positive elements of public service vocation, emphasizes the relationship between the desirable and the feasible. While the study of administrative culture may be done in a detached, relatively objective way, it raises the problem of the best way to treat values. Finally, without the presence of individual spirituality and a sense of duty, laws and codes of conduct would not create the environment for good government.

It is also clear that in the name of globalization, a certain dependence and continued reliance on the theory and methodology of Western-style administration is being fostered in the developing nations, with an emphasis on transplanting and replicating the ideas and institutions of the West. As more and more Western values and practices prevail everywhere, with standards of performance based on the indicators developed in the West, an imitative and replicative system of public management is emerging in the rest of the world, and public servants everywhere mirror the bureaucratic structures and mores in Washington DC, London, Paris, Bonn, and Ottawa. We should be ever vigilant in the field of public administration so that the diversity in administrative culture does not face the same fate as is happening with the declining of bio-diversity in the world. With this perspective, let us also worry about what is happening in the world around us:

1. For years, Western scholars have been unable to include alternatives in the form of non-Western contributions to administrative studies. Instead, it was expected that institutional imitation would easily produce similar results to those obtained in the West.
2. Ethnocentrism and ignorance in the West have continued to overshadow the need to appreciate the importance of local culture, traditions, and style of governance. It is their style of governance and the administrative culture that reflect the distinctiveness and complexity of various national identities, realities, and cultural diversities. These factors should be taken into consideration when imposing public service reforms and other conditionalities.
3. The public sector reform imposed by Western ideology has created, in its wake, skewed management styles and structures that are unrelated to the prevailing cultural norms, needs, and realities; these styles and structures reproduce the symbolism, but not the substance, of Western administration. It is also not surprising that the culture of governance in the Third World has tended to follow, or has been forced to replicate, the costly fads in the industrialized nations. Thus, efforts at administrative restructuring, "modernization," and other types of reforms must address first, either directly or indirectly, the question of the indigenous style, values, and culture of governance.

As culture and style of governance are the keys to understanding what makes a country function, it is imperative that any public sector reform imposed on developing nations draws from the local customs, culture, and traditions. When the local culture and traditions are discarded in the favor of Western-style management practices, and when not enough time is given to these nations to see if such a transplantation has germinated, a hodge-podge of two value systems start operating simultaneously with no one specific standard against which the conduct of public officials can be measured. For the West as well as for the Third World, a key to a just and sustainable world requires diversity in thought and action rather than the self-proclaimed universal relevance of Western originated paradigms and administrative culture. Finally, true globalization means the ability to decide with an open mind, to understand and to incorporate different and alternative cultural traditions into a common matrix, and to respect diversity all around. That ability to incorporate these new strains and challenges in the governing system of a nation will determine, to a large extent, the quality of life that ours and future generations will enjoy, or suffer.

MANAGEMENT MODELS IN THE PUBLIC ADMINISTRATION

When analyzing management in the public sector we start from a basic overview of the theoretical management directions mentioned in the previous chapter. From the developmental point of view two models of public administration, classic and new can be described. These two models represent for us different approaches and a different understanding of what the administration actually is and what tasks are performed and how it should be managed and organized.

Classical Model of the Public Administration

The classical model of the public administration is based on the theoretical foundations laid by John Stuart Mill, Woodrow Wilson and Max Weber, followed by F. Taylor, H. Fayol and others. Classical approach formulates certain basic administrative principles on which the general ideal model of the public administration is built.

These principles define the structure of the public sector, defining the motivation of employees of public institutions and define the public interest.

Principles of public administration according to the classical model:

1. The objectives and tasks of the public administration are determined by the political representation and performed by administrative officials. The fully rational decisions are achieved by this fact.
2. Management is based on written documents, which guarantees a central role in the performance of the governmental power to the administration.
3. The activities of the public administration are continuous and are based on a system of rules and regulations.
4. The rules by which the work is performed, may be technical in nature, or may have a legal form. In both cases it is necessary that the work is performed by a skilled workforce.
5. Tasks and functions are divided into various functional areas (departments), each of which is equipped with adequate powers and sanctions.
6. Officials and tasks are the part of a hierarchical system in which it is clearly defined the right to control and make complaint. Centralization is preferred.
7. There is one dominant interest within the public sector - the public interest - which defines the boundaries of the influence of individual interests in politics and administration.

Over the time, the classical model was rejected in the theoretical and practical levels. Hierarchically built bureaucratic management systems, top-down management, and operating under the Weber´s doctrines Weberovských stopped meeting the needs and demands that were placed on them.

New Management Model in the Public Administration

The classical model of public administration was criticized, among other things, on the ground that does not reflect the actual processes within the system. New approaches take into account the factor of human motivation and other factors of efficiency and effectiveness of the public administration at the same time. Such an approach is in accordance with the concept Hood also known by the acronym 3E - Economy, Efficiency, Effectiveness. All these factors play a role in the formulation of these principles.

Principles of the public administration – a new model:

1. Differentiation of the policy and administration is misleading and incorrect.

2. Public institutions do not work on the principle of the rational choice, only on the limited rationality.
3. Implementation of measures top-down does not work, and therefore the public sector is not able to automatically meet their targets.
4. Public administration is preferably performed by independently managed administration authorities.
5. Officials should not be bound by the procedural regulations, because the primary objective is to meet the challenges and effectiveness.
6. Centralization in the public sector may lead to rigidity and the hierarchy in the public administration can lead to the implementation deficit.
7. Employees in the public sector do not have a special motivation, but they behave so as to maximize their own interests, such as income, prestige and power.

Based on the study of the public administration, analysis of its behavior and efficiency started a wave of administrative reforms in the Western world then by the end of the 70s. They all had some common features at the beginnning - primarily they were management reforms or managerial ones.

After the oil crisis in the 70s, which ended in huge state budget deficits, it was obvious that the then Western models of welfare states (were unsustainable. Reduction of expenditure in the public sector required major changes. The reasons are thus obvious at the financial-economic level. Despite the different types of state administration, the establishment and the performance of power in the country there are roughly the same shifts, namely towards performance-oriented and less centralized public administration.

According to the OECD study there are eight basic trends in the development of the public administration:

1. The Release of an authority towards the greater flexibility.
2. Focus on performance, control, responsibility.
3. Focus On the competition and freedom of choice.
4. The provision of adequate services.
5. Emphasis on human resource management (position vs career system).
6. Optimization and implementation of information technologies.
7. The quality of management improvement.
8. Intensification of strategic management functions of centres.

The mentioned eight trends imply that new public, hence the state administration should be:

1. Controlled by certain variants of business techniques and principles (management by objectives, not according to the rules).
2. Focused on the client service.

How are these trends reflected in the real world? Reforms under the new model are reflected in each of the countries in diffent way with a different intensity. Generally speaking, though, the new model was considered to be an Anglo-American phenomenon of the Thatcher and Reagan era, a lot of emphasis on managerial reforms and performance orientation is given in the Nordic countries (e.g Sweden, Denmark), and the development towards such a defined administration was defined was registered in many other countries (including France and the Netherlands).

Management in the Public Administration

After the development of two basic models in the previous section, we will describe how they are understood and interpreted in different countries. We focus on three basic perspectives for the definition of the management in the public administration:

1. The British approach - with a slow evolution from the rigid government to nowadays managerial direction.
2. American approach - with a managerial culture and focus on taking over elements of the private sector.
3. The European approach - the gradual development with a focus on the application of the law and scientific management.

British Approach

There has been a significant shift in the understanding of the role of management and organization in the public sector in Britain since the 60s to nowadays. The original state can be characterized as follows:

1. The bureaucracy formed a closed group, almost "caste" in the society.
2. Officials with mostly classical humanities 'Oxbridge' education.

Officials did not pass the verification (input) skills and abilities. During the 60s to 80s, the British administration switched to a more open civil service with a strong emphasis on managerial skills. Since the 80swe have been talking directly about a new approach to the public administration and its functioning, which was called New Public Management (NPM)with its focus on the promotion of managerial techniques of organization and management taken over from the private sector was called New Public Management (NPM).

NPM distinguished the concepts of administration and management. Public Administration in the classical concept is the activity of the public service, public officials implement the politics defined by others. Public Management in the new concept then involves administration (administration is a part of the management) and at the same its organization to achieve the objectives in the most efficient way and clearly designated responsibilities. This means that managers in the public service, instead of just following the instructions and compliance with procedural rules and procedures (that is administration) focused on achieving results and are responsible for them. New Public Management can be characterized by the following elements:

1. Focus on effective use of resources to achieve high quality services.

2. The competitive environment between the public and private sectors in the provision of services.
3. A market-oriented approach, citizens are consumers of services.

NPM is more widespread in Britain than in continental Europe. Managers in Germany, France, Netherlands, for example, operate in strong legal environment and focus more on the application of law by a procedural form than to perform management functions.

On the other hand British NPM is significantly linked with the American managerialism and some authors believe that NPM originates just in the American approach.

Services in the public sector have had a long tradition in Britain. In the past, it was very different from the American individuality, anti state orientation and managerial culture. British public administration was by a definition the professional, apolitical, neutral, professional counseling service that is available to the political representation. Reforms of the system towards a market-oriented service management techniques and started with the onset of Margaret Thatcher in 1979.

The civil service gained a greater autonomy, bringing its service to become more efficient and better. A market and a competition, one of the fundamental elements of the New Public Management, was clearly reflected in the wave of privatization of state enterprises and institutions.

American Approach

The U.S. approach to the definition of the public administration is various and the definition of procedures in the public administration is not accurately established. The Idea of managerialism is the central idea of reforms here, as in the case of NPM. The high rate of adoption of private sector management methods and market orientation belong to the elements of the U.S. approach. The basic motive results for example from the following perception of the citizen – public services client:

Public service client (citizen) is a rational consumer, whose main influence comes from the possibility to refuse the service, if he chooses rationally between public and private providers, who are competing.

In the U.S., the reformist direction was called Reinventing Government by the works of one of the authors (David Osborne) who were engaged in reforms.

The United States are characterized by a managerial culture. The idea of the nation-state is not rooted, the culture of an individuality reigns here and they are not very good at administration and responsibility for common and public things things in a public common concept. The federal government has many constitutional and legal constraints that guarantee that it itself does not transfer too large share of power from the individual states. The postwar era of prosperity of the welfare state (Johnson - Great Society) after the oil shock was replaced by Reagan budget cuts and reforms. There was a drastic downsizing of the public sector and social programs during them.

Here the first took shape the movement toward the market-oriented public administration (according to the principle "works better, costs less" - "works better - costs less"), which operates on the principles of effective techniques of management and organization. It should be noted that a change of government (Clinton, then Bush) did not cause in any case a fundamental shift away from reforms lined up, just the opposite.

European Approach

The European approach is due to the adoption of management reforms more careful. Public administration in the European concept can be characterized by the following elements:

1. Public administration is part of the law and the legal framework of the state.
2. There Is the space where state employees work and create the state.
3. State employees serve to the state power and order.
4. Their task is to carry out state policy in a clear framework of laws and rules that aim hierarchically from the top to the bottom.

Another approach is the so-called Napoleonic (e.g. France, Italy), which is also different from the Anglo-American management approach. It is characterized by a strong centralist state. The government and the central administration are made up of an elite society which controls all the country from the center. Senior officials of such authorities in France are usually graduates of the hautes ecoles. Elitism of this type is common in public administration as well as in the policy. It is clear that in such an environment the managerial independence and autonomy of decision-making is difficult to accept.

PUBLIC ADMINISTRATION THEORY

Public Administration Theory is the amalgamation of history, organizational theory, social theory, political theory and related studies focused on the meanings, structures and functions of public service in all its forms. It often recounts major historical foundations for the study of bureaucracy as well as epistemological issues associated with public service as a profession and as an academic field.

Generally speaking, there are three different common approaches to understanding public administration: Classical Public Administration Theory, New Public Management Theory, and Postmodern Public Administration Theory, offering different perspectives of how an administrator practices public administration.

Important figures of study include: Max Weber, Frederick Winslow Taylor, Luther Gulick, Mary Parker Follett, Chester Barnard, Herbert A. Simon, and Dwight Waldo. Herbert Simon advanced a public administration theory that was informed by positivism. Notable Public Administration Theorist such as Max Weber expressed the importance of values in the development of public administration theory. However, theory cannot simply be derived from empirical observation of facts, it must be constructed using value judgements that direct our empirical observations and then guide out interpretation of those observations. Values are essential for the construction of public administration theories because it takes into account the meaningful ethical principles and philosophies of a culture which ensure appropriate theory practice. Public Administration theories are put into practice or considered through a few distinct strategies: Parallel, Transfer, or Collaboration also known as the theory-gap practice. This practice is used to transfer knowledge between practitioners and scholars.

Types of Public Administration Theory

Public Administration Theory recently has been divided into three branches. The three branches are, Classical Public Administration Theory, New Public Management Theory and Postmodern Public Administration Theory. Each of these three branches study Public Administration from a different perspective. These types of theories are some of the ways which an administrator can understand and exercise their duties as a public administrator.

Classical Public Administration Theory

Classical Public Administration is often associated with Woodrow Wilson and Max Weber. In the United States, Woodrow Wilson is known as 'The Father of Public Administration', having written "The Study of Administration" in 1887, in which he argued that a bureaucracy should be run like a business. Wilson promoted ideas like merit-based promotions, professionalization, and a non-political system. Sympathy can lead to downfall in an administration, means there should be pragmatism in bureaucracy.

New Public Management Theory

New Public Management asset of administrative practices,a consulting fad, and a body of theory that interprets recent developments in public administration. Many scholars argue persuasively that scholars should pay more attention to New Public management as a theory than as a fad. New public management is part and parcel of the massive intrusion of freemarket values into public space, which threatens to drive out political values altogether. It is worth noting that,in this sense, new public management is the radical opposite of the notion of migrating political values into "private" space in the interest of further democratizing society. However, new public management theory fails to addresses political questions in a meaningful way. This theory looks at public administration from its roots of capitalism, and goes on through the perspective of global capitalism. Intentional or not, new public management has served the interests of elites, particularly corporate elites, has degraded the ability of governments to address the public interest, and has served as a vehicle for elevating the apolitical governance of free trade and other supranational organizations,which have fully embraced the political philosophy of economic rationalism and new managerialism.

Post-modern Public Administration Theory

Post-modern public administration is referring to the inner workings of nearly every government entity in existence. Whether it is the congress men and women in Washington D.C. or the Department of Public Safety representatives located at any DPS office handling the paper work of applicants wanted to obtain a drivers license. The idea of public administration is broad enough to encompass all government positions that affect the public. Members of public administration come in different forms and quantities. When understanding the theory of postmodern public administration, it is important to make a differentiation between postmodern theory and the post-modern era as well as being able to differentiate between post-modernity (period of time) and postmodernism (theory/philosophy).

Postmodern theory evolves out of the postmodern era. Chuck Fox and Hugh Miller are two of the main contributors to postmodern theory because they were able to recognize the postmodern condition and how it was playing out in public administration and public policy. Fox and Miller argue that the traditional approach to public administration "robs public administration theorists of the independence required to imagine more emancipating conditions of work and governance." Miller proposes a network model based on economic utility which would explain events better than traditional approach to public administration. Miller states that "policy networks provide a way of processing dissension, articulating values, and airing possible policy implementation strategies. Maneuvering on behalf of the public interest in this complex politically subtle network is the task of post-progressive public administration." This theory began in the 1990s, even though this theory had been around in other disciplines for a while. An estimation of time could date back to Plato and his ideas of a public and communal government where there are policy making actions and steps through levels of democracy. This theory has since been revisited and changed through three intellectual movements, interrogating the loop model of democracy, which many have argued that it is largely a myth, showing the symbolic nature of policy and politics in the United States, and discourse theory. One of the downsides of this theory is that it is based on the slippery slope of relativism. This theory also provides people with the tools to rebuild our infrastructures of symbolic and social order. This theory addresses big questions of what is right and wrong and tries to address the issue to find antidotes for anomie and relativity.

The founding father of postmodern public administration is commonly referred to as Woodrow Wilson, while many can find his roots of inspiration from the works of Friedrich Nietzsche. Using Woodrow Wilson as a reference point, it can be shown that in his essay The Study of Administration, is it "traditionally accepted that with his study, Wilson applied positivist principles to public administration based on the belief that social reality would be objectively known with the separation of positivist traditional values from facts."

Public Administration Theory Development

Public Administration theory is derived from several contemporary theory building tools such as Max Weber's Ideal type method. Theories are also derived from studies of evolving governments around the world, such as China's expanding bureaucracy. Different aspects to take into account are: accountability, state-citizen relations, and services for all in times of fiscal scarcity. When developing theories, the most effective theories are the ones tailored for a particular country taking aspects such as values into account. When empirical evidence is the only aspect taken into account it leads to an ineffective policy because the theory will not reflect the values of the citizens, resulting in bad citizen- state relationships. The Theory-Gap Practice is used to analyze the correlations between Public Administration theory and practice. The three fields of the theory gap-practice that describe the relationship between scholars and practitioners are: Parallel, Transfer, and Collaboration strategy.

Max Weber's Ideal-type Method

The ideal-type method developed by Max Weber is a useful tool in contemporary public administration theory development because the method takes into account the culture of a society that is then integrated into a theory. Weber referred to it as cultural science or interpretive sociology, which, is to understand ideas and practices from within their own intellectual and cultural horizon and on the basis of categories that are grounded in a meaningful social and historical context. According to Margaret Stout, Ideal-type methods are used to frame observation and analysis and to evaluate what is found. Weber's method must be developed using value judgments that direct our empirical observations and then guide our interpretation of those observations. Through this theory building method, Weber insisted that all interpretations of meaning must remain at best "a peculiarly plausible hypothesis", as opposed to a claim of relevance of a theory. Weber's purpose for using this method is to clarify the importance of values in sense making, but how they are also extremely important for the conduct of meaningful social science. Weber's interpretive sociology employs a type of functional analysis that begins with the whole, proceeds to the parts, and then goes back from the parts to the whole. His ideal-type method is thereby simultaneously useful in both the study of social structure and social action. Social action is linked to subjective meaning at the individual level of analysis, and structural forms are a consequence or construction of social action. This combination is particularly valuable to public administration because the manner in which administrative action and the social structures of governance interrelate requires an approach that considers both. On the one hand, ideal-types enable consideration of things like alternative meanings of important concepts or alternative motivations held by social actors. On the other hand, they enable analysis of associated or resulting social structures. In this way, an ideal-type can concurrently help interpret the meaning of the administrative role as well as critique the institutions of governance.

Theory-gap Practice

Parallel: Proponents of this strategy of relating theory and practice believe that practical knowledge cannot be derived from theories. For the practitioners of this strategy, practice and theory remain separate components of knowledge. Practical knowledge aims to how to handle problems in particular situations while theory aims at handling a specific situation in a general set of principles. Advocates for the parallel strategy claim there can be a complementary relationship between practical and theoretical knowledge or that they can substitute each other in certain situations because particular situations will require practice and theory to work together. Thus advocates that champion parallel strategy argue that it is essential for management studies to maintain an autonomous communication system.

Transfer: This second strategy frames the theory-practice problem as one of translating and diffusing research knowledge into management. This strategy confronts the issue of public managers lack of interest or studying of the work of scholars. This is the result of the scholarly work not being easily applicable to practice, and the complexity of the journals, thus knowledge is not being transferred from theory to practice. The transfer strategy proponents claim the popularizing the scholarly work, and making it more relevant to current issues faced in public administration would enhance the transfer of knowledge from scholars to street level bureaucrats and public managers. However, some argue this approach falls short of expectations because many practitioners of public administration have little influence on the content of knowledge offered by scholars.

Collaboration: This strategy aims to enhance communication between scholars and practitioners before the theory is developed in order to build a dialectic method of inquiry, building on the idea that communication is necessary throughout the whole theory building process in order to have a well development practical theory. Scholars Van de Ven and P.E. Johnson put it as:

"Engagement is relationship that involves negotiation and collaboration between researchers and practitioners in a learning community; such a community jointly produces knowledge that can both advance the scientific enterprise and enlighten a community of practitioners."

Important Figures in Public Administration Theory

Max Weber

Max Weber, one of the many theorists.

Max Weber was a German political economist, social scientist, and renowned philosopher and is an important father to the theory of Public Administration and the bureaucratic side of it. He did extensive research studying ancient and modern states to gather a better perspective of bureaucracies in multiple eras for his Magnum Opus Economy and Society published in 1922. That piece of work has contributed countless insight into the Public Administration Theory. Max Weber considered bureaucracy to be the most rational form of administration yet devised by man. In his writings he asserts that domination is exerted through administration and that for legal domination to take place bureaucracy is required.

Woodrow Wilson

Thomas Woodrow Wilson, another one of the theorists of Public Administration.

Woodrow Wilson defined public administration as a detailed and systematic execution of public law, he divided government institutions into two separate sectors, administration and politics. According to him politics is dealt with policy formulation and questions regarding such, whereas administration is equipped with carrying said policies out. In his own words in his early essay, "The Study of Administration" he said "it is getting to be harder to run a constitution than to frame one." Wilson very much so tried to establish a distinction between politics and administration; he saw administration as a field of business which lies outside politics. He thought the theory of public administration existed simply because of technicalities and was around for the behind the scenes business aspect of politics.

Frederick Winslow Taylor

Frederick Taylor was an engineer by profession who saw much of life from a scientific aspect. He is a popular less conservative contributor to the Theory of Public Administration in that he produced his own, very popular, theory of traditional public administration, The Scientific Management Theory. He was concerned with finding the best and most efficient way to complete a task for a particular job, reducing the overall labor a worker had to exert with the least amount of movements. Frederick Taylors work approached motivation with a very authoritative, cold, scientific motivator which weighed heavy over any sort of humane aspect to scientific management. Overall many intricacies in Public Administration such as management, control and accounting are subject to scientific principles and Taylor draws on these to find his own, efficient theory approach to Public Administration Theory.

Public Administration Theory in Practice

Classical Public Administration - United States

Often considered the best way for organizing public sector work, it was used highly in the western world in the 19th and early 20th century. A differing proponent between America and Europe is the transferring of effective management methods between large private and public organizations. The first effective theory in America was Scientific Theory coined by Frederick W. Taylor in 1911. His work "Principles and Methods of Scientific Management" was used to implement ideas that would increase the efficiency of American government. Taylor's ideas of standardizing work, systematic control, and a hierarchical organization were perfect fits for the public sector of the 1940s.

New Public Management - United Kingdom

New Public Management was the prominent theory that inspired health care reforms for the United Kingdom. Its application to health care coincided with the growing expenditures that were being used due to the progress of technology and an aging population. The difference between private and public sectors in terms of budget process and ideology provided a clash of interest. 1990 saw the National Health Service create an internal market of separate care providers and hospitals. This creation of markets in turn stopped the State from being the funder and service provider simultaneously, to just primarily the funder. Although not privatized, these markets became competitive in nature. Assumption that the competition would lead to more empowerment, efficiency, and equity became rampant. Soon the publicly owned hospitals were granted a quasiautonomous status from the District Health Authorities leading to the competition for patients and funds. Their status acquired led to little if any interference in the everyday operations.

Postmodern Public Administration - United States

Postmodern Public Administration is linked to the capitalist model of the late 20th and 21st century. It relates to globalization, consumerism, and the fragmentation of authority and state. The concepts of science and reason are de-centered and viewed as the defining truths. It tends to negate any faith based actions.

ADMINISTRATIVE REFORMS

Human behaviour, outlook, attitude and many others are constantly changing and the impact of changes falls upon society in general and upon administration in particular. The public administration must make sincere and serious efforts to meet the new demands which are resultants of changes in outlook and behaviour. Viewed from this perspective the public administration can never remain static. In other words, the administrative system should be reformed so that it can meet the new demands of society. Here arises the necessity of reforming administration.

Let us define reform. It means to make changes, especially an institution or practice in order to improve it. This is the general meaning of reform. But reforming administration has separate connotation. The administrative system of a state can never be permanent or be applicable to all cases. Administrative reform is defined by Gerald Caiden as "the artificial inducement of administrative transformation against resistance". Caiden has further clarified the term reform- Reform is different from reorganisation or changes. But reorganisation is not ruled out of reform.

According to Harvey Mansfield, any organisation contemplates changes of some sort in an on-going activity, and, with it, ordinarily, some transfer of control. To secure a desired change it may be enough to issue an order or to make a persuasive suggestion to display a carrot or stick to the people already in place. Reorganisation presumes that these remedies may accompany or follow, but are not available or will not suffice to start the process of change. Instead it decrees a change in organisational structure or jurisdiction as a beginning and counts on this.

A recent critic says that there is difference between changes and reforms. All reforms are changes, but all changes cannot be considered as reforms. Changes are linked with piecemeal alternations and very often sporadic. The purpose of change is not to bring about large-scale or radical alternations – changes always do not have specific and positive purposes. Sometimes changes are introduced half-heartedly.

The changes may be reactionary. On the other hand, reforms aim at wide and sometimes radical changes in a system. Reforms are always normative and are introduced with specific purpose in mind. The Reformation Movement in Europe was launched with certain specific purposes and these were to reform the out-dated concepts and dogmas of Christianity. So reforms sometimes assume the character of movement. But the administrative reform does not fall in the category of movement.

It has already been noted that reforms are normative in nature. They are introduced for the attainment of specific purpose. It is generally said that the idea of introducing reforms arises only when the prevailing system appears to be unworkable or fails to meet the basic demands of society. The administrative reform falls in this category.

The purpose of administration is to meet the demands of people and execute the policies taken by the government. But when it is felt that the prevailing system of public administration fails to reach the target and to meet the demands of people then—and then only —the question of reforming administration arises. In other words, the prospect and the prevailing situation move in opposite direction. Reform becomes inevitable.

Origin of Administrative Reforms

Caiden in his Dynamics of Public Administration has said that the reform of public administration can be dated to the second half of the nineteenth century and in support of his contention he has advanced the following reasons. In his opinion (and in the opinions of large number of public administrationists) USA was the pioneer in the field of administrative reforms.

American capitalism started its progress from the middle of the nineteenth century and this resulted in the large amount of investments in various fields. But it was found that public investment and private initiative in the field of economic development must be accompanied by rapid and proper change in the field of public administration. But the public services and public administration lagged behind the growth of both private and public investments and a necessity for reforming the public administration was felt.

This may be regarded as the beginning of public administration. The capitalists and industrial magnates thought that, without proper public administration, investment proposals and public investments will never be successful. In other words, civil servants of high efficiency must be employed for the successful investment proposals.

There was another dark side of public administration in USA. What is generally called bureaucratic ethics was spectacularly absent in the administrative system. But it was felt that without morality and ethics the public administration can never achieve the goals for which it was ordained.

Let us quote few lines from Caidens' book: "public morality left much to be desired and frequent scandals and disasters hardly improved the public image of officialdom. Something had to be done to reform the administrative system of government more in keeping with contemporary needs to improve the standard of public service and root out the inefficiency and corruption".

Throughout the world there was a movement to reform the administration. The reform was felt primarily for two reasons. One is: the public administration must create a congenial atmosphere for the investment. The other reason was that, as far as practicable, the public administration must be efficient and moral or ethical.

Many scholars on public administration treat this article of Woodrow Wilson as the beginning of the reform of public administration. In his time the public administration was a branch or part of political science and Wilson claimed the separate existence of public administration as a discipline.

Towards the end of the nineteenth century it was enthusiastically advocated that the public administration has a special and very important role not simply for the maintenance of day-to-day administration but for better administration and development of society and if this goal is to be achieved the subject must be studied seriously and certain reforms are to be introduced so that it can meet the new demands of a changing society.

The reform movement gathered momentum and numerous scholars demanded that the movement for reforming public administration should be strengthened. But for that purpose huge amount of funds is required. All these happened towards the end of the nineteenth century.

We call the administrative reform as a special type of movement because various important aspects of public administration, were the consequences of the movement. We have already noted that America was the pioneer in the reform of administration. But UK can also claim certain amount of contribution in this field.

The contribution of America is, however, far greater than that of Britain. The American business community liberally donated huge sum for the research of administrative and management systems. The chief purpose of the administrative reform was to establish "an efficient, honest and morally irreproachable bureaucracy". Before the end of the nineteenth century several bold steps were taken to that end.

In the field of administrative reform Goodnow has a special place. He is regarded by many as the "Father of American public administration". He made few proposals or suggestions which were designed to reform administration. Goodnow suggested that special research institutes should be established for the continuous and effective research in public administration. He said that young and energetic graduates should come to do research in public administration.

The public administration should be made fully suitable for a changing society and, to achieve this goal, extensive research work should be started and continued. Bureaucracy is the root cause of many evils and for that reason it ought to be controlled. It is impossible to control it by ways of direct democracy. Naturally, the only way of controlling bureaucracy is by way of reforming public administration.

Reform based on Ideology

There is a close relation between administrative reform and ideology. At least many public administrators believe so. At first we shall briefly analyse what is ideology. According to one critic, "An ideology is a value or belief system that is accepted as fact or truth by some groups." In an ideology there are certain attitudes which are related to political, economic and social issues: The believers of an ideology thinks that through the application of the ideology which he supports his objectives can be achieved.

Through the application of an ideology social movement can be started and the reform of public administration falls within the category of social movement or the change of social system. The social system can be changed through the reform or radical change of the whole administrative system.

In what way an ideology helps the administrative reform. When an administration fails to meet the requirements of the people a movement is launched to highlight the inability of public administration and, simultaneously, movement is launched. The purpose of the movement is to explain the drawbacks or limitations of public administration to the general public.

The sponsors of the movement explain their purposes to the people. Common people may not always be aware of the complexities of public administration keeping this in mind the leaders of the reform movement explain everything to the public and, at the same time, place alternative proposals to the public. Strictly speaking many may object that this is not, strictly, ideology. But here we interpret it in a wider sense.

It is to be remembered that in order to ensure reform in administration large scale support of people is necessary. It is because of the fact that there may be some men who oppose reform. So in order to make administrative reform successful a movement is essential. On experience it has been found that there is strong link between movement and emotion. People shall be emotionally aroused in favour of administrative reform.

In this field, emotion has something to do. It has been maintained by a critic that ideology promotes solidarity — as is the case with Marxism and Leninism. Sorol's myth of the general strike is a classic example. Ideology provides a sense of orientation when one is lacking. It mirrors a universal picture and a reference point for individual actions as well as social policies. To sum up, ideology always plays an important role in the field of politics and public administration is an important part of politics.

Hence if any party or organisation wishes to have large scale reform in public administration it should be its duty to convince the people of the necessity of administrative reform. Without people's co-operation reform will remain a distant hope.

Some people say that in developed nations ideology does not always play a crucial role in the field of administrative reform. But in new nations or developing countries the ideology has been found to play a necessary role. In the developing nations "there is constant presence of industrialisation, modernisation and development and the greater part of this pressure falls upon public administration.

But since the concepts of industrialisation and modernisation are constantly changing the public administration will have to adjust with all these changes and hence the reform of public administration are essential. New nations generally follow certain norms or principles of ideology. In one way or other ideology enters into the picture."

In Marxism-Leninism there is special importance of public administration or management in the development process of society. It has been observed by Varlamov (Socialist Management and Leninist Concept): that human progress through management is becoming the motto of numerous scientific symposia, international congresses and conferences.

It is with management that administrators and politicians, theoreticians and practical workers, and specialists in the natural and social sciences link their hopes and projects, their plans and forecasts, and practical activities." Varlamov further writes, "The future of every country, if not of our entire planet, depends upon management, upon its objective, and social contents, functions and principles." So is the immense value of management in both social development and reconstruction. The point to note is that public administration or management cannot be separated from ideology.

At least socialist thinkers think in this line. So if ideology plays an important role in administration, we think, reforms will also be guided or influenced by the concept of ideology. It is generally said that the persons who want to introduce certain reforms must be influenced or guided by some sort of ideology. The influence of ideology upon administrative reform is not a Utopia, it is absolutely practical.

The government and public administrators introduced numerous administrative reforms to face the realities of changes that fell on public administration. It is observed that if science and technological progress are merged with public administration that will produce best results. But both science and technology are changing—so public administration will change and it is through reforms.

Incrementalism and Administrative Reform

In our earlier analysis of policy-making we have analysed the role of incrementalism. Incrementalism is based on limited rationality concept. Many people think that reforms in public administration should be introduced step by step. It is said that if all proposals for reforms are adopted at a time satisfactory results may not be obtained. That is why it has been suggested that it is better to proceed step by step.

A part of the proposals may be executed and the results will be observed and the next step will depend upon the results of the first step. Talking about this a critic makes the following observation: "Incrementalism is suspicious of a comprehensive view. Its argument is based on a limited rationality which is oriented towards direct and concrete experience rather a priori constructions or assumptions which claim to be self-evident."

The incrementalist approach to reform of administration asserts that a man's knowledge and farsightedness are highly limited and because of this he cannot predict every possible situation in a correct way. For this reason he will have to proceed cautiously and intelligently so that he can avoid mistakes. Herbet Simon once said that individual's capacity to collect information and to solve problems is very limited.

In this background he said: The central concern of administrative theory is with boundary between the rational and non-rational aspects of human social behaviour. Administrative theory is peculiarly the theory of intended and bounded rationality—of the behaviour of human beings who satisfied because they do not have the wits to maximise. What appears from this is the administrators or administrationists are not owners of unlimited knowledge, wits and capacity. Naturally they cannot foresee the future correctly.

Charles Lindblom's name is closely associated with the theory of incrementalism. But he is not the real originator of the doctrine. Karl Popper initiated an idea known as piecemeal planning for social and political change. Popper said that large- sized and ambitious planning does not always produce desired results and the best way is to divide planning and reform schemes into small parts and these are to be executed. If desired results are obtained the process should be continued. Popper thought that this was the best way.

Lindblom, following Popper built, up the fabric of his incrementalism. It is also called "muddling through" and "disjointed incrementalism". In his analysis of decision-making (reform proposals also fall in the category of decision-making) Lindblom makes a distinction between Branch Method and Root Method. Branch method means successive limited comparisons. The central idea of Root Method is rational comprehensive.

The branch method "continually building out from the current situation, step by step and by small degrees". In other words, the branch method is a piecemeal way of making policy —policy may be regarding management of organisation or reforming the public administration. Ambitious programme has hardly any place in an organisation. Everything starts from a preliminary stage and then moves to higher stage slowly. The successive limited comparison or Branch Method does not wish to travel in darkness. It capitalises the past experience and, after taking lessons from the past, it decides the future course of action. In a sense, it is a conservative method. Past guides the future.

Rational comprehensive model is another way of making policy regarding reforming public administration. It is also called synoptic problem solving.

This model assumes that decision maker:

1. Identifies, scrutinises and puts into consistent order those objectives and other values that he believes should govern choice of a solution to the problem,
2. This comprehensively surveys all possible means of achieving those values.

In all these methods there is a very crucial role of rationality. The policy-maker does not jump upon a new decision or project without carefully considering all the probable aspects of the policy if it is executed. The cautious stepping is the central concept.

Let us now briefly analyse the successive limited comparisons. Lindblom suggested the changes should be made incrementally. In his opinion incrementalism can be explained in the following way. It is a "method of social action that takes existing reality as one alternative and compare the possible gains and losses of closely related alternatives by making relatively small adjustments in existing reality or making larger adjustments about whose consequences approximately as much is known as about the consequences of existing reality or truth".

It has been asserted that incrementalism is a forceful way of reforming public administration. The administrator proceeds slowly but steadily to achieve his goal. He knows that without reforming public administration it cannot be used as a weapon for the attainment of people's demands. In this age of globalisation men's demands are changing and increasing. The public administration must keep note of this.

Reasons of Reforms

Why administrators and academics are so much concerned about the reforms of administration? It is not difficult to find out the reasons. To put it in other words, in every society there exists certain conditions which demand that the administrative system should be changed.

Otherwise it would not be able to meet the growing and changing requirements of the people:

1. An important reason or condition of reform is there is a clear gap between the existing system and what people or clients want. In other words, the prevailing structure of administrative system is incapable of meeting the demands of society naturally, the public administration must be reformed—it shall be made suitable for the new and demanding situation.

2. There is a second reason which is more weighty. The colonial powers of Europe administered the colonies of Asia and Africa following their own method, and rules and the chief purpose of colonial administration was to elongate the colonial rule. There was another purpose and it was to fulfill the aims of colonialism.

   After the colonies achieved political freedom, it was found that the colonial system of administration was not in a position to meet the requirements of the newly independent states. At the same time, the rulers of the new states realised that the old system of public administration could not be jettisoned. The necessary parts of the old colonial public administration can be kept and something new should be added to the old body to make the whole updated public administration suitable and meaningful. This can be treated as the starting point of administrative reform.

3. In order to incorporate the importance of ecological factors upon the public administration it is necessary that the prevailing system of administration should be changed or reformed. Fred Riggs is the first man who drew our attention to the immense importance of ecology on public administration. The reforms of public administration must be made in the background of the entire social system including ecology. Let us quote few lines from a critic: "It should be stressed that I do not suggest that reforms must necessarily be designed within the social content only as that would be self-defeating. The argument is that the reformers must be cognizant of these limitations and try to reform comprehensively. Any reform attempt should keep the entire social and political fabric as its target".

   The impact of ecology upon the society is so comprehensive that it cannot be ignored. But the old public administration did not feel it necessary to refurbish the public administration in the background of the entire social system including ecology. After Riggs succeeded in drawing our attention to the importance of ecology in public administration it was felt that the old structure of public administration should be reformed, otherwise it will have no relevance at all.

4. The public administration in general has been built up in the background of Weberian model of bureaucracy. But Weber built up his model of bureaucracy at the beginning of the last century. During the last one hundred years there have occurred sea-changes in the administrative systems and Weberian model has proved its incapability to face new situations. This inspired the public administrators to reform the public administration.

5. Globalisation and liberalisation have necessitated the reforms of public administration. The impact of globalisation or liberalisation is so far-reaching that the administrative system of a country cannot remain neutral. Particularly the public administration of developing nations is overwhelmingly influenced. The old public administration makes itself irrelevant for the new circumstances created by globalisation.

   The government or top executive feels the necessity of reforming administration. The economic systems of earlier centuries were interdependent, but their interdependence today has surpassed all previous records. If a state wants to survive it must accept the reality which means that the administrative system must be changed to make it relevant for the prevailing situation. This however, is not imaginary. The public administration of many countries has been force to reform in the light of changes that took place in the eighties and nineties of the last century.

6. No country today is thinking of direct democracy of the Athenian type. But there is no denying the fact that the advancement of democracy has made people very alert and they are endeavouring to influence administration. But the old Weberian model of bureaucracy does not fully encourage this. Naturally the old Weberian bureaucracy faces problems and the authority proceeds to reform.

There is no question of rejecting the old bureaucracy, simultaneously the new trend cannot be neglected. The net result is that the administration is to be reformed. It is to kill two birds with one stone. A state cannot run its administration without bureaucracy. Again, peoples' aspiration must be honoured.

Forms of Reform

The term reform is to some extent misleading. For example, it may mean partial reform or may mean complete reform. Naturally, the type of reform depends upon several factors. A newly independent country may start thorough reform. When a new political party with a definite political ideology comes to power, it will try to reform the administrative system in accordance with its own ideology. That reform may be partial or wide-ranging.

When the Bolshevik party in Russia came to power, its ambition was to convert Russia into a socialist state and to reach that ambitious goal. Lenin proceeded to reform administration in the light of Marxism. Even Lenin hesitated to uproot the bureaucracy of the Czar regime. But in one sense this reform was complete.

Reform may be a slow process, when new situation arises or problems crop up, the old administrative system becomes incapable to cope with it and the authority feels that some parts of public administration are to be reformed. New methods are adopted and these are allowed to function. If satisfactory results are not obtained then other new methods or reforms are introduced and in this way the reform process continues. We may say that reform is a slow and continuous process. When the situation calls for a reform or change in administration the authority responds.

There is a structural type of reform. The structure and working of public administration are reformed. New methods or systems are introduced. For example, decentralisation, delegation, or hierarchical methods are introduced for the betterment of public administration or it may be that the whole administrative system is divided into parts.

There is another type of reform which is called behavioural reform. It has been found that the public administrators or bureaucrats do not always behave properly with the people or clients. This may inflict adverse consequences upon the people or public administration. When the report of uncommon behaviour or unbecoming attitude reaches the proper authority it adopts precautionary measures.

The authority advises the person or department concerned to behave properly. This is called behavioural reform, or it may be that one department does not behave with another department and this affects the running of administration. The authority adopts measures which are tantamount to reform of public administration.

Another type of reform is organisation development. It belongs to open model of administration. Nicholas Henry defines it in the following way: "organisation development is a planned, organisation-wide attempt directed from the top that is designed to increase organisational effectiveness and viability through calculated interventions in the active workings of the organisation using knowledge from the behavioural sciences".

Here the whole organisation is not completely changed or the organisational system is not rejected. The internal management is sometimes reorganised to make it suitable for the new changes or situation. Legitimate claims or suggestions are accepted and incorporated into the administration of organisation. The chief aim is to develop the administrative system to satisfy the needs of clients or people. The team management or the relations among the various departments are reorganised. In this way the organisation is developed.

Implementation of Reforms

Reforming public administration is essential because time outlook of people, society — all are changing. Naturally, public administration or administrative system will also change. In other words, the public administration of every state is reformed. But the problem is to propose reforms and to implement them are quite separate. Again, there are several methods of implementing them. Caiden the noted author of public administration, thinks that there are several ways of executing reform.

The important way of implementing the reform is political revolution. In Russia, China and in several other countries public administration was thoroughly changed or reformed after revolution. The revolutionaries, in order to execute their policies, schemes and ideas changed the old administrative system. But complete change or abolition of old administration are not possible or advisable. After coming to power Lenin kept the bureaucratic system but he was forced to follow Marxist principle and ideology. However it is admitted on all hands that revolution is a very important way of reform.

When the old system of public administration proves its incapability to cope with the new situation or changes the old, public administration is reformed. This is a normal procedure and it is adopted everywhere. There is a famous proverb-old order changed yielding place to new. To put it in other words, various sorts of change such as change in political sphere, change outlook. Changes in behaviour force the authority to change or reform public administration. The administrative system cannot or should not be rigid. The rigidity in public administration will create chaos or discontent among the citizenry. It should not be allowed to persist.

Public administration is reformed through legal ways. There are different legal ways of reforming public administration. Sometimes the legislature enacts a law for specific purpose. That purpose is served but that law indirectly aims at changing certain aspects of public administration. Originally it was not the purpose of law to reform administration. But the execution of law reforms the public administration.

Sometimes the decisions of judges indirectly reform the administration. It is to be remembered here that the judges had no intention to change any part of public administration, but his judgement has done the job indirectly. This very often happens in USA and India.

The personal behaviour or attitude is a potent cause of the change of public administration. A very powerful person or a man of high imagination comes to power and he wanted to implement the dreams which he nourished in mind intended to execute them. In this case the person concerned must be courageous and he must have sufficient hold over the whole administrative system.

The authority is sometimes forced to implement or introduce reforms being pressurised by public or pressure groups or interest groups. Particularly in liberal democracies various types of groups are quite active and elites want to satisfy their needs. All these force the authority to reform public administration. The outlook and political philosophy of a party is another cause of reform and that reform is forthwith implemented in order to keep the election pledges.

New Areas of Administrative Reforms

Administrative reform is a broad term and naturally its area is quite wide. The true administrative reform does not mean piecemeal reforms that take place here and there in the vast body of public administration. Every issue that concerns the government may also come under the umbrella of administrative reform. Viewed from this perspective we can say that administrative reform includes numerous issues. It is because the chief aim of public administration is to help the state in achieving its goals.

Caiden in his Dynamics of Public Administration says that a true public administration must consider the following issues as its subjects. He says: "Public administration no longer stops at the housekeeping end of these and other public activities, such as forestry, laboratory administration, gallery administration, archives and engineering". According to Caiden the subject matter of public administration is very wide and it is concerned with all sorts of public authorities. If so, whenever an attempt is made to reform public administration all the important subjects and areas must come under the purview of administrative reform.

It has been suggested that whenever attempts are made to reform public administration the following areas should be included:

1. Population growth and control, family planning, public hygiene, sex education.
2. Drug control should be the subject of administrative reform. The term drug control is a very wide term. The public administration should see that the sale and distribution of harmful drugs must be banned. Intoxicants and smoking be prohibited.
3. The public administration must keep an eye on space laws and related problems.
4. In any society there are various forms of public service providers. It is the duty of central public administration to see that the service centres are performing their duties sincerely and properly. If this is not done the administrative reform must try to put everything in proper form.
5. Though academic institutions enjoy autonomy, they are not outside the purview of general public administration. The state administrative authority keeps an eye over the activities of these institutions, If the functions of educational institutions adversely affect the public morality law and order the public administration must try to take steps against this tendency. If the prevailing system fails to do the needful, the reform in public administration must be made.

6. Foreign affairs do not remain outside the general public administration. Two centuries ago there was practically no existence of international relations in today's sense and the public administration had no serious concern about the on-going of international relations. Today the situation has changed completely. The state administration must see that the incidents at international level do not go against the core interests of state. If there is anything wrong public administration takes steps and if it is not capable it must be reformed Caiden has suggested the reforms of public administration from this perspective.
7. An important area of administrative reform is electoral system. In all democratic countries elections are held periodically. But electoral system and election are ruled by certain laws and procedures and it is known to all that these are framed by the general public administration under the guidance of government or the concerned minister. Parliament enacts laws and public administration implements them. Necessary changes and amendments are done by the public administration department.

Problems of Administrative Reform

Change and reform are both essential for every system and especially very important for public administration. But the essentiality of reform does' not mean that its attainment and implementation are very easy tasks and naturally can be smoothly implemented. Here lies the problem of administrative reform.

This we can analyse from number of angles and some are stated briefly:

1. The situation for administrative reform appears to be imminent. The prevailing system of public administration is unable to cope with the changes that have engulfed the society. In other words, there has developed a very big gap between the capacity of public administration and the growing demands and requirements.

   In other words, the public administration is unable to meet the needs of people or clients and, in that case, reform appears to be indispensable. But the problem is the reform may not be able to satisfy the demands of people and in that situation reform will be unsuccessful.
2. The administrative reform is not a day to day affair. That is, public administration cannot be reformed frequently. When to reform and how much to be reformed pose big problems and these cannot be solved easily. The authority will start reforming public administration when the necessity will be fully ripe. Men will ardently desire a reform in public administration. But here is a problem again. A section of the society wants reform while the other section may feel that it is unnecessary. The reconciliation between the two opposing groups may prove an impossibility.
3. A reform must be a long-term process. But the problem is it is not possible for the administrators to anticipate the future. The result is today's reform may appear to be irrelevant in the near future. But an administration cannot be reformed frequently. None can overcome this problem. Reform is essential and future irrelevancy is certain.
4. An important objective of administrative reform is to ensure the support of the clients for the reform and participation of people in administration. Here lies a very big problem.

> Without people's support a reform proposal can never be executed. Particularly in a country where there are large number of parties and the relation between them is far from cordial. When the party in power proceeds to introduce certain reforms in public administration other parties will or may object.

Again, in a class society where there are two powerful classes any reform that aims to give some special privileges to a class working class, the capitalist class will strongly object; or if any reform goes against the interests of elites or any powerful interest groups others will object and try to scuttle the reform proposals. Party rivalry or anti-government attitude stands on the way of the implementation of reforms.

This happens in democracy. This is the issue of participation of people in administration. But participation of men in public administration cannot always be ensured. A participation must always be preceded by political socialisation which, briefly stated, means that people must have interest in political affairs and must have desire to participate.

Even if a reform scheme is accepted its implementation may create problems. People may not cooperate with the authority. In a transitional state the backwardness of people in outlook, thought and behaviour may force the authority from executing the reforms. We hold the view that reforming administration is essential, but the reforms may not be successful if these are not accepted by the people.

In the light of the above analysis we say that the success of administrative reforms depends upon certain preconditions and some are briefly stated:

1. The authority must be serious and sincere about the reforms. That is, the authority is adamant that for the betterment of society public administration must be reformed.
2. The authority is sure that the reforms in public administration will bring about desired and improved results. If not, the authority should not try to reform.

The authority, through its machinery, should try to gauge the attitude or mentality of the people about the reform proposals. In a democracy nothing can be imposed upon the people by applying coercive measures. The authority shall try to anticipate what people actually want and what the reforms are prepared to offer. There shall be a conciliation between the two.

The authority must be able to prove or establish that the present form of public administration is not able to satisfy the requirements of the general public. The public will also agree with the authority. When this happens, administrative reform will be able to achieve success. There is also the problem of implementation. For the successful implementation of reform, an efficient government machinery is essential.

People's cooperation is also deemed as a precondition. Even various forces -both national and international may try to scuttle the reform proposals. In this regard utmost alertness on the part of authority is required. Finally, we hold the view that it is the duty of the authority to create a favourable atmosphere for the reform proposals so that the general public can accept it easily.

References

- What-is-public-administration: managementstudyguide.com, Retrieved 13 April, 2019
- Principles-of-public-administration, public-administration, topic: britannica.com, Retrieved 14 May, 2019
- Myrick, Darrel. "Frederick Taylor as a Contributor to Public Administration" (PDF). Unisa. Mediterranean Journal of Social Sciences. Retrieved 2015-11-17
- Approaches-to-public-administration: managementstudyguide.com, Retrieved 15 June, 2019
- Institutional-approach-to-public-administration: managementstudyguide.com, Retrieved 16 July, 2019
- Özcan, Kerim (Sept. 2010). "Traces of Postmodernism in the New Public Management Paradigm" (PDF).www.todaie.edu. Retrieved April 13, 2016
- Administrative-reforms-meaning-origin-problems-and-other-details, dministrative-reforms, public-administration: yourarticlelibrary.com, Retrieved 17 August, 2019

2

Fundamental Aspects of Public Administration

Some of fundamental components of public administration are administrative law, administrative discretion, public interest, decentralization, advocacy evaluation, public service, civil service and bureaucracy. This chapter has been carefully written to provide an easy understanding of these key components of public administration.

ADMINISTRATIVE LAW

Administrative law refers to the legal framework within which public administration is carried out. It derives from the need to create and develop a system of public administration under law, a concept that may be compared with the much older notion of justice under law. Since administration involves the exercise of power by the executive arm of government, administrative law is of constitutional and political, as well as juridical, importance.

There is no universally accepted definition of administrative law, but rationally it may be held to cover the organization, powers, duties, and functions of public authorities of all kinds engaged in administration; their relations with one another and with citizens and nongovernmental bodies; legal methods of controlling public administration; and the rights and liabilities of officials. Administrative law is to a large extent complemented by constitutional law, and the line between them is hard to draw. The organization of a national legislature, the structure of the courts, the characteristics of a cabinet, and the role of the head of state are generally regarded as matters of constitutional law, whereas the substantive and procedural provisions relating to central and local governments and judicial review of administration are reckoned matters of administrative law. But some matters, such as the responsibility of ministers, cannot be exclusively assigned to either administrative or constitutional law. Some French and American jurists regard administrative law as including parts of constitutional law.

The law relating to public health, education, housing, and other public services could logically be regarded as part of the corpus of administrative law; but because of its sheer bulk it is usually considered ancillary.

Principles

One of the principal objects of administrative law is to ensure efficient, economical, and just administration. A system of administrative law that impedes or frustrates administration would clearly be bad, and so, too, would be a system that results in injustice to the individual. But to judge whether administrative law helps or hinders effective administration or works in such a way as to deny justice to the individual involves an examination of the ends that public administration is supposed to serve, as well as the means that it employs.

In this connection only the broadest generalities can be attempted. It can be asserted that all states, irrespective of their economic and political system or of their stage of development, are seeking to achieve a high rate of economic growth and a higher average income per person. They are all pursuing the goals of modernization, urbanization, and industrialization. They are all trying to provide the major social services, especially education and public health, at as high a standard as possible. The level of popular expectation is much higher than in former ages. The government is expected not only to maintain order but also to achieve progress. There is a widespread belief that wise and well-directed government action can abolish poverty, prevent severe unemployment, raise the standard of living of the nation, and bring about rapid social development. People in all countries are far more aware than their forefathers were of the impact of government on their daily lives and of its potential for good and evil.

The growth in the functions of the state is to be found in the more-developed and in the less-developed countries; in both old and new states; in democratic, authoritarian, and totalitarian regimes; and in the mixed economies of the West. The movement is far from having reached its zenith. With each addition to the functions of the state, additional powers have been acquired by the administrative organs concerned, which may be central ministries, local, provincial, or regional governments, or special agencies created for a particular purpose.

Distinctions between Public Administration and Private Action

Activities such as traffic control, fire-protection services, policing, smoke abatement, the construction or repair of highways, the provision of currency, town and country planning, and the collection of customs and excise duties are usually carried out by governments, whose executive organs are assumed to represent the collective will of the community and to be acting for the common good. It is for this reason that they are given powers not normally conferred on private persons. They may be authorized to infringe citizens' property rights and restrict their freedom of action in many different ways, ranging from the quarantining of infectious persons to the instituting of criminal proceedings for nonpayment of taxes. To take another example, the postal laws of many countries favour the post office at the expense of the customer in a way unknown where common carriers are concerned. Again, a public authority involved in slum clearance or housing construction tends to be in a much stronger legal position than a private developer.

The result of the distinction between public administration and private action is that administrative law is quite different from private law regulating the actions, interests, and obligations of private persons. Civil servants do not generally serve under a contract of employment but have a special status. Taxes are not debts, nor are they governed by the law relating to the recovery of debts by private persons. In addition, relations between one executive organ and another, and between an executive organ and the public, are usually regulated by compulsory or permissive powers conferred upon the executive organs by the legislature.

The law regulating the internal aspects of administration (e.g., relations between the government and its officials, a local authority and its committees, or a central department and a local authority) differs from that covering external relations (those between the administration and private persons or interests). In practice, internal and external aspects are often linked, and legal provisions of both kinds exist side by side in the same statute. Thus, a law dealing with education may modify the administrative organization of the education service and also regulate the relations between parents and the school authorities.

Another distinction exists between a command addressed by legislation to the citizen, requiring him to act or to refrain from acting in a certain way, and a direction addressed to the administrative authorities. When an administrative act takes the form of an unconditional command addressed to the citizen, a fine or penalty is usually attached for failure to comply. In some countries the enforcement is entrusted to the criminal courts, which can review the administrative act; in others the administrative act itself must be challenged in an administrative court.

Need for Legal Safeguards

Statutory directions addressed to the executive authorities may impose absolute duties, or they may confer discretionary powers authorizing a specified action in certain circumstances. Such legislation may give general directions for such activities as factory inspection, slum clearance, or town planning. The statute lays down the conditions under which it is lawful for the administration to act and confers on the authorities the appropriate powers, many of which involve a large element of discretion. Here the executive is not confined merely to carrying out the directions of the legislature; often it also shares in the lawmaking process by being empowered to issue regulations or ordinances dealing with matters not regulated by the statute. This may be regarded either as part of the ordinary process by which the legislature delegates its powers or as an inevitable feature of modern government, given that many matters are too technical, detailed, or subject to frequent change to be included in the main body of legislation—legislation being less easy to change than regulations.

Whatever the source of the executive's rule-making power, safeguards against misuse are necessary. For instance, the regulation must not exceed the delegated powers; its provisions must conform with the aims of the parent statute; prior consultation with interests likely to be affected should take place whenever practicable; and the regulations must not contravene relevant constitutional rules and legal standards. In some countries regulations are scrutinized by a type of watchdog known as the council of state before they come into force; in others, by the parliamentary assembly; and in yet others, by the ordinary courts.

In most countries the executive arm of government possesses certain powers not derived from legislation, customary law, or a written constitution. In the United Kingdom there are prerogative powers of the crown, nearly all of which are now exercised by ministers and which concern such matters as making treaties, declaring war and peace, pardoning criminals, issuing passports, and conferring honours. In Italy, France, Belgium, and other continental European countries, certain acts concerning the higher interests of the state are recognized as actes de gouvernement and are thereby immune from control by any court or administrative tribunal. In the German Empire, the principle that an administrative act carried its own legal validity was accepted at the end of the 19th century by leading jurists. This led to the doctrine that administration was only loosely bound to the law. The doctrine was rejected in the Federal Republic of Germany, however, and efforts were made to reduce the area in which the executive was free to act outside administrative law.

Bureaucracy and the Role of Administrative Law

An inevitable consequence of the expansion of governmental functions has been the rise of bureaucracy. The number of officials of all kinds has greatly increased, and so too have the material resources allocated to their activities, while their powers have been enlarged in scope and depth. The rise of bureaucracy has occurred in countries ruled by all types of government, including communist countries, dictatorships and fascist regimes, and political democracies. It is as conspicuous in the former colonial states of Africa and Asia as among the highly developed countries of western Europe or North America. A large, strong, and well-trained civil service is essential in a modern state, irrespective of the political character of its regime or the nature of its economy.

Fear of the maladies that tend to afflict bureaucracy has produced a considerable volume of protest in some countries; and, even in those where opposition to the government or the party in power is not permitted, criticism and exposure of bureaucratic maladministration are generally encouraged.

Bureaucratic maladies are of different kinds. They include an overdevotion of officials to precedent, remoteness from the rest of the community, inaccessibility, arrogance in dealing with the general public, ineffective organization, waste of labour, procrastination, an excessive sense of self-importance, indifference to the feelings or convenience of citizens, an obsession with the binding authority of departmental decisions, inflexibility, abuse of power, and reluctance to admit error. Many of these defects can be prevented or cured by the application of good management techniques and by the careful training of personnel. A whole range of techniques is available for this purpose, including effective public relations, work-study programs, organization and management, operational research, and social surveys.

Administrative law is valuable in controlling the bureaucracy. Under liberal-democratic systems of government, political and judicial control of administration are regarded as complementary, but distinct. The former is concerned with questions of policy and the responsibility of the executive for administration and expenditure. The latter is concerned with inquiring into particular cases of complaint. Administrative law does not include the control of policy by ministers or the head of state.

Judicial Review of Administration

Judicial review of administration is, in a sense, the heart of administrative law. It is certainly the most appropriate method of inquiring into the legal competence of a public authority. The aspects of an official decision or an administrative act that may be scrutinized by the judicial process are the competence of the public authority, the extent of a public authority's legal powers, the adequacy and fairness of the procedure, the evidence considered in arriving at the administrative decision and the motives underlying it, and the nature and scope of the discretionary power. An administrative act or decision can be invalidated on any of these grounds if the reviewing court or tribunal has a sufficiently wide jurisdiction. There is also the question of responsibility for damage caused by the public authority in the performance of its functions. Judicial review is less effective as a method of inquiring into the wisdom, expediency, or reasonableness of administrative acts, and courts and tribunals are unwilling to substitute their own decisions for that of the responsible authority.

Judicial review of administration varies internationally. Sweden and France, for instance, have gone as far as subjecting the exercise of all discretionary powers, other than those relating to foreign affairs and defense, to judicial review and potential limitation. Elsewhere, a preoccupation with procedure results in judicial review deciding only whether the correct procedure was observed rather than examining the substance of the decision.

It is of course impractical to subject every administrative act or decision to investigation, for this would entail unacceptable delay. The complainant must, therefore, always make out a prima facie case that maladministration has occurred.

Judicial review cannot compel the state to act in a particular way because the courts concerned cannot impose sanctions on the government, which itself controls the use of force. Such remedies as an injunction, an order for specific performance, or an order for mandamus will not lie against the central government. These inhibitions, however, are of less practical importance than might be supposed. Nevertheless, nearly all governments (even revolutionary ones) are eager to proclaim the lawfulness of the regime and seldom disregard the decisions of an authorized court or tribunal.

In judicial review of administration at a national level, a country's history, politics, and constitutional theory all play their part. There are, broadly, three major systems: the common-law model; the French, or council of state, model; and the procurator model.

Common-law System

The common-law system originated in England in the Middle Ages. In the 17th century relations between the courts and the executive developed into a constitutional struggle between the Stuart kings and the judges over the judges' right to decide questions affecting the royal power and even to pronounce an independent judgment in cases in which the king had an interest. Francis Bacon, in his essay Of Judicature (written in 1612), put forth the royalist point of view when he declared that the judges should be "lions, but yet lions under the throne." "It is a happy thing in a state," he wrote, "when kings and states do often consult with judges; and again, when judges do often consult with the king and state: the one, when there is matter of law intervenient in business of state; the other, when there is some consideration of state intervenient in matter of law." The subordination of the judicature to the royal will was strongly resisted by Chief Justice Sir Edward Coke, Bacon's great rival, who refused to comply with James I's wishes in a number of cases in which the royal prerogative was involved. The King harangued the judges more than once on their duty to respect the royal prerogative and power.

In the constitutional conflict that took place a generation later, the judges and the lawyers made common cause with Parliament against Charles I, and eventually the independence of the judges was established. Henceforth there was to be one system of law to which all would owe obedience. As a result, the executive possessed no inherent powers other than those subject to the rule of law inasmuch as legislation now had to emanate from the crown in Parliament. In addition, the judges were expected to protect the subject against the executive. A more intangible consequence was the belief that "government" and "law" were often thought to be opposed to one another. The earlier conflict between crown and judges survived to become an antagonism between the legal profession and the executive, particularly the civil service.

These developments established the principle that the executive should never interfere with the judiciary in the exercise of its functions. This was, indeed, almost the only strict application in England of the doctrine of the separation of powers. On the other hand, it was regarded as right and proper that the judiciary should interfere with the executive whenever a minister or a department was shown to have acted illegally. In this way the concept of the rule of law came gradually to be identified with the idea that the judges, in ordinary legal proceedings in the ordinary courts, could pronounce upon the lawfulness of the activities of the executive. Any attempt to divide the seamless web of the law, any suggestion of a distinction between public and private law, appeared destructive of the law's universality and its power to keep the executive within bounds.

The principle that all public authorities are liable to have the lawfulness of their acts and decisions tested in the ordinary courts was applied everywhere the common law prevailed, including the United States, despite the much stricter interpretation given by the Founding Fathers there to the doctrine of the separation of powers—a doctrine embodied in the federal and state constitutions. A complete separation of powers was not considered feasible by the framers of the Constitution, and they therefore introduced checks and balances, whereby each of the three branches of government would be prevented from growing too powerful by the countervailing power of the others. This actually strengthened the power of the courts to review the actions of the executive. Elsewhere in the common-law world, the extended role of the courts in reviewing administration was adopted without any public debate concerning the separation of powers or the need to protect liberty by a system of checks and balances. This absence of an explicitly defined role for courts led, in the early post-World War II years in Britain, to real fears that the courts would be unable or unwilling to question the expanded powers of governmental bodies.

Modification of the Common-law System

The common-law system was extensively modified in the course of the 20th century. Until then it did not correspond to the realities of the situation in Britain because, prior to the Crown Proceedings Act (1947), it was not possible to sue ministers and their departments in tort; government ministers in Britain are considered ministers of the crown, and an ancient legal doctrine holds that "the king can do no wrong." Moreover, the development of state-provided social services has been accompanied by the creation of a large number of administrative tribunals to determine disputes between a government department and a citizen. The jurisdiction of these tribunals is of a specialized and narrowly circumscribed character and relates to such functions as social insurance and social assistance, the National Health Service, rent control, assessment of property for local taxation, the compulsory acquisition of land by public authorities, and the registration of children's homes. Since 1958 a permanent Council on Tribunals appointed by the lord chancellor has exercised a general supervision over about 40 tribunal systems, but they remain an unsystematic and uncoordinated movement. However, they provide a method of administrative adjudication far cheaper, more informal, and more rapid than that offered by the courts; the members are persons possessing special knowledge and experience of the subject dealt with; they do not have to follow the strict and complex rules of evidence that prevail in the courts; and it is possible to introduce new social standards and moral considerations to guide their decisions. These tribunals have won general approval for the quality and impartiality of their work. An appeal on a question of law lies in most instances from the decision of an administrative tribunal to the High Court of Justice. There is still no comprehensive administrative jurisdiction in Britain permitting judicial review over the whole field of executive action and decision.

In Australia a similar movement took place with the growth of a large number of administrative tribunals that regulate many different spheres of public administration, such as industrial conditions; the award of pensions, allowances, and other state grants; town planning; censorship of films; fair rents; the licensing of occupations calling for special skills or public responsibility; trade, transport, and marketing; the assessment of national taxes, local taxes, or duties; the protection of industrial design, patents, and copyrights; and compensation for interference with private-property rights in the public interest. From 1975 these tribunals were managed by the Administrative Appeals Tribunal.

In the United States the courts review administration much more comprehensively than in Britain. Nevertheless, much adjudication is now performed by public authorities other than the courts of law. The movement toward administrative tribunals began with the Interstate Commerce Act (1887), establishing the Interstate Commerce Commission to regulate railways and other carriers. This law introduced a new type of federal agency, outside the framework of the executive departments and largely independent of the president. Other regulatory commissions followed: the Federal Trade Commission, the Federal Communications Commission, the Securities and Exchange Commission, the National Labor Relations Board, and the Occupational Safety and Health Administration. These bodies have had administrative, legislative, and judicial functions delegated to them by Congress, and the doctrine of the separation of powers can no longer be successfully invoked to challenge the constitutionality of such legislation. The regulatory commissions are often described by American jurists as administrative tribunals.

Thus, in the United States, as in other parts of the Anglo-American common-law world, the concept of the exclusive exercise by the ordinary courts of all judicial powers and of the absence of special administrative tribunals has been substantially modified by these developments.

Council of State System

French System

In France the separation of powers was given a place of honour in the Declaration of the Rights of Man and of the Citizen. In the French view, however, if a court were permitted to review an administrative act or decision, it would contravene the separation of powers as much as if the executive could override the decision of a court. Just as an appeal from a court lies to a higher court, the reasoning goes, so an appeal from an administrative authority should lie to a higher administrative authority. Only thus would the true separation of powers be observed.

Herein lies the explanation of administrative law as a system of law separate from the body of law administered in the courts. A law of August 1790 declared that the judiciary was distinct from and would always remain separated from the executive. It forbade judges, on pain of dismissal, to interfere in any way with the work of administrative bodies. In October 1790 a second law stated that under no circumstances should claims to annul acts of administrative bodies fall within the jurisdiction of the courts. Such claims should be brought before the king as head of the general administration.

The Conseil du Roi of the ancien régime, with its functions as legal adviser and administrative court, is generally considered to be the precursor of the Conseil d'État. The basic structure of the Conseil d'État was laid down by Napoleon, however. Among the functions accorded to it by the constitution of the year VIII was that of adjudicating in conflicts that might arise between the administration and the courts. It was also empowered to adjudicate any matters previously left to the minister's discretion that ought to be the subject of judicial decision. In 1806 a decree created a Judicial Committee of the Conseil to examine applications and report thereon to the General Assembly of the Conseil. These enactments laid the foundation of an administrative jurisdiction that was not clearly established until May 24, 1872, when a law delegated to the Conseil d'État the judicial power to make binding decisions and recognized the Conseil as the court in which claims against the administration should be brought.

The Conseil d'État is and always has been part of the administration. It has for long had the task of giving legal advice to the government on bills, regulations, decrees, and administrative questions. It is this that long led foreign jurists into believing that, when sitting as a court, its decisions would inevitably be biased in favour of the executive. Nothing could be further from the truth, and today the Conseil is universally recognized as an independent court that provides French citizens with exceptionally good protection against maladministration. Suits that are directed against the French administration are heard in the Section du Contentieux, or Judicial Division, the successor of the Judicial Committee after restructuring in 1872.

The Conseil d'État is the final authority in administrative disputes. Owing to the immense volume of work falling on it, the former prefectural councils, which served as administrative courts subordinate to the Conseil d'État, were transformed in 1953 into administrative tribunals of first instance, and the professional qualifications and career prospects of their members were improved. The great majority of cases go before these tribunals, and the Conseil d'État is the court of first and last instance only in those exceedingly rare cases when it is specially designated for that purpose.

If difficulty or doubt arises as to whether a case falls within the administrative jurisdiction or that of the ordinary courts, the question is resolved by the Tribunal des Conflits. This is a court specially established for the purpose, consisting of five judges from the Cour de Cassation (the highest civil court) and five from the Conseil d'État. The minister of justice, in his capacity as keeper of the seals (garde des sceaux), may sometimes preside and cast a tie-breaking vote.

Several other countries have followed France in establishing councils of state. Among them are Italy, Greece, Belgium, Spain, Turkey, Portugal, and Egypt. It must be stated, however, that in no other country has a council of state acquired such high status, powers, authority, or prestige as in France.

German System

Germany traditionally has had no council of state, but it does have a fully articulated system of special administrative courts. In the states, or Länder, there are lower administrative courts and superior administrative courts, and for the federation there is the Federal Administrative Court, which acts mainly as a court of appeals from the superior administrative courts in the Länder and even from the lower administrative courts in certain circumstances. The Federal Administrative Court serves also as a court of first and last instance in disputes not involving questions of constitutionality between the federation and the Länder or between two or more Länder; it hears petitions by the federal Cabinet on declarations that an association is prohibited under the Basic Law of the Federal Republic, petitions against the federation in matters concerning the diplomatic or consular service, and cases concerning the business of the Federal Intelligence Service.

A Land administrative court possesses jurisdiction concerning the acts of the Länder administrative authorities and also complaints against officers of the federal government located in the Länder. Some of the highest federal organs are exempt from the Länder courts. Few cases go beyond the Länder supreme administrative courts.

Recourse to an administrative court is available for public law disputes unless the matter has been assigned to another court by federal legislation. (Public law governs the relationship between the state and executive in the exercise of their governmental authority and the individual—insofar as the relationship is not commercial). The Administrative Courts Code holds that property claims arising from services for the common good and restitution claims arising from violation of duties under public law shall be heard by the ordinary courts. In other words, the German system is complicated by the rule that only the ordinary civil courts can award damages against an official or the executive arm of government. As a consequence, the distinction between the ordinary courts and the administrative courts depends on the remedy sought and not on the subject matter of the dispute or the nature of the parties. The jurisdiction of the administrative courts in Germany is therefore less comprehensive and clear-cut than in France.

Procurator System

The third system for ensuring administrative legality, called the Procuracy, was founded in Russia by Peter the Great in 1722, who intended it to be the "eye of the tsar." Catherine II issued a directive in 1764 stating that the procurator general and his staff were to supervise the execution of the laws in the provinces, ensure justice, and prevent abuses. This was designated general supervision. In 1864, however, the Procuracy was relieved of its responsibility for supervising administration, its functions being confined to judicial matters, such as acting as public prosecutor in all criminal cases and conducting them on behalf of the government and the law.

The Procuracy was abolished in November 1917 but revived in 1922. The Soviet constitution charged the procurator general with the general duty of supervising the observance of the law by all ministries and institutions subordinate to them as well as by individual officials and citizens. The procurator general was appointed by the Supreme Soviet for five years. He appointed subordinate procurators at all administrative levels, from union republic to district and town.

The functions actually performed by the procurator underwent many fluctuations and vicissitudes after 1922. The role as a public prosecutor continued, but it was exercised mainly to enforce party policies or programs on recalcitrant citizens rather than to punish public officers or authorities for breaches of the law. Sometimes the task of general supervision was emphasized; at other times it was abandoned in favour of more urgent tasks, as in World War II. Finally, the position of the Procuracy was laid down in a union law of May 24, 1955, and a decree of the Presidium of the Supreme Soviet made on April 7, 1956.

The procurator was not the president of a court or a tribunal but rather a watchdog of legality. His organization comprised a department for general supervision; a bureau of investigation for the supervision of preliminary inquiries in criminal matters; a department for the supervision of investigations carried out by the KGB (Committee for State Security); departments to supervise criminal and civil proceedings in the courts; a department to supervise prisons, compulsory-labour centres, and the like; and departments for statistics, administration, and research.

General supervision was defined by Soviet writers on administrative law as meaning supervision by the procurators over legality in administration. Procurators were expected to see that the laws were strictly observed, to oppose their violation by anyone whatsoever, to protect the citizens, and to ensure that they fulfilled their duties. The law of May 24, 1955, required the Procuracy to ensure that the regulations or decisions issued by ministries, departments, their subordinate establishments and enterprises, and cooperative and other public organizations strictly conformed to the constitution and laws of the Soviet Union and the republics as well as to the decrees of the Council of Ministers of the Soviet Union and the republics. They were also to ensure strict execution of the laws by officials and citizens. The procurator was concerned solely with the legality of administrative action.

After the mid-1960s a change took place in the role of the procurator from the handling of complaints by citizens against government bodies to the handling of "economic" complaints (e.g., violations such as filing fraudulent plan fulfillment records) and the monitoring of economic performance. The decline in the number of individual citizens' grievances handled by the Procuracy, as well as the economic and coercive purposes for which it was used, make direct analogy between the procurator and an ombudsman misleading.

Since the Procuracy was not a court, it could not make a binding decision. This point was emphasized by Article 58 of the 1977 constitution, giving citizens the right to take complaints against administrative actions to the courts. The normal procedure (apart from cases of dereliction involving a criminal prosecution) was for the procurator to protest against any illegality that he detected or that was brought to his notice or to initiate disciplinary action against an erring official. Every citizen had a right to lodge a complaint with the procurator, and denunciation and exposure of bureaucratic abuses were officially encouraged by the Communist Party. The fact that the Procuracy could not make a binding decision did not necessarily prevent it from being an effective organ for securing administration according to law. Neither the French Conseil d'État nor the courts in any country can enforce judgments against the central government, but this does not prevent the decisions of the Conseil or declaratory judgments of the courts from being observed almost as a matter of course.

The former Communist regimes of eastern Europe established procuracies based on the Soviet model. In Poland an additional institution to maintain administrative legality was the Supreme Chamber of Control, which was independent of the government and subordinate only to the legislature and the Council of State, a political body quite different from the French model. The functions of the Supreme Chamber of Control involved exercising general supervision over public administration and took into account legality, economy, and opportuneness.

Ombudsman

The ombudsman is a part of the system of administrative law for scrutinizing the work of the executive. He is the appointee not of the executive but of the legislature. The ombudsman enjoys a large measure of independence and personal responsibility and is primarily a guardian of correct behaviour. His function is to safeguard the interests of citizens by ensuring administration according to law, discovering instances of maladministration, and eliminating defects in administration. Methods of enforcement include bringing pressure to bear on the responsible authority, publicizing a refusal to rectify injustice or a defective administrative practice, bringing the matter to the attention of the legislature, and instigating a criminal prosecution or disciplinary action.

When Sweden created the office of ombudsman in the constitution of 1809, the holder of that office was occupied with civil affairs and was appointed by the legislature. He was independent of both executive and judiciary and had full powers to inquire into the details of any administrative or executive act and into certain judicial activities if reported to him by individuals as an abuse of rights. He had effective authority to prosecute civil servants and other public officials—including, on occasion, ministers themselves.

The Swedish ombudsman's responsibility now comprises civil affairs, including the judicature, the police, prisons, and the public administration, both central and local, but excluding ministers and the monarch. He can act as a public prosecutor (although he does not often do so); as a receiver of complaints from aggrieved citizens; or as an inspector of such institutions as jails, mental hospitals, homes for delinquent children, and retreats for alcoholics to discover if they are being administered in accordance with the law.

The institution of ombudsman was first adopted in other Scandinavian countries and then—especially from the 1960s—in many countries throughout the world, including New Zealand, the United Kingdom, Israel, Portugal, the Netherlands, and Spain. Australia, the United States, and Canada have ombudsmen at the state or provincial level, and in the United States several cities have municipal ombudsmen. In Britain there is an ombudsman to investigate complaints against local government, the National Health Service, and administration in Northern Ireland, in addition to the ombudsman operating at the national level. Some specialized ombudsmen have been appointed in the United States to safeguard the rights of prisoners to medical treatment. In Israel the police have an office of public complaints, and there is a military ombudsman; there is also a state controller, who issues annual reports on executive procedures.

There is no doubt about the value of the ombudsman in the states in which the institution has been established. Part of the ombudsman's usefulness lies in his ability to reassure citizens who believe they have been unjustly treated that careful inquiry into their complaints shows their suspicions to be groundless. In most countries the ombudsman has little positive power other than the right to inspect and to demand the fullest information. He may, however, recommend a particular interpretation of, or a particular modification of, the law. He can also recommend that the government pay compensation to a complainant.

Administrative Procedure

An orderly procedure, besides being efficient, allows responsibility to be fixed on a particular officer or body at each stage of the administrative process. It can safeguard the rights of citizens and protect the executive against the criticism of having acted in an arbitrary manner. It can ensure regularity and consistency in the handling of individual cases. Much depends, however, on the quality and purpose of the procedural requirements. Most countries possess only an uncodified mass of administrative law prescribing procedure. Much of it is to be found in the laws and regulations governing particular functions of government, such as taxation, public health, education, and town planning.

Rules of administrative procedure cover such matters as the setting of administrative machinery in motion; methods for lodging appeals; the rights of interested persons; the time limits that must be observed; the conditions to be satisfied by objectors; and the right of legal representation. The leading treatise on U.S. administrative law devotes many chapters to such procedural topics as rule making, requirement of opportunity to cross-examine and rebut, adjudication procedure, examiners, bias, evidence, official notice, findings, reasons, and opinions.

Some countries have a general code of administrative procedure embodied in legislation. Among them are Austria, Poland, Spain, and the United States.

In common-law systems, the doctrine of natural justice influences administrative procedure in two ways: That a person may not be judge of his own cause, and that a person shall not be dealt with to his material disadvantage, whether of person or property, or removed from or disqualified for office, without being given adequate notice of what is alleged against him and an opportunity to defend himself.

An indirect result of the second principle is the public hearing, widely used by government departments (and in the United States by regulatory commissions) in deciding matters involving individual or corporate rights. In the United Kingdom a public inquiry is now a common means of handling appeals to the Department of the Environment against the decisions of local authorities in such matters as planning applications and compulsory purchase of land.

In 1957 the Franks Committee was appointed by the British lord chancellor to study administrative tribunals and such procedures as the holding of a public inquiry. The committee declared that the work of administrative tribunals and of public inquiries should be characterized by openness, fairness, and impartiality, and their report applied these aims in great detail. The recommendations of the committee were largely accepted and resulted in the Tribunals and Enquiries Act of 1958.

ADMINISTRATIVE DISCRETION

Administrative discretion refers to the power to choose between courses of conduct in the administration of an office or a duty pertaining thereto. It is the exercise of professional expertise and judgment, as opposed to strict adherence to regulations or statutes, in making a decision or performing official acts or duties.

It is an admitted fact that the modem legal systems of the world recognize the conferment of administrative discretion to the instrumentalities of the State. The responsibility is cast, for the enforcement of public policy, on the executive branch of the government. In practice such responsibility is managed to be discharged by the large number of administrators who exercise power of decision making. Legislature, while making law to the nation, prescribes the procedure to be followed and the guidelines to be adhered to in the exercise of discretionary powers. There is a presumption that administrative authorities have to exercise the discretionary powers in the course of its action with reasonable amount of care. The government may make rules to cany out the purpose of the Act, depending upon the complexities of the problem, and their varying nature. Large amount of discretions are left to be exercised by the administrative authorities. The legislature, however, specifies exhaustively the ways in which discretion may be exercised. In fact, legislation is generally sketchy or skeletal, leaving many gaps for conferring powers on administration to discharge their duties and functions by using discretion.

The significance of discretion is increasing day-by-day as the administration is required to apply vogue and indefinite statutory provisions. Moreover, it has become very difficult to cope with the present day problems within the general rule of comprehensive nature. What is true is that the life is growing more and more complex and correspondingly numerous problems are arising making it difficult for the administrator to cope with such difficult situations. Task of the administrator becomes more and more difficult in the absence of discretion. Sometimes, the enacted law falls short to find measures to solve the complicated problems. This, therefore, expands the scope of discretion.

In modem times, the state has to concern itself with the welfare of the community in addition to classical functions. To achieve the constitutional goal of establishing a welfare state has further compelled the government to take steps for ameliorating the plight of the poor people in the field of education, health, housing and other civic facilities. It may be noticed that the administration is required to respond effectively to tackle these problems. In the process of growth towards the well-being of the society, the scope of discretionary power is gradually expanding and becoming inevitable to accomplish the cherished goals. All this has, in fact, necessitated in the conferment of the discretionary powers on the administration and its instrumentalities. The fact is that case-to-case approach is disadvantageous as the administrator may not find it possible to have a general rule or norm to be adopted. There is an ever increasing danger of discrimination leading to abuse of power. Moreover, it would be a time consuming process to select the best course of action in each individual case. Hence, the appropriate way to deal with these cases is to somewhat standardize the administration, leaving only a residual margin for adjustability, in the realm of fact situations, in practical cases.

There is a need to evolve the basic principles to govern the exercise of discretionary power. What is important is that the discretion must be exercised by the authority to which it is committed. It must act in good faith and give regard to all relevant considerations and must not be swayed away by irrelevant considerations. To quote Smith: "The authority in which the discretion is vested can be compelled to exercise the discretion, but not to exercise in any particular manner. In general, a discretion must be exercised only by the authority to which it is committed. That authority must genuinely address itself to the matter before it. It must not act under the dictation of another body or disable itself from exercising a discretion in individual case. It must act in good faith, must have regard to all relevant consideration and must not be swayed away by irrelevant consideration, must not seek to purpose alien to the letter and spirit of the legislation that gives it power to act, and must not act arbitrarily and capriciously". The hands of the administrative authority need to be tightened limiting to act within the bounds of law. It cannot exercise the power to frustrate the broad policy of law under which it is exercised. It is imperative to see that administrative agencies do not act as a free agent of the discretionary powers given by the statute. The spirit is that power cannot be used for an ulterior motive, not authorized by law. The administrator must justify his action on valid ground of public interests and statutory provisions.

Nomenclature of Discretionary Power

The term 'discretion' implies power to make a choice between alternative courses of action or inaction. In its ordinary meaning the word 'discretion' signifies unrestrained exercise of choice or will freedom of according to one's jdugement; unrestrained exercise of will; the liberty or power of acting without control other than one's own judgement. It has a reference to 'power' or 'right' conferred upon the public authority empowering them to act officially in certain circumstances according to the dictates of their own judgement and conscience, uncontrolled by the judgement or conscience of others Tomlin's Law Discretionary defines the word 'discretion' as to discern between right and wrong, and therefore, whoever has power to act in discretion is bound by rule of reason and law. Discretion, in general, is discernment of what is right and proper. It denotes knowledge and prudence, that discernment which enables a person to judge critically of what is correct and proper united with caution; nice discernment, and judgement directed by circumspection; deliberate judgement; soundness of judgement; a science of understanding to discern between falsity and truth, between wrong and right, between shadow and substance, between equity and colourable glosses and pretences and not to do according to the will and private affection of the persons. When it is said that something is to be done within the discretion of the authorities that something is to be done according to the rules of reason and justice, not according to private opinions; according to law and not rumour. It is not to be arbitrary, vague and fanciful but legal and regular to be exercised within the limit, to which an honest, competent to the discharge of his office to confine himself.

'Discretion' implies 'choice'. It is submitted that the choice is not unlimited but guided by statutory policy and object. The choice is amongst alternative courses of action as circumscribed by the statute itself. Davis rightly advocated that unnecessary discretionary powers shall be confined, structured and checked. Lord Wrenbury rightly suggests that a person in whom is vested a discretion must exercise his discretion on reasonable ground. It does not empower a man what he likes mere because he is minded so - he must in the exercise of his discretion not to do what he likes but what he ought. Discretion may mean absence of already articulated standard that can be readily and easily applied to be a situation that confronts the executants of a legislative enactment. Consequently, the primary responsibility is on the legislature and such responsibility appertains to at least articulation of statutory intent, purpose, policy and objective. Failure or perfunctory discharge of this responsibility by the legislature, if not subject to the judicial disapprobation, can only provide a fertile gorund for breeding administrative arbitrariness, culminating ultimately, in administrative despotism.

Lord Comdan defines the word 'discretion' as an exercise of judgemet, skill or wisdom distinguished from folly, unthinking or haste. The world in itself implies vigilant circumspection and care; therefore, where the legislature concedes discretion, it also imposes a heavy responsibility.

To sum up, discretionary power is a 'Sacred Trust' meant for effectuating the statutory policy, purpose and objects and that, this 'sacred trust' is not to be exercised for ulterior purposes. Grant of discretion is no legislative licence for indulging in discriminatory purposes. It may, however, be submitted here that discretion is not limited to what is authorized but includes all that is within, "the effective limits" of the officer's power. Another facet of the discretion is that a choice to do nothing - or to do nothing now - is included. What is apparent is that discretion includes interim choices as well as final one and procedural choices as well as substantive one. It extends to methods, forms, timing, degree of emphasis, many other subsidiary factors.

Need for Administrative Discretion

Administrative discretion is by-product of intensive form of welfare government. During the last century, the role of government has changed worldwide, from laissez-faire to paternalism and from paternalism to materialism, state is expected today to take care of its citizens from cradle to the grave. People demand that it is a duty of the government to solve their problems rather than merely to show lolly-pop in the form of merely defining their rights. Regulations of patterns of ownership, production and distribution is considered a responsibility of government to guarantee the maximum good of maximum number. Moreover, phenomenal growth in science and technology have burdened the modem government with more and more duties to satisfy the conflicting claims of its people.

Modernisation and technological development have brought great structural changes and have given birth to crucial problems such as cultural conflicts, haphazard urbanization, ruthless exploitation of natural resources, environmental pollution, rapid transport and traffic chaos, automation and consequential unemployment, irate production and distribution, concentration of economic power, dismal health, education, incessant labour strikes and lockouts, staggering inflation, accelerated smuggling, pervasive corruption, adulteration, tax evasion, violence and many others, 8 All these problems have resultantly necessitated to solve the arising complex problems in the light of the commitment of a welfare state which is possible only when more and more administrative authorities are created and clothed with guided discretionary power enabling them to find ways and means to solve the complexities of problems through administrative action.

We do hardly find any government and any legal system in the world which do not involve the exercise of discretion. What is important is that elimination of discretion has become not only difficult but impossible when the state has ushered in an era of ever expanding welfare activities to devise and carry out various welfare schemes it become inevitable to confer vast discretionary powers in the hands of the administrative authorities. It may be submitted here that inadequacy of traditional courts to respond to the new challenges has necessarily compelled the government to confer more and more discretionary powers upon the administrative bodies. The traditional administration of justice is technical, expensive and dilatory. Therefore, in cases where the need is fair disposition and not merely disposition of file, administrative authorities need to be invested with discretion.

It is imperative to mention here that public opinion, being powerful because of the strong media, has forced the government to undertake a variety of welfare functions such as public health, social insurance, housing, etc. This has involved the growth of wide discretionary powers in the hands of government in the lives of the individuals and the community. It has become after all, a necessity that the administrative authority is entrusted with the discretion to carry out the ultimate task of promoting welfare of the community. Issues involving safety measures in coal-mines, summary abatement of public nuisance which endanger public health or safety are the areas in which the administrative authorities are required to be strengthened with wide discretionary powers as immediate action is necessary to safeguard the rights of the individual. These cases can be dealt with by the administration in a befitting manner if large degree of discretion is allowed to them.20 As a matter of fact, without the exercise of discretion nothing can be done. The need for discretion is much greater in modem welfare society. It is well established that the abandonment of the laissez faire policy, the assumption of positive role by the state, industrialization, the dawn of an era of globalization have given rise to the culture of conferment of more and more discretionary powers on the administrative authorities. To devise and carry-out various welfare activities, there is no den3dng the fact, it has become necessary to confer vast discretionary powers in the hands of administration. What is true is that the legislature may not be able to enact a comprehensive legislation because it is not always possible for the legislature to foresee each and every problem. In such situation wide discretionary powers are to be entrusted to the administration to seek a solution through their own wisdom and rationality. Moreover, mechanical application of a rule of law, in fact, may lead to injustice in many circumstances. Therefore, in order to avoid such situation, or at least, to minimise them, it becomes necessary to leave an area of freedom on law-free zone to administrative authorities to solve the problems in accordance with the expediency of policy.

To sum-up it may be mentioned here that the need for conferment of the discretionary powers on the administrative body has arisen, briefly speaking, because of the reasons: that present day problems which the administration is called upon to solve are so complex that it is difficult to comprehend them within the scope of general rule. In order to deal with these problems effectively, it has become necessary to leave an area of freedom of action to administrative authorities, that it is not always possible for the legislature to foresee each and every problem because of the complexity of time and situation and hence to deal with such situation wide discretion has to be entrusted to administrative authorities to search a solution through their creativity; and that legislature may not know the techniques to solve the problems because of the lack of previous experience and absence of technical knowledge. Accordingly, there arises a need to adopt to the device of delegation by which it tells the delegate its mind and then leave it to the discretion of the delegate and accordingly the delegate may, through the case-to-case consideration, endeavour to solve the problem.

PUBLIC INTEREST

The public interest is a concept that can be defined in several ways. It is often treated as an ideal standard to which appeals for validation of political claims and policies are directed. References to the public interest commonly occur in editorials, political speeches, and other utterances of an admonitory or edifying character. The term is also often encountered in judicial and regulatory pronouncements. The significance of the conception is normative rather than analytical.

In efforts made to define the term systematically, several categories appear. There is the formal meaning wherein the public interest is viewed as the objective of the duly authorized organs of government or as the expression of majority rule. In substantive or policy terms, the public interest may be envisaged as embracing those activities necessary to the safety of the state and the welfare of the community: Defense, police protection, education, and public health and sanitation. The public interest has no a priori content waiting to be revealed. Public responsibilities regarded as being in the public interest in one setting may not be so regarded in a different context. The fact that the concept is elastic and relative rather than fixed and absolute makes it of greater utility in the quest for a supporting consensus as social changes occur and efforts at accommodation are made. The public interest then serves to remind the parties immediately concerned that there are considerations extending beyond their own goals or their particular rivalries or negotiations. Thus in labor-management disputes, or when subsidies or favorable tariff rates are sought for special groups, the consumer interest may be identified as the public interest. The individual may find himself in one role seeking to advance his self-interest and in another capacity allied with the larger good. Hence the term, whether for manipulative ends or for hortatory or inspirational purposes, is neither the device nor exclusive goal of any one group or class. As an aim to be articulated or an ideal to be enunciated, the public interest stands for the broad versus the narrow, the more inclusive versus the limited.

Indeed the very existence of the state as a collectivity would seem to prompt the formulation of basic common purposes. Thus the public interest is akin to the statements of ultimate ends that characterize political philosophy, varying from Plato's concern with the moral development of citizens as the purpose of the city-state to Hobbes's emphasis on order, Locke's protection of natural rights, and the utilitarian's assertion of the greatest good for the greatest number. As these illustrations indicate, the existence of a common interest is an implicit assumption, although its more specific manifestation cannot always be readily agreed upon. Yet both in traditional political thought and in contemporary organization theory, it has been noted that despite uncertainty about exactly what the shared interests may be, some measure of sharing exists for every human association.

The public interest can be visualized as a continuum that represents the values, aspirations, and objectives of the community or polity. There are values that are clearly central, such as health; and there are objectives that are controversial, such as fluoridation of water or discouragement of cigarette smoking. There are aspirations that are nearly universal, such as world peace; but there are numerous policy objectives to this end, which are subjects for debate. It is impossible to state with precision where any given item belongs on the continuum, yet there is general acceptance that a range of activities and goals exists above irrational or selfish individual interests.

Granted that a wide consensus supports freedom, justice, and compassion, the problem is to objectify these ideals in public policies bearing concretely on such areas as civil rights, race relations, juvenile delinquency, or narcotics addiction. The public interest cannot be thought of as a compromise struck between the desires of dope addicts and moralists or between hoodlums and the police. The public interest is clearly more than the sum of competing interests. It is an insistent reminder that morality must have a central place in any society that respects the freedom of its members. The concept of public interest holds the ultimate ethical justification for the demands that the state makes on the individual. The high value placed upon freedom and justice calls for the readiness of the citizen to make sacrifices if necessary and to share responsibility for sustaining the values of the polity.

The concerns of the philosopher and the needs of the official and the politician will call for continuing reference to the public interest if for no other purpose than as a symbol, as a shorthand device for directing attention to considerations that transcend the immediate, the selfish, and the merely expedient.

The public interest, as a concept, seems to be employed in situations that involve a conflict of interests or a problem of defending or interpreting broader or longer-range considerations against special or more immediate factors. Thus T. H. Green in his Lectures on the Principles of Political Obligation refers to the "common good" in analyzing the rights and duties of the state and the citizen. Brief reference is made to the public interest in the following context: "If the injured individual were likely to fail in the institution of proceedings for his own redress or defence, the public interest would require that the matter should be taken out of his hands".

Similarly Robert Maclver in The Web of Government refers to the general welfare and community, but when he describes the conflicting interests of modern industrial states, he writes that "government cannot afford to sit by while the disputants bring economic pressure to bear on one another. In the public interest it must devise whatever measures are expedient to prevent any interruption of vital services".

Uses of the Concept

The fact that the term is imprecise does not mean it is disappearing from ordinary usage; this is evident from the frequent references to the public interest in political polemics and in day-today discussions of public policy. The term then is justified as a useful working hypothesis: if it were abolished today, some other polar term would be coined to contrast the selfish goals of the few with the larger good, or sheer majority power with the proper rights of a minority. The occasional debasement and abuse of the term, it is argued, is no reason for its rejection. And as for ambiguity: Is "individual freedom"any more precise than "public interest"?

The concept of the public interest has won acceptance in the context of a functionally differentiated political system and a modern, industrial, and bureaucratized society that has a strong tradition of constitutionalism and rule of law.

The term is closely associated with the growth and professionalization of the civil service. The existence of a "neutral bureaucracy,"officeholders neither subservient to the will of a monarch nor dependent upon a political party, calls for some focus of loyalty. The public interest helps to meet such a need.

Felix Frankfurter, in his The Public and Its Government, uses the concept in referring to the public officials "pitted" against the utilities experts, for whom they are no match "except for occasional men of great capacity and exceptional devotion to the public interest". There are also occasions when officials are accused of exceeding their authority to the detriment of the public interest.

Where clearly distinguishable interests compete and policies can be seen as expressions of group desires, the public interest can be determined with some degree of specificity. Industrialization and improved means of communication and transportation have brought about conditions of complexity requiring more competence and expertise to determine the public interest in particular cases.

In negative terms one can list the efforts made to protect the public interest from threats to public order, safety, and morals (laws and ordinances with respect to crime, accidents, vice) and in the economic sphere regulations applying to fraud, monopolies, vote fixing, fair employment practices, and consumer protection.

Institutionally and procedurally, legislative bodies must rely upon special agencies to discover and protect the public interest within their respective jurisdictions.

From the standpoint of jurisprudence it would appear that the concept has a firm position. According to one spokesman, "the lawmen have a vested interest in 'the public interest' as an operational concept: They would be tongue-tied without it". Nor have judges refrained from definition: "Public interest means something in which the public, the community at large, has some pecuniary interest, or some interest by which their legal rights or liabilities are affected. And Munn v. Illinois states, "Property does become clothed with a public interest when used in a manner to make it of public consequence, and affect the community at large. When one devotes his property to a use in which the public has an interest, he must submit to be controlled by the public for the common good". Technological development and economic growth have resulted in industries whose activities go beyond the owners, shareholders, employees, competitors, and direct customers and affect the interests of a wide community, as in the case of the railroads and power companies.

The literature of recent years indicates a wide range of views concerning the significance of the concept. The differences of opinion result from the varying emphases with respect to its normative aspects and questions concerning its usefulness for analytical purposes. Since there is no generally accepted definition of the term, several different formulations are offered.

According to Walter Lippmann, "the public interest may be presumed to be what men would choose if they saw clearly, thought rationally, acted disinterestedly and benevolently".

Alfred Verdross regards the public interest as "the establishment of social conditions under which individual persons are able to build, through industry and productive work, a life which is in consonance with the dignity of the human being".

The ideal of the public interest calls on men, despite their egoism, to set their preferences side by side with the preferences of others and to examine them all with the same disinterestedness and impartiality. It asks them to seek as tolerable and comprehensive a compromise among these interests as is possible. And it reminds them that every decision they make is a limited one, that some interests may have been overlooked, that something better may be possible.

Stephen Bailey calls public interest "the central concept of a civilized polity. Its genius lies not in its clarity but in its perverse and persistent moral intrusion upon the internal and external discourse of rulers and ruled alike". He also notes: "There is perhaps no better example in all language of the utility of myth than the phrase the public interest".

The work of nearly a score of writers on the public interest is collected in Nomos No. 5 under the editorship of Carl J. Friedrich, who notes that it is not possible to discern "any distinctly philosophical, legal or political-scientific approach, though some of the authors lean more in one direction, some more in the other".

Frank J. Sorauf has given thoughtful attention to "the conceptual muddle"concerning the "public interest"; his conclusions are as follows:

No single criterion or standard, such as the public interest, can subsume or encompass all that is good and desirable for society—regardless of the system of values one prefers or propounds. The matter of the goals of a contemporary industrial society consists in reality of a series of specific, policy-centered questions which involve the entire range of our concern, from a realistic approach to the emerging nationalism of Africa, through care for the ill among the aged, to the resolution of domestic racial conflict and tension. The answers to these policy questions will be hammered out painfully and pragmatically, and they will certainly be expressed in alternatives and wisdom considerably more specific and vastly less grandiose than the all-encompassing guise of a "public interest."If one argues that a public interest exists in all these problem areas, and if he can go the next step and identify it, all well and good.

That the "public interest "has meaning for some public officials and interest groups is an incontestable fact. That it may in these terms affect the shaping and administration of public policy is equally incontestable. Observation of American politics will also afford instances of its effective use as a unifying symbol and a social myth. Even should scholars reject the public interest for their own analysis, they must observe and record its prevalence and influence in the political system. But it is only as political datum that the public interest has a definable relevance to the study of politics and public policy, Glendon A. Schubert has reviewed definitions and usage in an effort to discover whether the term could be used as a standard susceptible to empirical verification. His conclusion, if practicable, would point to a wide range of investigations:

If we assume that the peaceful adjustment of conflicting interests is not only the consummate art of the politician, but that it is also the fundamental task of all policy processes in a democratic polity, then a model of administrative due process would be empirically verified if, in practice, the decisions actually made resulted in the maximal accommodation of the affected interests, in comparison with the relative capacities of alternative structures for making the same decisions, and measured by a reciprocally minimal recourse to other centers for public policy change (i.e., the legislature, the chief executive, courts, etc.). There would be technical problems in the construction of realistic models, and there would be practical problems in inducing political support for the translation into actuality of any models that went beyond the description of existing agencies and processes.

Schubert concludes that in spite of these difficulties the task is worthwhile. In a later paper, however, he suggests that political scientists might do better to concentrate on concepts other than the public interest, concepts that promise more usefulness as scientific tools.

Research Needs and Opportunities

From an analytical viewpoint, the concept of the public interest may be best understood when viewed within a specific context or continuum. There is ample opportunity for research into decisions of regulatory bodies and judgments by the courts where the concept is interpreted in the light of specific issues.

Inquiry into the purposes to which the concept is put, by whom, under what conditions, and with what consequences may lead to a clear understanding of the dilemmas and choice points that face opinion leaders, legislators, officials, judges, and all others who would engage in the contest of politics. A history of the usage of the concept might well be undertaken. What relationship can be traced between the public interest and ideas of the general welfare or the national interest? Have significantly different shades of meaning or emphasis occurred? Moreover, international civil servants have yet to classify the public or publics they serve and the interests to which their energies are dedicated. Many of these problems can currently be examined in the new "modernizing"countries where officials are uncertain of their status and their standards.

While a civil servant may feel that the public interest has been served if he follows the inner check of conscience or the course dictated by the highest technical or scientific standards of his profession, the problem of responsibility is not thereby resolved. The community's values are also involved in the public interest: Public debate, discussion by the press, and legislative action or judicial intervention may be called for before an equilibrium is reached that appears to satisfy the articulate elements. There can obviously be no definitive adjustment "in the public interest"but rather a temporarily acceptable accommodation of interests and values. In this process of interaction there is opportunity for innovation and creativity and the public interest may be newly forged. The frontiers of scientific inquiry and problems of foreign aid in exotic cultures, for example, confront civil servants (and military officers) with necessities and opportunities for seeking fresh solutions for policy problems and unprecedented courses for governmental decision and activity.

A fresh perspective is gained if the public interest concept is viewed against the conditions that obtain in the developing countries. The problem of governance begins in the identification and articulation of interests. In traditional societies the peasant is a spectator or a pawn rather than a self-conscious participant. In the absence of effective interest groups, the charismatic leader rather than the politician qua broker has full opportunity. An underdeveloped society by definition lacks a well-defined infrastructure, and leaders accordingly are prone to make emotional appeals to a mass public and to stimulate nationalistic sentiments. Moreover, problems are not met through legal processes and administrative procedures of an essentially rationalistic character. Governmental sanctions are to be found in custom or in the will of the ruler or the authority of a dominant class rather than in appeals to the public interest. The ruler is the symbol or expression of power; governance is not thought of as a process of formulating issues and of analyzing, negotiating, manipulating, and adjusting special interests to reach generally acceptable outcomes and thereby to articulate the public interest. As Lucian Pye writes:

Although in transitional societies there is generally a somewhat greater awareness of the potentialities of politics as a means of rationally solving social problems than there is in traditional systems, the expressive aspects of politics usually continue to occupy a central place in determining the character of political behavior. The peculiar Western assumption that issues of public policy are the most important aspect of politics, and practically the only legitimate concern of those with power, is not fully accepted in non-Western politics. Indeed, in most non-Western societies the general assumption is not that those with power are committed to searching out and solving problems, but rather that they are the fortunate participants in an exciting and emotionally satisfying drama.

Lippmann has argued that "the art of governing well has to be learned. If it is to be learned, it has to be transmitted from the old to the young, and the habits and the ideas must be maintained as a seamless web of memory among the bearers of the tradition, generation after generation".

New nations, for example in Africa, need governmental institutions to provide justice and order. They need wise public policy to provide education, employment, and social welfare services for their rapidly growing populations. Here are newly enfranchised voters aspiring to the fruits of modernity but arriving at the status of citizenship without the historical experience or traditions out of which grew the polities of the West. Can the concept of the public interest be introduced; or can these new societies get along without such a unifying and disciplining concept? One answer offered is the theory of "one party rule."Loyalty to the leader of a single party can be quickly though not always permanently imposed, as Nkrumah and many other leaders have demonstrated. Acceptance of the public interest as a guiding belief would mean restraint on the ambitions of politicians and limits to the demands of the electorate.

In the developing countries, as industry advances, problems of administrative discretion can emerge, but whether the public interest will become an influential concept is uncertain. Will the civil service be motivated to serve the public? Will the courts be called upon to bring large economic enterprises within their jurisdiction? Will a recognition of individual rights requiring adjudication between adversary parties lead judges to apply criteria of public interest? Will the ties of kinship or loyalty to village tribe, community, or region permit an awareness of the larger configuration of "public"? Will the acceptance of tradition stand in the way of the rational pursuit of "interest"? Does the concept strengthen nationalism? Dictatorship? The answers to such questions will determine whether the term public interest has a universal applicability or whether it will remain a feature of Western jurisprudence and political thought.

The rule of law, due process, a free press, a loyal opposition, and the public interest are all valueladen concepts the limits and substance of which are difficult to define with precision, but all are significant in the maintenance of democratic government. Sport without the idea of fair play would lose zest—so, too, politics bereft of appeal to the public interest. The task of the umpire, in both situations, is probably made easier psychologically by reliance on such abstractions; but the responsibility of decision is in no way lessened, and the readiness of participants to question and of other observers to object remains.

The public interest is a concept that leaves open the way to change, as general acceptance for new policies is won and officials remain accountable for their decisions. Since there are many ways for seeking public acceptance and for safeguarding administrative responsibility within a democratic polity, it is doubtful that anything would be gained by insistence upon a precise definition of the public interest.

Public interest law is the work done by lawyers on behalf of poor individuals, unrepresented interests, and the general good. Public interest law services are usually provided at no cost to the beneficiaries, who are either too poor to pay or are not organized in ways that would allow them to retain lawyers. Public interest lawyers work in the courts, agencies, legislatures, and also through the media and community organizations. Although only a small number of American lawyers participate in these activities, public interest law reflects the American legal profession's commitment to values not fully served by the normal fee-for-service system of legal practice.

There is an intimate relationship between public interest law and the Constitution. First, the governmental structure created by the Constitution makes public interest law both necessary and possible. Second, without public interest law, many constitutional protections might be ineffective. Finally, the broader American tradition of constitutionalism depends on institutions like public interest law.

The governmental structure created by the Constitution makes legal advocacy important for the pursuit of many individual and collective interests. United States government is one by representation, not by direct participation. Although, in theory, citizens are supposed to be knowledgeable about public issues and elected representatives are supposed to take account of the interests of all constituents, in fact, most decisions are made in remote arenas and officials often are not aware of all affected interests. As a result, direct advocacy by professionals will make a difference in outcomes. If all such advocacy must be purchased in the marketplace, the system will be skewed toward the interests of the "haves." The presence of public interest advocates, at least to some degree, offsets marketplace bias.

The special role our written Constitution plays in American political life makes subsidized advocacy all the more important. Americans resolve many fundamental issues—from slavery to reproductive freedom—through consitutional litigation. If free legal services are not sometimes available in these struggles, the results can be seriously skewed.

Although the constitutional structure thus makes public interest law necessary, it also helps make it possible. Of course, there is a constitutional right to counsel in criminal cases. In addition, several constitutional protections have been given to public interest lawyers. In naacp v. button the Supreme Court ruled that litigation on behalf of a disadvantaged group was constitutionally protected speech and overturned Virginia's efforts to penalize NAACP lawyers. This ruling was extended by In re Primus, where the Court made clear that nonprofit groups representing protected interests were exempt from normal bans on solicitation by lawyers.

The rights granted by the Constitution usually are not self-enforcing. Without legal representation, many would remain a dead letter. Protections for criminal defendants remain mere paper promises unless the accused are represented by competent lawyers. Because of the serious consequences of a deprivation of these rights, the Constitution itself guarantees counsel. But there are many other areas in which public interest law, although not constitutionally guaranteed, is equally essential. Many efforts to curb free speech, for example, would have gone unchallenged if public interest groups like the american civil liberties union were not available to defend this interest. The guarantee of equal protection of the law might still sound completely hollow to African Americans if the subsidized services of NAACP lawyers and other public interest advocates were not available.

Public interest law spans the political spectrum. Some of the more notable liberal public interest law groups include the ACLU, the naacp legal defense and educational fund, and the Commission on Law and Social Action of the american jewish congress. Public interest law groups of a conservative persuasion include the Pacific Legal Foundation, which brings suits against governmental regulation; the Rutherford Institute, which litigates cases involving equal access for religious groups and defends nonviolent protestors in the antiabortion movement; and the Washington Legal Foundation, which pursues a grab bag of causes, including judicial review of redistricting and lawsuits by crime victims.

A major aspect of American political culture is our "constitutionalism": The belief in higher values protected by the Constitution. Often, marginal and subordinated groups have looked to higher law and constitutional values as guides and inspiration for their struggle for inclusion in the American commonwealth. Women, blacks, and other groups have looked beyond existing law and institutions to a penumbra of constitutional values that, they believed, entitled them to fuller participation in economic, social, and political life. Public interest law, as idea and institution, is a reflection of this faith in the redemptive power of law and legal institutions. To be sure, law does not always fulfill the promises Americans put in it. Public interest law is often weak and ineffective; legal solutions may not lead to real gains. But public interest lawyers have won real victories and made some difference for subordinated groups. As long as America's basic political institutions remain unchanged, public interest law will be essential: it ensures that forces of the market and status quo do not overshadow democracy and constitutional values and helps preserve constitutionalism as a real force in our political life.

DECENTRALISATION

The term "decentralization" embraces a variety of concepts which must be carefully analyzed in any particular country before determining if projects or programs should support reorganization of financial, administrative, or service delivery systems.

Different types of decentralization should be distinguished because they have different characteristics, policy implications, and conditions for success.

Decentralization is the assignment of fiscal, political, and administrative responsibilities to lower levels of government in a prevalent but controversial institutional reform.

According to L.C. Smith it refers to delegation or devolution of central state powers of policy making and decision taking to lower levels of government.

Smith sees it as reversing the concentration of administration at the single center and conferring powers on local government.

It is the transfer of authority and responsibility for public functions from the central government to subordinate or quasi-independent government organizations and/or the private sector – It is a complex multifaceted concept.

Process by which a central government formally transfers powers to actors and institutions at lower levels in a political- administrative hierarchy.

It therefore involves the transfer of power, functions, means and competencies from central government to the sub-national structures.

Purpose of Decentralization

- Failure of centralized systems to deliver efficiently,
- Decentralization has the potential to ensure a more equitable distribution of resources,
- It is part of the good governance/democratisation agenda,
- It is supposed to engender popular participation in decision-making.

Types of Decentralization

Various forms of decentralization have implications for delivery of water and sanitation services, as our experiences have indicated:

- De-concentration,
- Delegation,
- Privatization,
- Devolution.

Administrative Decentralisation

Transfer of public service delivery functions from central government to local governments, field offices of MDAs, etc.

Two main types:

- Delegation,
- Deconcentration.

Deconcentration

It refers to situations where the national government shifts some administrative power to its own ministry offices at the local level.

Delegation

It is when the national government delegates administrative authority to 'parastatal' organizations at the local or regional level.

Privatization

Transfer of economic planning, production, distribution or other economic functions from government to voluntary, private or non-governmental institutions.

Devolution

- Transfer of political power from central government to lower-tier authorities. It is the ultimate form of political decentralization.
- Full transfer of resource mobilization and allocation responsibilities from central government to an quasi-autonomous, sub-national public authority that is fully independent of the devolving authority.
- Usually culminates in the establishment and empowerment of local governments that is accountable to the local population.
- Usually involves the establishment of a legal and regulatory framework.

Devolution refers to national governments handing over administrative authority to legally recognized, geographically identifiable units of local government with their own elections.

Fiscal Decentralisation

- Financial responsibility is a core component of decentralization.
- If local governments and private organizations are to carry out decentralized functions effectively, they must have an adequate level of revenues –either raised locally or transferred from the central government– as well as the authority to make decisions about expenditures.
- The restructuring of existing systems of resource mobilization and allocation with the aim of empowering local government authorities to perform their decentralized functions.

Fiscal Decentralisation may include:

- Formulas for transferring revenue to local govts.
- Legally empowering local govts to collect and retain some taxes, fees, etc.
- Legally empowering local govts to prepare their own budgets and disburse funds.
- It is a key ingredient for successful devolution.

Fiscal decentralization can take many forms, including:

- Self-Financing or cost recovery through user charges.
- Co-financing or co-production arrangements through which the users participate in providing services and infrastructure through monetary or labor contributions.
- Expansion of local revenues through property or sales taxes, or indirect charges.
- Intergovernmental transfers that shift general revenues from taxes collected by the central government to local governments for general or specific uses.
- Authorization of municipal borrowing and the mobilization of either national or local government resources through loan guarantees.

In many developing countries local governments or administrative units possess the legal authority to impose taxes, but the tax base is so weak and the dependence on central government subsidies so ingrained that no attempt is made to exercise that authority.

Political Decentralization

Political decentralization aims to give citizens or their elected representatives more power in public decision-making.

It is often associated with pluralistic politics and representative government, but it can also support democratization by giving citizens, or their representatives, more influence in the formulation and implementation of policies.

Advocates of political decentralization assume that decisions made with greater participation will be better informed and more relevant to diverse interests in society than those made only by national political authorities.

The concept implies that the selection of representatives from local electoral jurisdictions allows citizens to know better their political representatives and allows elected officials to know better the needs and desires of their constituents.

Political decentralization often requires constitutional or statutory reforms, the development of pluralistic political parties, the strengthening of legislatures, creation of local political units, and the encouragement of effective public interest groups.

Administrative Decentralisation

Transfer of public service delivery functions from central government to local governments, field offices of MDAs, etc.

Ghana's Decentralization Policy

- Re-demarcation of administrative jurisdictions (metropolitan areas, municipalities and districts).
- Establishment of Metropolitan, Municipal and District Assemblies.
- Establishment of sub-district structures: Town/Area Councils, Unit Committees.
- Restructuring of resource allocation & resource sharing b/n central & local govts.
- E.g. District Assemblies Common Fund, land rates and minerals royalties, grants, transfers, and external credits to local governments.
- Designating MLGRD as the agency responsible for implementation of the decentralisation policy.
- Establishment of NDPC to co-ordinate decentralised development planning.
- Establishment of structures and mechanisms to enhance probity, accountability and transparency in public administration at all levels of government.

Main Components of Ghana's Decentralization Policy:

- Political decentralisation.
- Administrative Decentralisation.
- Decentralized Development Planning.
- Fiscal decentralization.

Political Decentralisation

- Re-demarcation of the country into districts.
- Establishment and empowerment of the RCCs, MMDAs & the Sub-District Structures to perform various functions.
- Establishment of the MMDAs as legislative, administrative, planning.
- Service delivery, budgeting and rating authorities.
- Sub-district structures to facilitate resource mobilization and popular participation.

Administrative Decentralisation

- Restructuring of ministerial institutions and transferring defined functions, Powers and resources to local govts.
- Integration of sectoral programmes, resources and assets into the Assembly system.
- Restructuring of 22 depts into 16, 13 and 11 depts under the Metropolitan, Municipal and District Assemblies respectively.
- Passage of a Local Govt Service Act to bring all employees of the MMDAs into the public service.

Decentralised Development Planning

- A bottom-up, integrated and participatory development planning system.
- Planning at district level, sub-district and sectoral levels coordinated by the DPCU.
- RPCUs responsible for harmonising and synchronising district devt plans based on national development policy framework and guidelines issued by NDPC.
- Development of service centres as well as rational, efficient and sustainable settlement and land use patterns.

Fiscal Decentralisation

- Meant to enhance the Assemblies' access to resources.

- Creation of the DACF, allocated based on a formula prepared by the Administrator of DACF and approved by Parliament.
- Establishment of 'MPs Common Fund'.
- Ceding of income tax payable by informal sector operators, vehicle operators, and betting, entertainment and advertising companies to the MMDAs.
- IGF sources of the MMDAs: user fees, rates (basic and property), licenses, investment incomes, loans/overdrafts, etc.
- Submission of MMDA budget to the RCCs for harmonisation, co-ordination and collation and approval of by Min. of Finance.

Benefits of Decentralization

- Improved delivery of basic services for citizens at the local level.
- Through engagement of user groups more citizens' participation in delivery and quality of service; Better administrators suited to the locality; users' monitoring of services.
- Contribution to developing the local economy Engagement of local people as service-providers; opportunities to raise revenues to delivery high quality services; contribution to the economy.
- Framework for effective local level democracy local leaders engage with marginalized groups and promote accountability, inclusion and participation, the representation of citizens.
- A robust local governance strengthening linkages between local stakeholders in pursuit of the common services and priorities with sharing of roles, responsibilities and risks.

Importance of Decentralization: Political

- Increase political stability and national unity by giving groups in different parts of the country the ability to participate more directly in decision making.
- Increases their local commitment to maintaining the political system.
- National government policies can be effectively brought down to the local level, especially the rural areas through which they will understand government plans and support it.
- It ensures greater representation of various political, religious, ethnic and tribal groups in development decision-making that will lead to greater equity in the allocation of government resources.
- It serves as training ground for political applicants (MPs).

Economic

- The planning of development taking into cognizance local needs.

- Mobilization of local resources for development programmes, especially labor therefore reduces cost.
- The people are motivated to work harder.
- Development of local capabilities to take over functions initially performed by central government.
- It reduces cost and ensures efficiency as the economy and government grows, this leads to increases in the number of public goods and services that can be produced at lower cost.

Social

- It brings the local people together as they plan and implement programmes for their development.
- The opportunity of taking part in national decision-making process offers them recognition.
- Pride in steering their interest in the work which encourages them to put in their best.

Administrative

- Officials are able to aggregate and tailor development plans to the needs of the people on local basis throughout the country.
- The reassignment of government officials to local levels, increases their sensitivity to local needs.
- Development of greater administrative capability among local governments officers who have the opportunity to develop their managerial and technical skills.
- It provides a structure through which the activities of training central government ministries, departments or agencies involved in development could be co- coordinated more effectively.
- It ensures that flexible and creative administrative innovations can easily be tested and new policies experienced.

Challenges: Centralizing Elements

- All by-laws are approved by the Minister of LGRD.
- The President has the power to dissolve defaulting or non-performing Das without consulting the electorate.
- The minister of LGRD has power to issue guidelines, in respect of fees to be charged by the DAs for the service and facilities provided, licenses and permits issued/rates levied.
- According to Section 88 of the Local Government Act, Act 462, the DAs require central government guarantee to raise loans in excess of 25,000 cedis.

- As a result the effectiveness of the DAs in discharging their functions as the highest political authority in the district are undermined, and their responsibilities have been restricted to local issues only.
- Instead of minimizing central government control over the local governments, DACF has been used as a tool to increased the control of centre over DAs' functions.
- The decisions of the DACF have been usurped by the central government so that the DAs remain talking shops without finance to implement their decisions.
- For instance, deductions at source without the knowledge of the Das.
- Continued central control has prevented the DACF being an effective instrument of decentralization and democratization.
- The introduction of the DACF meant to serve as an incentive to mobilize resources locally has rather become as source for relegating on its local resource mobilization efforts.
- DACF is also suffering from irregularity in disbursement of funds, lack of transparency and lack of discretion afforded to district authority over the allocation of funds.

Fiscal Decentralization

Composite budgeting has not been implemented because of the unwillingness of the Ministry of Finance.

In addition, centralized laws on fiscal policies of Ghana such as the Financial Administration Decree (FAD), 1979 and Financial Administration Regulation (FAR) Financial Memorandum of Local and Urban Councils, 1961 and even the Local Government Act do not promote a segregation of DA budget from that of the central government.

Personnel

DAs are confronted with lack of technical and competent personnel.

While devolution of authority imposes increasing demands for services at the local level and requires well-trained local functionaries, the economic conditions of Ghana, administrative and structural reforms suggest less government spending on human resources and fewer government agents.

Lack of autonomy to recruit and fire personnel without the interference of the ministry is not only frustrating but an impediment to effective decentralized local governance.

Other Challenges

- Inadequacy of fiscal, and human resources over interference of central government.
- Lack of a political process that promotes accountability, responsiveness and representation at the local government level.
- Unwillingness of the leadership of decentralized departments and agencies to cede power to the local government leadership and refusing full integration.
- Weak ability of local authority to initiate and implement policies and programs.

ADVOCACY EVALUATION

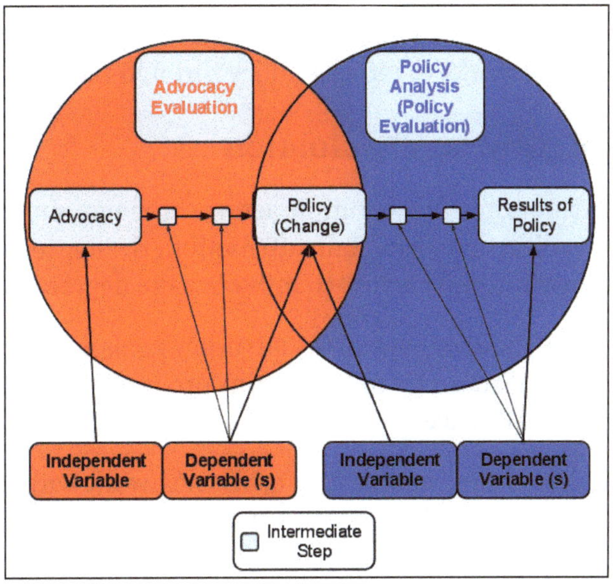

Advocacy evaluation.

Advocacy evaluation, also called public policy advocacy design, monitoring, and evaluation, evaluates the progress or outcomes of advocacy, such as changes in public policy. This is different from policy analysis, which generally looks at the results of the policy, or mainstream program evaluation, which assesses whether programs or direct services have been successful. Advocacy strives to influence a program or policy either directly or indirectly; therefore, the influence is being evaluated, rather than the results of that influence. Advocacy evaluators seek to understand the extent to which advocacy efforts have contributed to the advancement of a goal or policy. They do this in order to learn what works, what does not, and what works better in order to achieve advocacy goals and improve future efforts.

Goals of Advocacy (Dependent Variables)

In order to evaluate something, one must know the goals of the program/activity, in this case - advocacy efforts. Policy advocacy evaluation focuses on the contribution towards achieving policy, and not on the results of that policy. Policy advocacy evaluators look at these dependent variables (many of which interrelate significantly with movement in the policy cycle):

Intermediate Goal Examples:

- Increased awareness of constituents about the need for policy (Problem Identification - Agenda Setting).
- Change in rate of key-words use by politicians, sometimes starting from 0 (Problem Identification - Agenda Setting).
- Increase in ratio of policy being implemented according to the adopted legislation (Adoption - Implementation).
- Developed capacity of advocacy actor or network of actors to conduct advocacy efforts.

Ultimate Goals:

- Policy change itself in the desired direction (of the policy cycle). This is the highest level intermediate outcome, and as an inherent best practice, is the goal of most policy advocacy efforts. Policy Advocacy works to move a policy through the policy cycle.

Distinct Challenges of Advocacy Evaluation

- Contribution vs. attribution: Since multiple actors campaign simultaneously for and against any given policy, it is difficult to ascertain attribution. Evaluating contributions is preferred in this case as it allows multiple actors to influence the degree of success.
- Long term nature of advocacy: Since many advocacy goals are long term, measuring impact can be a challenge. Instead, outcomes, interim progress, and intermediary goals are the preferred measures of influence.
- Shifting strategies: Since the context that advocates work within is ever-changing, advocates adapt their strategies, which creates a difficult environment in which to monitor progress.
- Complexity and theories of change: Logic models and theories of change for advocacy campaigns are inherently complex; for example: protests+lobbying+media campaigns - contribution to policy change. These kinds of theories of change have so many layers, nuances, and uncontrollable factors to them that intra and inter organizational agreement is difficult, making strategic planning, and evaluation all the more challenging.

Typology of Policy Advocacy

Direct Advocacy (Directly trying to influence policy makers):

- Lobbying (also known as direct lobbying) is the act of attempting to influence decisions made by government officials, most often legislators or members of regulatory agencies. Various people or groups, from private-sector individuals or corporations, fellow legislators or government officials, or advocacy groups use lobbying.

Indirect Advocacy (Indirectly influencing policymakers by getting their constituents to advocate):

- Grassroots lobbying (also known as indirect lobbying) is a form of lobbying that focuses on raising awareness of a particular cause at the local level, with the intention of reaching the legislature and making a difference in the decision-making process. Grassroots lobbying is an approach that separates itself from direct lobbying through the act of asking the public to contact legislators and government officials concerning the issue at hand, as opposed to conveying the message to the legislators directly.
- Activism consists of intentional efforts by citizens or citizen groups, towards policymakers, to promote or prevent social, political, economic, or environmental change. Activism can take a wide range of forms including, from writing letters to newspapers or politicians, political campaigning, rallies, street marches, strikes, sit-ins, and hunger strikes.

- Astroturfing supports political, organizational, or corporate agendas, and is designed to give the appearance of a "grassroots" movement. The goal of such campaigns is to disguise the efforts of a political and/or commercial entity as an independent public reaction to some political entity—a politician, political group, product, service, or event.

PUBLIC SERVICE

Public service is a service which is provided by government to people living within its jurisdiction, either directly (through the public sector) or by financing provision of services. The term is associated with a social consensus (usually expressed through democratic elections) that certain services should be available to all, regardless of income, physical ability or mental acuity. Even where public services are neither publicly provided nor publicly financed, for social and political reasons they are usually subject to regulation going beyond that applying to most economic sectors. Public policy when made in the public's interest and motivations can provide public services. Public service is also a course that can be studied at a college or university. Examples of public services are the fire brigade, police, air force, and paramedics.

Sectors

Public services are associated with fundamental human rights (such as the right to water). The Volunteer Fire Dept. and Ambulance Corps. are institutions with the mission of servicing the community. A service is helping others with a specific need or want. Here, service ranges from a doctor curing an illness, to a repair person, to a food pantry.

In modern developed countries, the term "public services" (or "services of general interest") often includes:

- Courts,
- Electricity,
- Education,
- Emergency services,
- Environmental protection,
- Health care,
- Military,
- Public transportation,
- Public buildings,
- Social services,
- Telecommunications,
- Urban planning,

- Transportation infrastructure,
- Waste management,
- Water supply network.

Characteristics of Public Services

A public service may sometimes have the characteristics of a public good (being non-rivalrous and non-excludable), but most are services which may (according to prevailing social norms) be under-provided by the market. In most cases public services are services, i.e. they do not involve manufacturing of goods. They may be provided by local or national monopolies, especially in sectors which are natural monopolies.

They may involve outputs that are hard to attribute to specific individual effort or hard to measure in terms of key characteristics such as quality. They often require high levels of training and education. They may attract people with a public service ethos who wish to give something to the wider public or community through their work.

Nationalization and Privatization

A group of Chilean 'Damas de Rojo', volunteers on their local hospital.

Nationalization

Nationalization took off following the World Wars of the first half of the twentieth century. In parts of Europe, central planning was implemented in the belief that it would make production more efficient. Many public services, especially electricity, gas and public transport are products of this era. Following the Second World War, many countries also began to implement universal health care and expanded education under the funding and guidance of the state.

Privatization

There are several ways to privatize public services. A free-market corporation may be established and sold to private investors, relinquishing government control altogether. Thus it becomes a private (not public) service. Another option, used in the Nordic countries, is to establish a corporation, but keep ownership or voting power essentially in the hands of the government. For example, the Finnish state owned 49% of Kemira until 2007, the rest being owned by private investors. A 49% share did not make it a "government enterprise", but it meant that all other investors together would have to oppose the state's opinion in order to overturn the state's decisions in the shareholder's meeting. Regulated corporation can also acquire permits on the agreement that they fulfill certain public service duties. When a private corporation runs a natural monopoly, then the corporation is typically heavily regulated, to prevent abuse of monopoly power. Lastly, the government can buy the service on the free market. In many countries, medication is provided in this manner: the government reimburses part of the price of the medication. Also, bus traffic, electricity, healthcare and waste management are privatized in this way. One recent innovation, used in the UK increasingly as well as Australia and Canada is public-private partnerships. This involves giving a long lease to private consortia in return for partly funding infrastructure.

CIVIL SERVICE

Civil service refers to the body of government officials who are employed in civil occupations that are neither political nor judicial. In most countries the term refers to employees selected and promoted on the basis of a merit and seniority system, which may include examinations.

Appointment

In earlier times, when civil servants were part of the king's household, they were literally the monarch's personal servants. As the powers of monarchs and princes declined and as, in some countries, their sovereignty was denied them, appointment became a matter of personal choice by ministers and heads of departments. The influence senior civil servants may wield over policy and the need for them to work in close harmony with ministers induce all governments to insist on complete freedom of choice in appointments, even when, as in Great Britain, the freedom is rarely invoked. In some countries, notably the United States, senior advisers usually are replaced whenever a new administration takes office.

In Europe in the 19th century, appointment and promotion frequently depended on personal or political favour, but tenure was common in the lower and middle ranks once an appointment had been made.

Dependency on a superior's favour led civil servants to ally themselves with liberal public opinion, which was critical of the waste and corruption involved in political patronage. Pressure for reform led to official formulations of basic qualifications for different posts; appointments and promotions boards were established within each department to prevent or obstruct overt political favouritism and nepotism; and salary scales were introduced for different grades to provide a civil servant with increments for good service while still holding the same post. In many countries civil service commissions were set up to ensure impartiality in selection procedures and to lay down broad principles for personnel management in the civil service. Recruitment in many European countries corresponded to the national educational systems: the highest class of civil servants entered service after graduation from a university, the executive class after full completion of secondary school, the clerical class after the intermediate school examination. The manual workers in the service were mainly recruited from persons of mature age who had left school after primary education or, in such countries as France and Germany, from military veterans. As public administration became more complex in the 20th century, specialized categories of civil servants were created to bring into the service doctors, scientists, architects, naval constructors, statisticians, lawyers, and so on. In several countries the establishment of these special classes caused some difficulties because their salary scales had to be linked with those of competing professional groups outside the service. The distinction between foreign service and home service personnel has sometimes caused difficulty because of inadequate liaison between overseas representatives and the makers of foreign policy at home. In the United States, the Rogers Act of 1924 unified the overseas service itself, but the civil servants of the State Department in Washington, D.C., continued to be regarded as part of the federal civil service.

The posts that fall under the rules of the U.S. merit system are not grouped into a small number of general classes but have individual job specifications and entry qualifications. Although designed to select entrants with special knowledge or skills for individual posts, this system has been criticized for failing to make the best use of the talent available to the government. In 1978 the Senior Executive Service was created to achieve more effective promotion and deployment.

All countries base appointments on some kind of competition. In some countries great emphasis is placed on formal written examinations supplemented by interviews. Such is the situation in France, where entry into the higher civil service is channeled through specialist schools, or grandes écoles, of which the École Nationale d'Administration and the École Polytechnique are the most important. In Great Britain, traditionally one of the great advocates of entry by formal examination, the Civil Service Commission relies more on informal tests and a series of interviews and observations and tends to measure the candidate's intellectual competence by the quality of his university degree. The conventional written examination is dispensed with also in such European countries as Finland, Switzerland, the Netherlands, and Portugal, as well as the German Länder, or states. In the Länder the qualifications and references of all candidates are compared, whereupon the most eligible are interviewed by a departmental board. Candidates are expected to have completed a lengthy program of academic work for professional qualification and a period of subsequent training in a variety of public institutions under official supervision. If successful in their interviews, candidates are recommended to the minister, who makes appointments to higher grade posts, or to the heads of department, who handle the middle and lower categories. On the face of it, this method offers fewer guarantees of impartiality than does the formal written examination, but a civil service career is less attractive now than formerly and the civil service has to compete, usually at lower salaries, with business and the professions for the best available talent. In Sweden a constitutional provision requires that nearly all public documents (including the proceedings of authorities that make appointments) be open for public inspection, thus providing a check upon corruption or favouritism.

Most federal and culturally diverse countries try to ensure an equitable distribution of posts among their constituent elements. In Switzerland the federal authorities try to maintain a balance of posts not only between the cantons but also between the political parties, religions, and languages. The federal civil service in Germany draws on the public service officers in the Länder, and some degree of proportional representation is attempted. There was considerable pressure in Canada in the 1970s to ensure a more equitable distribution of federal civil service posts between the English- and French-speaking populations. It is also clear that many African states are compelled to recognize regional and tribal origins in their appointments to the civil service.

Conditions of Service

The forerunners of civil servants, being members of the royal household, had duties but no rights. The first attempts to formalize methods of appointment and conditions of service were among the administrative innovations introduced in Prussia in the 18th century. Elsewhere attempts were frustrated by political and public objections. Increased formal regulation of conditions of service came about when civil servants organized themselves into professional groups, sometimes barely distinguishable from trade unions. The fact that civil servants are agents of the public power, providing services on which law, order, and public health depend, has raised the question whether they should be permitted to strike; if they cannot lawfully strike, they are deprived of the main weapon in pressing for improvements in their conditions of service. Thus, there have developed special arrangements for reviewing conditions of service periodically and for settling contentious issues. In particular, it has been necessary to have a properly recognized system for regulating conduct and discipline. In the United Kingdom, traditional standards are supplemented or revised to accord with recommendations from periodic commissions of enquiry, which pay special attention to official conduct in relation to political activities and business dealings. In France and Germany these codes of conduct have been based mainly upon the rules of administrative law and the jurisprudence of administrative courts, although certain civil service rights and duties are specified in constitutional law. In other countries, particularly in the United States and India, conduct and discipline are regulated by administrative rules and codes promulgated by executive order after discussion and enquiry.

The standards placed upon a civil servant's conduct are partly those to be expected of any loyal, competent, and obedient employee and partly those enjoined upon a public employee. Ideally, the civil servant should be above any suspicion of partiality and should not let personal sympathies, loyalties, or interests affect the performance of duties; for example, a civil servant is obliged to be circumspect in private financial dealings. As a general rule, a civil servant is not allowed to engage directly or indirectly in any trade or business and may engage in social or charitable organizations only if these have no connection with official duties. There are always strict limits on a civil servant's right to lend or borrow money, and they are prohibited from accepting gifts.

Civil Servants and Politics

There are different attitudes about the extent to which civil servants may engage in political activities. One view is that a civil servant has the same constitutional rights as other citizens and that it is therefore unconstitutional to attempt to limit those rights other than by the common law. The opposing view is that, since civil servants are engaged in the unique function of national government, their integrity and loyalty to their political masters might be affected by active participation in political affairs, and public confidence in their impartiality could be shaken. Broadly speaking, those countries that traditionally expect civil servants to behave with complete impartiality and to conform to ministerial policy with energy and good will, whether they agree with the policy or not, expect all civil servants to behave with circumspection in political affairs. The United Kingdom has a total ban on its senior civil servants' engaging in any form of political activity. The prohibition becomes progressively less strict, however, for the medium and lower grades of the service.

Another group of countries, including France and Germany, have deemed policy and administration to be so intimately connected that all top posts are filled at the discretion of the government of the day; thus, civil servants are allowed greater scope in political activities. They are nevertheless expected to act with greater discretion and public decorum than private citizens, and an excess of power or an abuse of office for political purposes renders a civil servant instantly liable both to statutory regulations and to severe internal disciplinary proceedings.

Civil Servants and Unions

Traditionally, governments have been hostile toward civil service unions, and in the past repressive laws made strike action unlawful. Strikes nevertheless occurred, and governments eventually adopted an attitude of open encouragement toward trade unionism. Most governments accept, in theory at least, that the state should be a model employer. It follows that, if the state genuinely pursues a policy of discussion and negotiation with civil servants and attempts properly to fulfill agreements with them, it should in return be freed from the threat of strike action. Mindful that the withdrawal of civil servants from some public services would lead to chaos, many governments have found it prudent to establish permanent channels for negotiating such matters as salaries and discipline. Organizations representing the staff and a management side of senior officials representing the state mirror the employer-employee relationship of private industry, although a higher percentage of public- than private-sector employees are members of unions. The United Kingdom was the first country to establish negotiating machinery for civil servants. Following a report in 1917, organizations known as Whitley Councils were set up, consisting of equal numbers of medium and lower staffs on the one hand and directing and supervisory staffs on the other. These councils operate within the ministries, and a National Whitley Council performs central advisory functions for the government. They have no powers of decision, however, only of recommendation, because governments are never prepared to surrender their ultimate responsibility for determining the public interest. The councils have done a good deal to provide a sense of common purpose and joint responsibility within the civil service as a whole, although pay restraints from the early 1970s generated great friction between civil service unions and government.

In France each department has a comparable consultative body, but its work is broader in scope in that it can scrutinize recruitment, personnel records, promotions, and disciplinary procedures. There is also a national council, presided over by the prime minister or a specially nominated minister for civil service affairs, which is concerned with general personnel policy, conditions of service, and coordination of departmental committees.

Until after World War II, the commonly accepted view in the United States was that expressed by Pres. Calvin Coolidge: "There is no right to strike against the public safety by anybody, anywhere, at any time." Although federal employees are still forbidden to strike, a rule illustrated by the dismissal of striking air traffic controllers in 1981, consultation has increased, and in many federal departments appeals committees comprising departmental heads and one or more members of the Merit Systems Protection Board may now hear appeals from civil servants against decisions adversely affecting their careers. These committees are also consulted on general matters of departmental interest, such as job classifications, pension schemes, promotion policies, and office procedures.

Patterns of Control

The expansion of public services, as well as the development of permanent civil service career structures, raised fears that civil services were becoming autonomous powers in their own right, no longer subject to the traditional forms of control. This view is associated with the sociologists Max Weber, who criticized the bureaucracy of imperial Germany, and Robert Michels, who formulated the "iron law of oligarchy." Michels's law suggested that every organization with a permanent staff produces an oligarchy running the organization according to the interests and values of the bureaucratic group. In addition, the growing complexity of modern government has greatly augmented the informal power of senior civil servants who act as advisers to ministers. This is particularly the case in countries (usually the more democratic ones) where ministries frequently change hands.

In the 19th century civil services were normally restricted to maintaining law and order and minor economic regulations such as those concerning weights and measures and factory laws. The subordination of civil servants to their political masters and their political masters' responsibility to the courts and legislatures seemed to provide an adequate safeguard against arbitrary administrative actions. But in some countries, notably Germany, France, and Austria, civil services became endowed with much greater authority, operating as part of the police power. This caused concern because civil servants were exempt from normal legal processes when performing their official functions. In response, special administrative courts were set up to which private citizens or corporations could appeal against administrative acts. Jurisdiction was limited, however, and redress was frequently slow. The courts themselves remained specialized institutions of the executive rather than normal parts of the judiciary.

Sweden provided a marked contrast. Before the constitution of 1809 the executive power had been absolute. Afterward, not only did it become subject to control by the legislature, but this control also was reinforced by the creation of a special post of ombudsman.

World War I brought increased governmental activity almost everywhere. The area in which administrative discretion could be exercised grew; civil servants became as much adjudicators as administrators, and their influence upon economic life increased. By World War II the state had become, even in many conservative countries, an economic regulator, an industrial producer of overwhelming importance, and a conciliator between competing interests. In all of these matters civil servants were the effective agents of the state.

Responses to Civil Service Power

In the United States, Congress created an institution to counter the threatened increase in civil service power. As far back as the late 19th century Congress, when legislating for new areas of government, assigned powers to agencies or commissions, specifying their powers, competence, and composition and freeing them from direct presidential control. In this way large areas of government escaped the control of the executive branch of government, including the federal civil service. These independent regulatory agencies have covered major economic fields and have included the Interstate Commerce Commission, the Federal Communications Commission, the Tennessee Valley Authority, and the Nuclear Regulatory Commission. This policy has laid Congress open to the charge that it has created a headless fourth branch of government, but it has successfully prevented the emergence of a monolithic federal civil service.

To counter charges that the U.S. civil service was encroaching on the powers of the judiciary, the Administrative Procedure Act of 1946 laid down detailed provisions to safeguard citizens' rights where the administration had powers of adjudication. These rights included the right to ample previous notice of proceedings, the right to submit evidence, the right to have independent hearing officers (to the exclusion of investigating or prosecuting officers), and the right to a decision based solely on testimony and papers actually entered in the proceedings.

Other democratic countries have been concerned about the growing powers of the civil service and about whether traditional forms of judicial and ministerial control are adequate. Many European countries have modeled their instruments of administrative jurisdiction and jurisprudence on the French Conseil d'État. In the United Kingdom the creation of a special administrative jurisdiction of this kind has been opposed by both parliamentary and judicial opinion, but it was because of mounting criticism of civil service immunity from detailed control that Parliament created the special office of parliamentary commissioner, or ombudsman. Public access to the office is by way of a member of Parliament, and the commissioner is excluded from inquiring into matters of policy, local government authorities, or lower judicial bodies.

Civil Servants and Communism

Special problems of control arose in communist countries, where the main preoccupation of the regime, which was under the direct control of the Communist Party, had been to ensure the civil service's continual loyalty. Impartiality and objectivity in the administrative machine's dealings with the public were not of such high priority as in pluralist societies. A body of administrative procedure was built up, but this was always subordinated to the directives of the party leadership. Communist countries also had to establish new ways of judging performance, since the state monopoly of political power and means of production ensured that traditional incentives and yardsticks could not be applied.

Yet in their own way, communist countries had elaborate controls. In the Soviet Union all ministries had a special section staffed by, and responsible to, operatives from the Ministry of Internal Affairs. This section provided security control over the ordinary civil servants, and its personnel were not part of that ministry's official structure. The Communist Party maintained further control through the party apparatus, and it closely supervised senior appointments.

Communist planning, financial, and personnel controls of a technical kind resembled those in democratic countries, but in the Soviet Union there were two additional special supervisory agencies. The Commission of State Control was responsible for vigilance over state property and administration. Its departments paralleled the different branches of state administration and maintained audits of their work. Its officers had the right of access to all administrative records and could issue directives to other institutions. They had powers to prosecute civil servants for criminal offenses, and they could apply a formidable range of disciplinary measures to civil servants, either by direct action or through the responsible minister.

The second agency of control arose because of the difficulty of reconciling disputes between production units and their controlling ministries in an economy that lacked the traditional forms of market discipline and could not rely upon an enforceable law of contract. A special system of compulsory arbitration operated through the State Arbitration Tribunal (known as Gosarbitrazh) under the Council of Ministers and through arbitration tribunals responsible to the councils of ministers in each of the republics. It settled all disputes concerning contracts, quality of goods, and other property disputes between various state enterprises. The system was staffed by civil servants charged with enforcing "contractual and plan discipline," but it was supported by technical experts qualified in economic and industrial matters.

International Civil Service

The elements of an international civil service first appeared in the Universal Postal Union. Some four and a half decades later the League of Nations and the International Labour Organization (ILO) were founded. They required a staff of almost 600 experts and subordinate personnel, which took the form of a true international civil service. It drew mainly on British, French, and Swiss personnel, but more than 40 states contributed members in order to spread recruitment as widely as possible. There were no formal methods of selection for the higher personnel; the secretary-general of the League used personal contacts. The staff fell into three divisions: administrative, supervisory and clerical, and custodial. The history of the League shows that, at any rate as far as a secretariat was concerned, a broad measure of international loyalty could be achieved. The staff of the ILO was maintained after the League's disbandment in 1946.

Until World War II the League of Nations was the only major international organization of its kind. Since then, international organizations have multiplied, and compared with most of them the League had a small staff. The postwar organizations include the United Nations, the Organization of American States, the European Community (EC; ultimately succeeded by the European Union [EU]), and the Organisation for Economic Co-operation and Development. By the mid-1980s there were nearly 20,000 smaller bodies, ranging from the Nordic Council to small research institutes.

International organizations have evolved into two general types. In the first—an example of which is the EU—a genuinely supranational civil service exists; its members have a career structure within the organization and can identify with it. In the second (the UN, for instance), officials undertake a particular job for a limited period and seldom develop a career within the organization. In the EU the civil service is divided into several grades, recruitment to the service generally being through competitive examination. After recruitment a period of training follows. Each agency within the UN operates its own recruitment system. By far the majority of senior appointees assigned to the UN at any one time have served there for less than 15 years.

In both types of international organization, there is a danger that officials will promote the interests of their own country to the detriment of internationalism. In the UN a quota system operates by which each country is allocated a number of appointments in proportion to its UN budget contribution. As a result, some national governments are in a strong position to influence recruitment. In contrast, the statutes governing the EU's civil service forbid quotas, but an unofficial system has developed whereby a relatively high proportion of senior officials are from the more populous states. Such practices risk sacrificing meritocracy to nationalism.

Some countries do expect their nationals working at the UN to promote national interests. But the quota system—and this is one of the arguments for it—leads to administrators from at least the more prosperous countries competing with fellow nationals rather than with colleagues from other countries. Moreover, it is unlikely that decisions, whether biased or not, will be made in the bureaucracy alone. And since officials' national origins are no secret, partiality is fairly difficult to conceal.

BUREAUCRACY

Bureaucracy is specific form of organization defined by complexity, division of labour, permanence, professional management, hierarchical coordination and control, strict chain of command, and legal authority. It is distinguished from informal and collegial organizations. In its ideal form, bureaucracy is impersonal and rational and based on rules rather than ties of kinship, friendship, or patrimonial or charismatic authority. Bureaucratic organization can be found in both public and private institutions.

Characteristics and Paradoxes of Bureaucracy

The foremost theorist of bureaucracy is the German sociologist Max Weber, who described the ideal characteristics of bureaucracies and offered an explanation for the historical emergence of bureaucratic institutions. According to Weber, the defining features of bureaucracy sharply distinguish it from other types of organization based on nonlegal forms of authority. Weber observed that the advantage of bureaucracy was that it was the most technically proficient form of organization, possessing specialized expertise, certainty, continuity, and unity. Bureaucracy's emergence as a preferred form of organization occurred with the rise of a money-based economy (which ultimately resulted in the development of capitalism) and the attendant need to ensure impersonal, rational-legal transactions. Instrumental organizations (e.g., public-stock business firms) soon arose because their bureaucratic organization equipped them to handle the various demands of capitalist production more efficiently than small-scale producers.

Contemporary stereotypes of bureaucracy tend to portray it as unresponsive, lethargic, undemocratic, and incompetent. Weber's theory of bureaucracy, however, emphasizes not only its comparative technical and proficiency advantages but also attributes its dominance as a form of organization to the diminution of caste systems (such as feudalism) and other forms of inequitable social relations based upon a person's status. In the pure form of bureaucratic organization universalized rules and procedures would dominate, rendering personal status or connections irrelevant. In this form, bureaucracy is the epitome of universalized standards under which similar cases are treated similarly as codified by law and rules, and under which the individual tastes and discretion of the administrator are constrained by due process rules. Despite the widespread derogatory stereotypes of bureaucracy, a system of government grounded in law requires bureaucracy to function.

Nevertheless, the words bureaucracy and bureaucrat are typically thought of and used pejoratively. They convey images of red tape, excessive rules and regulations, unimaginativeness, a lack of individual discretion, central control, and an absence of accountability. Far from being conceived as proficient, popular contemporary portrayals often paint bureaucracies as inefficient and lacking in adaptability. Because the characteristics that define the organizational advantages of bureaucracy also contain within them the possibilities of organizational dysfunction, both the flattering and unflattering depictions of bureaucracy can be accurate. Thus, the characteristics that make bureaucracies proficient paradoxically also may produce organizational pathologies.

Jurisdictional Competency

Jurisdictional competency is a key element of bureaucratic organization, which is broken into units with defined responsibilities. Fundamentally, jurisdictional competency refers to bureaucratic specialization, with all elements of a bureaucracy possessing a defined role. The responsibilities of individuals broaden with movement upward through an organizational hierarchy. The organizational division of labour enables units and individuals within an organization to master details and skills and to turn the novel into the routine. Although the division of labour is highly efficient, it can lead to a number of harmful organizational pathologies; for example, units or individuals may be unable to identify and respond adequately to problems outside their competency and may approach all problems and priorities exclusively from the purview of a unit's specific capabilities. This feature of bureaucracy also can lead organizational units to shirk responsibility by allowing them to define a problem as belonging to some other unit and thereby leave the issue unattended. Alternatively, every unit within an organization is apt to put a face on a problem congenial mainly to its own interests, skills, and technologies.

Command and Control

Bureaucracies have clear lines of command and control. Bureaucratic authority is organized hierarchically, with responsibility taken at the top and delegated with decreasing discretion below. Because of the risk of organizational parochialism produced by limited and specific jurisdictional competencies, the capacity to coordinate and control the multiplicity of units is essential. Authority is the glue that holds together diversity and prevents units from exercising unchecked discretion. Yet, few features of bureaucratic life have received so much adverse attention as the role of hierarchical authority as a means for achieving organizational command and control. Popular criticisms emphasize that hierarchical organization strangles creative impulses and injects hyper-cautious modes of behaviour based on expectations of what superiors may desire. Command and control, which are necessary to coordinate the disparate elements of bureaucratic organization, provide for increasing responsibility upward, delegation, and decreasing discretion downward.

Continuity

Continuity is another key element of bureaucratic organization. Rational-legal authority necessitates uniform rules and procedures for written documents and official behaviour. A bureaucracy's files (i.e., its past records) provide it with organizational memory, thereby enabling it to follow precedent and standard operating procedures. The ability to utilize standard operating procedures makes organizations more efficient by decreasing the costs attached to any given transaction. Organizational files record procedures, antecedent behaviour, and personnel records. They also allow an organization to be continuous and, thus, independent of any specific leadership. On the whole, continuity is vital to an organization's capacity to retain its identity and even its culture. Without its records, it would be impossible to maintain transactions grounded in legality. Yet continuity also has a dysfunctional side, leading organizations to behave predictably and conservatively or, worse perhaps, merely reflexively. Continuity also may lead a bureaucracy to repeat regularly activities that may be inaccurate and whose inaccuracies thereby cumulate.

Professionalization

Professionalization of management, another basic element of bureaucracy, requires a full-time corps of officials whose attention is devoted exclusively to its managerial responsibilities. In government, professionalization is vested in the corps of civil servants whose positions have generally been obtained through the passage of tests based upon merit. The civil service is sometimes considered a permanent government, distinct from the transient politicians who serve only for a limited time and at the pleasure of the electorate in democratic political systems.

In businesses and in other nongovernmental bureaucratic organizations, there is also a professional cadre of managers. Professionalization increases expertise and continuity within the organization. Even when organizations are temporarily leaderless or experience turmoil in their top leadership positions, the professional cadre helps to maintain an organizational equilibrium. The virtues of professionalization are clear; without a professional corps, organizations would suffer from crises induced by incompetency. Professionalization thus contributes to the superior technical proficiency that Weber claimed was the hallmark of bureaucratic organization.

Despite its virtues, professionalization also carries potential risks. Often the professional corps of managerial experts itself becomes a covert source of power because it has superior knowledge compared to those who are its nominal but temporary superiors. By virtue of greater experience, mastery of detail, and organizational and substantive knowledge, professional bureaucrats may exercise strong influence over decisions made by their leaders. The existence of powerful bureaucrats raises issues of accountability and responsibility, particularly in democratic systems; bureaucrats are supposedly the agents of their leaders, but their superior knowledge of detail can place them in a position of indispensability. In addition, although a permanent corps of officials brings expertise and mastery of detail to decision making, it also deepens the innate conservatism of a bureaucracy. The permanent corps is usually skeptical of novelty because the essence of bureaucratic organization is to turn past novelties into present routines. Professional bureaucrats, be they in the civil or private sector, also tend to favour the organizational status quo because their investments (e.g., training and status) are tied to it. Consequently, the more professionalized the cadre becomes, the more likely it is to resist the intrusion of external forces.

Rules

Rules are the lifeblood of bureaucratic organization, providing a rational and continuous basis for procedures and operations. An organization's files provide the inventory of accumulated rules.

Bureaucratic decisions and—above all—procedures are grounded in codified rules and precedents. Although most people dislike rules that inhibit them, the existence of rules is characteristic of legal-rational authority, ensuring that decisions are not arbitrary, that standardized procedures are not readily circumvented, and that order is maintained. Rules are the essence of bureaucracy but are also the bane of leaders who want to get things done their way instantly.

Rules restrain arbitrary behaviour, but they also can provide formidable roadblocks to achievement. The accumulation of rules sometimes leads to the development of inconsistencies, and the procedures required to change any element of the status quo may become extraordinarily onerous as a result of the rule-driven character of bureaucracy. One perspective holds that the strict adherence to rules restricts the ability of a bureaucracy to adapt to new circumstances. By contrast, markets, which can operate with very few rules, force rapid adaptation to changing circumstances. Yet, most major business organizations are arranged in bureaucratic form because hierarchy and delegated responsibility reduce the transaction costs of making decisions.

Thus, the most basic elements of pure bureaucratic organization are its emphasis on procedural regularity, a hierarchical system of accountability and responsibility, specialization of function, continuity, a legal-rational basis, and fundamental conservatism. The emergence of capitalism and the emphasis on standard currency transactions over and above barter systems created the need for bureaucratic forms of organization in both the private and public sectors. However, the critical elements of the bureaucratic form of organization also can conflict with one another and are often at the base of criticisms that regard bureaucracies as dysfunctional. In sum, what makes bureaucracy work also may work against it.

Bureaucracy and the State

All forms of governance require administration, but only within the past few centuries has the bureaucratic form become relatively common. Although Weber observed bureaucratic forms of administration in ancient Egypt, during the later stages of the Roman Empire, in the Roman Catholic Church, and in imperial China, the rise of the modern nation-state was accompanied by a commensurate elevation in the status of its administration, the bureaucratization of the administration, and the indispensability of its permanent officialdom. The bureaucracy, in service to the crown, was the manifestation of the state. Building the state essentially was identified with the increasing proficiency of its bureaucratic apparatus and the status of its permanent officials.

The development of public bureaucracy generally accompanied the capacity of a state to extend its reach and to unite its territories under a single sovereignty. The establishment of a full-time administrative cadre was a sign of a government's administrative unity and its capacity to implement its writ. The bureaucratization of the state, odd as it may initially seem, typically provided the basis for its democratization because it eliminated feudal, plutocratic, and patrimonial bases of administration. Some states, typically those that experienced a struggle to break the power base of a provincial aristocracy, developed a strong professional bureaucracy to serve the crown and unify the state. During the reign of Louis XIV, France established a strong professional corps of officials responsible for public works, extracting revenues, and otherwise supporting the ambitions of the crown. The term bureaucracy was coined (as bureaucratie) in the mid-18th century by French philosophe Vincent de Gournay, derived from the French bureau, meaning writing desk, and -cratie, meaning government. In the 19th century the Meiji Restoration in Japan, motivated by powerful modernizing ambitions, centralized the state, weakened the aristocracy, and created a powerful bureaucracy. By contrast, Britain's more powerful aristocracy continued to wield amateur administrative functions until well into the 19th century, when a professionalized civil service eventually emerged. In the United States a professional civil service was not created at the federal level until 1883, and in many of its states and localities not until much later. The actual realization of a modern bureaucracy at the federal level in the United States was a patchwork, reflecting responses to specific problems and its complicated system of political authority.

Traditionally, governments have reformed their administrative operations in response to evident failures (e.g. the inability to deal with crises or to function effectively in warfare) and the need to create universal systems of benefits (e.g. pensions, health care, and education), both of which require revenue extraction by an efficient institution. Until the end of the 20th century, administrative reforms generally strengthened the meritocratic and universalistic bases of administrative organization to guard against the malignant influences of corruption, a lack of accountability, and patronage. However, by the 1980s reform efforts in established democracies gained momentum, emphasizing decentralization and market-based decision making and, in some instances, even the replacement of full-time civil servants with managers on contract. In order to increase flexibility and adaptability and to make the public sphere leaner and performance-oriented, the debureaucratization of the state's administrative apparatus became fashionable, if not comprehensively applied. These reforms often fall under the rubric of what is called New Public Management.

The administrative apparatus of the state in developing countries, however, rarely has come close to achieving the impersonal, rule-based status that Weber depicted. Nor has it generally been able to produce the level of proficiency that Weber claimed was characteristic of bureaucracy. Often the lack of sufficient resources to pay officials in resource-scarce societies has led to corruption and, at the very least, shirking on the job so that officials can tend to other, more remunerative ventures. The absence of a strong professionalized corps of officials in such settings has meant that the civil service is often a source of patronage, allowing leaders to pay off supporters or deter the formation of an opposition. As these countries generally lack adequate resources, the state bureaucracy has less to extract to allow for the proficient delivery of services.

Many of the problems identified in developing countries, of course, affect even the most affluent countries, though usually to a lesser degree. The extent to which bureaucracy performs in accordance with the Weberian characterization is related to the external circumstances governing its capabilities. As a consequence, when these resources are lacking or when there is little basis for the rule of rational-legal authority, the state bureaucracy is unable to act in ways that may make it accountable, proficient, or rule-based. Further, when pay is low and educational resources limited, the officials responsible for running the administrative machinery may have inadequate skills and become susceptible to corruption and shirking. Thus, the fact that the administrative apparatus of a state is casually referred to as "the bureaucracy" (or its officials as "bureaucrats") says little about how proximate to or distant from the Weberian ideal of bureaucracy it is.

In developing countries ideas about administrative reform often move in the direction of the more formalistic Weberian ideal—particularly the creation of universalistic standards, regular procedures, and accountability. By contrast, in more-affluent countries, there is some emphasis, particularly but not exclusively in the largely English-speaking democracies, to reduce administrative formalism associated with bureaucracy, diminish the number of rules, and increase discretion and performance accountability lower down in organizations. Whereas in developing countries the main need is the reduction of corruption, in more established countries the reform motif is focused on rapid adaptability and performance. In settings where the state bureaucracy is believed to have been essential to the identity and performance of the state itself (e.g. France and Germany), there is more resistance to the introduction of market criteria to evaluate the state administrative apparatus or to disrupt prevailing patterns of civil service recruitment and training.

Trends in Bureaucratic Organization

Empirical studies of ostensibly bureaucratic organizations have often revealed a rich informal life within them that is at odds with the formal chain-of-command depictions. The classic work Administrative Behavior, originally published in 1947 from the doctoral dissertation of Herbert Simon, dissected the vintage bureaucratic paradigm and concluded that it was frequently inconsistent with psychological and social realities. Workers on production lines, for example, often generated their own norms that produced suboptimal results for the organization. In reality, the Weberian ideal of bureaucratic organization is frequently imperfect.

The terms bureaucracy and bureaucrat are often loosely employed as interchangeable with any form of administrative organization, however distant its pattern of behaviour from the Weberian model. Frequently, therefore, criticisms of bureaucracy and bureaucrats are criticisms of administrative behaviour that departs significantly from the ideals of bureaucratic organization and the professionalism of its corps of officials. Still, bureaucracy has been challenged by more informal and adaptive modes of organization (e.g markets, networks, and other less hierarchical or rules-driven modalities of organization). As no other form of organization allows for the regularity and accountability characterized by the bureaucratic form, however, it is unlikely that the bureaucratic form of organization will be supplanted.

References

- Administrative-law, topic: britannica.com, Retrieved 18 January, 2019
- Ovsey, Dan (27 May 2014). "Public sector stigma: The 100,000 workers Tim Hudak removes from the provincial payroll could have a tough transition to the private sector". Financial Post. Retrieved 16 January 2016
- Public-interest, law, social-sciences-and-law: encyclopedia.com, Retrieved 19 February, 2019
- Anderfuhren-Biget, Simon; Varone, Frédéric; Giauque, David (December 2014). "Policy Environment and Public Service Motivation". Public Administration. London. 92 (4): 807–825. Doi:10.1111/padm.12026
- Civil-service, topic: britannica.com, Retrieved 20 March, 2019
- Bureaucracy, topic: britannica.com, Retrieved 21 April, 2019

3

Public Policies

The principled guide to action taken by the administrative executive branches of the state in relation to a class of issues in accordance to the law and institutional customs is termed as public policy. Some of the major domains within public policy are agricultural policy, commercial policy, cultural policy, domestic policy, foreign policy, etc. This chapter closely examines these key types of public policies to provide an extensive understanding of the subject.

"Policy" is a consistent and purposeful way of doing something. Individuals, families and businesses can have policies that are private and self governed. The term "public policy" refers to a course of action taken by a government to address a public issue. Public policy is created in the interest of a larger group of people and is the outcome of government processes that include the enactment of laws and regulations, and the allocation of resources. Some of the issues that are addressed by public policy include health, education, social welfare, crime, transportation and international relations.

Individuals and groups commonly attempt to influence public policy through advocacy, education and the formation of special interest organizations. The ability of citizens to shape public policy is defined by a nation's form of government, with the public in democracies having far more impact on policy than in nations with other types of political systems. In a democracy, policymakers are often faced with competing interest groups who are advocating for opposing policies. For public officials, the formulation of public policy requires the ability to rigorously examine public issues and to implement ethical solutions that support the common good.

Law is a major component of public policy. Specific legislation enacted in the context of a nation's constitution or international law will determine how a policy is implemented and how services related to the policy are funded. Once a policy has been adopted through legislation, one or more agencies are put into place to enforce that policy.

The concept of public policy can be extended to include the policy decisions of any organization outside of government that addresses public issues, including nonprofit organizations, cultural institutions and religious organizations. Although these organizations are not capable of enacting public laws, they often provide solutions to public policy issues through internal policies that are in keeping with local and national laws. These organizations also use advocacy and education to promote public policy changes that support the goals of their organization.

As an academic discipline, the study of public policy is differentiated from economics or political science in its emphasis on applying theory to practice. Public policy schools provide instruction in policy analysis, political economy, public administration, public affairs and urban planning. In the past, public policy degrees were focused exclusively on the study of national policy. Economic globalization has led to many programs instituting tracks that focus on international policy, especially as it relates to global issues such as climate change, nuclear proliferation, terrorism and economic development.

Features of Public Policy

- Goal-oriented: All public policies have the ultimate aim to fulfil certain goals the government has in mind. The reason for the formation and implementation of these policies is the welfare of the citizens of the nation. So the government can use public policies to implement government programs to achieve their goals. For example, the current government has a financial inclusion policy. They wish to enlist the majority of our rural population in banks through the Jan Dhan Yojna.
- Result of government action: Public policy is the result of the collective of all government actions. So the actions and activities of all government officials collectively integrate to form public policy. The entire legal structure of our country stands on the collective actions of its representatives. From the actions of the highest judge in the land to that of lawyers and clerks forms the basis of our judiciary.
- Can take various forms: Public policy forms by the decision of the government to do something, or even to not do something. The decision of the government can represent itself in many forms like law, notices, ordinances, judicial decisions, executive orders, and judgments etc.
- Depicts concern of the government: Public policy is the solution to a problem the society is facing. This means the solution for the betterment of society has the sanction of the government. So it is of great importance to entrepreneurs and businessmen in a country. They need assurance that the government is looking after their concerns and economic interests as well. And if the government refuses to take any action it reflects their ignorance or disconcert. This will warn its citizens of the government's lack of empathy and concern.

AGRICULTURAL POLICY

Agricultural policy describes a set of laws relating to domestic agriculture and imports of foreign agricultural products. Governments usually implement agricultural policies with the goal of achieving a specific outcome in the domestic agricultural product markets. In relation to the forgoing, Akarowhe propounded that agricultural policies are pathways of improving the activities involve in cropping, livestock, forestry, processing and marketing of agricultural product. Agricultural policies are predetermined goals, objectives and pathway set by an individual or government for the purpose of achieving a specified outcome, for the benefit of the individual(s), society and the nations' economy at large. Agricultural policies take into consideration the primary, secondary and tertiary processes in agricultural production. Outcomes can involve, for example, a guaranteed supply level, price stability, product quality, product selection, land use or employment.

Policy Tools

An agricultural subsidy is a governmental subsidy paid to farmers and agribusinesses to manage the agricultural industry as one part of the various methods a government uses in a mixed economy. The conditions for payment and the reasons for the individual specific subsidies varies with farm product, size of farm, nature of ownership, and country among other factors. Enriching peanut farmers for political purposes, keeping the price of a staple low to keep the poor from rebelling, stabilizing the production of a crop to avoid famine years, encouraging diversification and many other purposes have been suggested as the reason for specific subsidies.

Price floors or price ceilings set a minimum or maximum price for a product. Price controls encourage more production by a price floor or less production by a price ceiling. A government can erect trade barriers to limit the quantity of goods imported (in the case of a Quota Share) or enact tariffs to raise the domestic price of imported products. These barriers give preference to domestic producers.

Objectives of Market Intervention

National Security

Some argue that nations have an interest in assuring there is sufficient domestic production capability to meet domestic needs in the event of a global supply disruption. Significant dependence on foreign food producers makes a country strategically vulnerable in the event of war, blockade or embargo. Maintaining adequate domestic capability allows for food self-sufficiency that lessens the risk of supply shocks due to geopolitical events. Agricultural policies may be used to support domestic producers as they gain domestic and international market share. This may be a short term way of encouraging an industry until it is large enough to thrive without aid. Or it may be an ongoing subsidy designed to allow a product to compete with or undercut foreign competition. This may produce a net gain for a government despite the cost of interventions because it allows a country to build up an export industry or reduce imports. It also helps to form the nations supply and demand market.

Environmental Protection and Land Management

Farm or undeveloped land composes the majority of land in most countries. Policies may encourage some land uses rather than others in the interest of protecting the environment. For instance, subsidies may be given for particular farming methods, forestation, land clearance, or pollution abatement.

Rural Poverty and Poverty Relief

Subsidising farming may encourage people to remain on the land and obtain some income. This might be relevant to a third world country with many peasant farmers, but it may also be a consideration to more developed countries such as Poland. It has a very high unemployment rate, much farmland and retain a large rural population growing food for their own use.

Price controls may also be used to assist poor citizens. Many countries have used this method of welfare support as it delivers cheap food to the poorest in urban areas without the need to assess people to give them financial aid. This often goes at the cost of the rural poor, who then earn less from what is often their only realistic or potential source of income: agriculture. Because in almost all countries the rural poor are poorer than the urban poor, cheap food policies through price controls often increase overall poverty.

The same often counts for poverty relief in the form of food aid, which (unless while during severe drought) drives small producers in poor countries out of production. It tends to benefit lower middle class groups (sub-urban and urban poor) at the expense of the poorest 20 percent, who as a result remain deprived of customers.

Organic Farming Assistance

Welfare economics theory holds that sometimes private activities can impose social costs upon others. Industrial agriculture is widely considered to impose social costs through pesticide pollution and nitrate pollution. Further, agriculture uses large amounts of water, a scarce resource. Some economists argue that taxes should be levied on agriculture, or that organic agriculture, which uses little pesticides and experiences relatively little nitrate runoff, should be encouraged with subsidies. In the United States, 65% of the approximately $16.5 billion in annual subsidies went to the top 10% of farmers in 2002 because subsidies are linked to certain commodities. On the other hand, organic farming received $5 million for help in certification and $15 million for research over a 5-year time period.

Fair Trade

Some advocate Fair Trade rules to ensure that poor farmers in developing nations that produce crops primarily for export are not exploited or negatively impacted by trade policies, practices, tariffs, and agreements which benefit one competitor at the expense of another - which advocates consider a dangerous "race to the bottom" in agricultural labor and safety standards. Opponents point out that most agriculture in developed nations is produced by industrial corporations (agribusiness) which are hardly deserving of sympathy, and that the alternative to exploitation is poverty.

Much of what developing countries export to the rich world, also comes from industrial corporations. The reason for that is, that rich countries have put up elaborate quality demands, most of whom make no factual health contribution. Small farmers often in effect meet these demands, but are rarely able to prove that in western standards. Therefore, the biggest impediment to growth of small farming and therefore of fare trade in sectors beyond coffee and bananas, is these quality demands from the rich world.

Arguments against Market Intervention

Dumping of Agricultural Surpluses

In international trade parlance, when a company from country A sells a commodity below the cost of production into country B, this is called "dumping". A number of countries that are signatories to multilateral trade agreements have provisions that prohibit this practice. When rich countries subsidize domestic production, excess output is often given to the developing world as foreign aid.

This process eliminates the domestic market for agricultural products in the developing world, because the products can be obtained for free from western aid agencies. In developing nations where these effects are most severe, small farmers could no longer afford basic inputs and were forced to sell their land.

"Consider a farmer in Ghana who used to be able to make a living growing rice. Several years ago, Ghana was able to feed and export their surplus. Now, it imports rice. From where? Developed countries. Why? Because it's cheaper. Even if it costs the rice producer in the developed world much more to produce the rice, he doesn't have to make a profit from his crop. The government pays him to grow it, so he can sell it more cheaply to Ghana than the farmer in Ghana can. And that farmer in Ghana? He can't feed his family anymore."

According to the Institute for Agriculture and Trade Policy, corn, soybeans, cotton, wheat and rice are sold below the cost of production, or dumped. Dumping rates are approximately forty percent for wheat, between twenty-five and thirty percent for corn (maize), approximately thirty percent for soybeans, fifty-seven percent for cotton, and approximately twenty percent for rice. For example, wheat is sold for forty percent below cost.

According to Oxfam, "If developed nations eliminated subsidy programs, the export value of agriculture in lesser developed nations would increase by 24 %, plus a further 5.5 % from tariff equilibrium. Exporters can offer US surpluses for sale at prices around half the cost of production; destroying local agriculture and creating a captive market in the process." Free trade advocates desire the elimination of all market distorting mechanisms (subsidies, tariffs, regulations) and argue that, as with free trade in all areas, this will result in aggregate benefit for all. This position is particularly popular in competitive agricultural exporting nations in both the developed and developing world, some of whom have banded together in the Cairns Group lobby. Canada's Department of Agriculture estimates that developing nations would benefit by about $4 billion annually if subsidies in the developed world were halved.

Agricultural Independence

Many developing countries do not grow enough food to feed their own populations. These nations must buy food from other countries. Lower prices and free food save the lives of millions of starving people, despite the drop in food sales of the local farmers. A developing nation could use new improved farming methods to grow more food, with the ultimate goal of feeding their nation without outside help. New greenhouse methods, hydroponics, fertilizers, R/O water processors, hybrid crops, fast-growing hybrid trees for quick shade, interior temperature control, greenhouse or tent insulation, autonomous building gardens, sun lamps, mylar, fans, and other cheap tech can be used to grow crops on previously unarable land, such as rocky, mountainous, desert, and even Arctic lands. More food can be grown, reducing dependency on other countries for food.

Replacement crops can also make nations agriculturally independent. Sugar, for example, comes from sugar cane imported from Polynesia. Instead of buying the sugar from Polynesia, a nation can make sugar from sugar beets, maple sap, or sweetener from stevia plant, keeping the profits circulating within the nation's economy. Paper and clothes can be made of hemp instead of trees and cotton. Tropical foods won't grow in many places in Europe, but they will grow in insulated greenhouses or tents in Europe. Soybean plant cellulose can replace plastic (made from oil). Ethanol from farm waste or hempseed oil can replace gasoline. Rainforest medicine plants grown locally can replace many imported medicines. Alternates of cash crops, like sugar and oil replacements, can reduce farmers' dependency on subsidies in both developed and developing nations.

Market interventions may increase the cost to consumers for agricultural products, either via hidden wealth-transfers via the government, or increased prices at the consumer level, such as for sugar and peanuts in the US. This has led to market distortions, such as food processors using high fructose corn syrup as a replacement for sugar. High fructose corn syrup may be an unhealthy food additive, and, were sugar prices not inflated by government fiat, sugar might be preferred over high fructose corn syrup in the marketplace.

Developed World Cases

Agriculture Policy Concerns

An example of the breadth and types of agriculture policy concerns can be found in the Australian Bureau of Agricultural and Resource Economics article "Agricultural Economies of Australia and New Zealand" which says that the major challenges and issues faced by their industrial agriculture industry are:

- Marketing challenges and consumer tastes.
- International trading environment (world market conditions, barriers to trade, quarantine and technical barriers, maintenance of global competitiveness and market image, and management of biosecurity issues affecting imports and the disease status of exports).
- Biosecurity (pests and diseases such as bovine spongiform encephalopathy (BSE), avian influenza, foot and mouth disease, citrus canker, and sugarcane smut).
- Infrastructure (such as transport, ports, telecommunications, energy and irrigation facilities).
- Management skills and labor supply (With increasing requirements for business planning, enhanced market awareness, the use of modern technology such as computers and global positioning systems and better agronomic management, modern farm managers will need to become increasingly skilled. Examples: training of skilled workers, the development of labor hire systems that provide continuity of work in industries with strong seasonal peaks, modern communication tools, investigating market opportunities, researching customer requirements, business planning including financial management, researching the latest farming techniques, risk management skills).
- Coordination (a more consistent national strategic agenda for agricultural research and development; more active involvement of research investors in collaboration with research providers developing programs of work; greater coordination of research activities across industries, research organisations and issues; and investment in human capital to ensure a skilled pool of research personnel in the future).

- Technology (research, adoption, productivity, genetically modified (GM) crops, investments).
- Water (access rights, water trade, providing water for environmental outcomes, assignment of risk in response to reallocation of water from consumptive to environmental use, accounting for the sourcing and allocation of water).
- Resource access issues (management of native vegetation, the protection and enhancement of biodiversity, sustainability of productive agricultural resources, landholder responsibilities).

Poverty Reduction

Agriculture remains the largest single contributor to the livelihoods of the 75% of the world's poor who live in rural areas. Encouraging agricultural growth is therefore an important aspect of agricultural policy in the developing world. In addition, a recent Natural Resource Perspective paper by the Overseas Development Institute found that good infrastructure, education and effective information services in rural areas were necessary to improve the chances of making agriculture work for the poor.

Biosecurity

The biosecurity concerns facing industrial agriculture can be illustrated by:

- The Threat to poultry and humans from H5N1; possibly caused by use of animal vaccines.
- The threat to cattle and humans from bovine spongiform encephalopathy (BSE); possibly caused by the unnatural feeding of cattle to cattle to minimize costs.
- The Threat to industry profits from diseases like foot-and-mouth disease and citrus canker which increasing globalization makes harder to contain.

Avian Influenza

Use of animal vaccines can create new viruses that kill people and cause flu pandemic threats. H5N1 is an example of where this might have already occurred. According to the CDC article "H5N1 Outbreaks and Enzootic Influenza" by Robert G. Webster et al.: "Transmission of highly pathogenic H5N1 from domestic poultry back to migratory waterfowl in western China has increased the geographic spread. The spread of H5N1 and its likely reintroduction to domestic poultry increase the need for good agricultural vaccines. In fact, the root cause of the continuing H5N1 pandemic threat may be the way the pathogenicity of H5N1 viruses is masked by co-circulating influenza viruses or bad agricultural vaccines." Dr. Robert Webster explains: "If you use a good vaccine you can prevent the transmission within poultry and to humans. But if they have been using vaccines now [in China] for several years, why is there so much bird flu? There is bad vaccine that stops the disease in the bird but the bird goes on pooping out virus and maintaining it and changing it. And I think this is what is going on in China. It has to be. Either there is not enough vaccine being used or there is substandard vaccine being used. Probably both. It's not just China. We can't blame China for substandard vaccines. I think there are substandard vaccines for influenza in poultry all over the world."

In response to the same concerns, Reuters reports Hong Kong infectious disease expert Lo Wing-lok indicating that vaccines have to take top priority. Julie Hall, who is in charge of the WHO's outbreak response in China, claimed that China's vaccinations might be masking the virus. The BBC reported that Dr Wendy Barclay, a virologist at the University of Reading, UK said: "The Chinese have made a vaccine based on reverse genetics made with H5N1 antigens, and they have been using it. There has been a lot of criticism of what they have done, because they have protected their chickens against death from this virus but the chickens still get infected; and then you get drift - the virus mutates in response to the antibodies - and now we have a situation where we have five or six 'flavours' of H5N1 out there."

Bovine Spongiform Encephalopathy

Bovine spongiform encephalopathy (BSE), commonly known as "mad cow disease", is a fatal, neurodegenerative disease of cattle, which infects by a mechanism that surprised biologists upon its discovery in the late 20th century. In the UK, the country worst affected, 179,000 cattle were infected and 4.4 million killed as a precaution. The disease can be transmitted to human beings who eat or inhale material from infected carcasses. In humans, it is known as new variant Creutzfeldt–Jakob disease (vCJD or nvCJD), and by June 2007, it had killed 165 people in Britain, and six elsewhere with the number expected to rise because of the disease's long incubation period. Between 460,000 and 482,000 BSE-infected animals had entered the human food chain before controls on high-risk offal were introduced in 1989.

A British inquiry into BSE concluded that the epidemic was caused by feeding cattle, who are normally herbivores, the remains of other cattle in the form of meat and bone meal (MBM), which caused the infectious agent to spread. The origin of the disease itself remains unknown. The current scientific view is that infectious proteins called prions developed through spontaneous mutation, probably in the 1970s, and there is a possibility that the use of organophosphorus pesticides increased the susceptibility of cattle to the disease. The infectious agent is distinctive for the high temperatures it is able to survive; this contributed to the spread of the disease in Britain, which had reduced the temperatures used during its rendering process. Another contributory factor was the feeding of infected protein supplements to very young calves instead of milk from their mothers.

Foot-and-mouth Disease

Foot-and-mouth disease is a highly contagious and sometimes fatal viral disease of cattle and pigs. It can also infect deer, goats, sheep, and other bovids with cloven hooves, as well as elephants, rats, and hedgehogs. Humans are affected only very rarely. FMD occurs throughout much of the world, and while some countries have been free of FMD for some time, its wide host range and rapid spread represent cause for international concern. In 1996, endemic areas included Asia, Africa, and parts of South America. North America, Australia, New Zealand and Japan have been free of FMD for many years. Most European countries have been recognized as free, and countries belonging to the European Union have stopped FMD vaccination.

Infection with foot-and-mouth disease tends to occur locally, that is, the virus is passed on to susceptible animals through direct contact with infected animals or with contaminated pens or vehicles used to transport livestock. The clothes and skin of animal handlers such as farmers, standing water, and uncooked food scraps and feed supplements containing infected animal products can harbor the virus as well. Cows can also catch FMD from the semen of infected bulls. Control measures include quarantine and destruction of infected livestock, and export bans for meat and other animal products to countries not infected with the disease.

Because FMD rarely infects humans but spreads rapidly among animals, it is a much greater threat to the agriculture industry than to human health. Farmers around the world can lose huge amounts of money during a foot-and-mouth epidemic, when large numbers of animals are destroyed and revenues from milk and meat production go down. One of the difficulties in vaccinating against FMD is the huge variation between and even within serotypes. There is no cross-protection between serotypes (meaning that a vaccine for one serotype won't protect against any others) and in addition, two strains within a given serotype may have nucleotide sequences that differ by as much as 30% for a given gene. This means that FMD vaccines must be highly specific to the strain involved. Vaccination only provides temporary immunity that lasts from months to years. Therefore, rich countries maintain a policy of banning import from all countries, not proven FMD-free by US or EU standards. This is a point of contention.

Although this disease is not dangerous to humans and rarely fatal to otherwise healthy animals, it reduces milk and meat production. Outbreaks can be stopped quickly if farmers and transporters are forced to abide by existing rules. Therefore, (besides temporary discomfort to the animals), any outbreak in the rich world should not be much more as a localized, cyclical economic problem. For countries with free roaming wildlife it is nearly impossible to prove that they are entirely free of this disease. If they try they are forced to erect nationwide fences, which destroys wildlife migration. Because detecting and reporting of FMD have enormously improved and sped up, almost all poor countries could now safely create FMD-free export zones. But rich countries refuse to change the rules. In effect, many poor tropical countries have no chance to meet current rules, so they are still today banned from exporting meat, even if many of them are FMD-free.

The result is that if drought hits, the poor try to cope by selling their few animals. This quickly saturates regional demand. The export ban then destroys the value of these animals, in effect destroying the most important coping mechanism of several hundreds of millions extremely poor households. The rules around meat exports have been changed many times, always to accommodate changing circumstances in rich countries, usually further reducing meat export chances for poor countries. For that reason Kanya and many other countries find the rules very unjust. They are however discouraged to file a formal complaint with WTO by diplomats from rich countries.

Citrus Canker

Citrus canker is a disease affecting citrus species that is caused by the bacterium *Xanthomonas axonopodis*. Infection causes lesions on the leaves, stems, and fruit of citrus trees, including lime, oranges, and grapefruit. While not harmful to humans, canker significantly affects the vitality of citrus trees, causing leaves and fruit to drop prematurely; a fruit infected with canker is safe to eat but too unsightly to be sold. The disease, which is believed to have originated in South East Asia, is extremely persistent when it becomes established in an area, making it necessary for all citrus orchards to be destroyed for successful eradication of the disease. Australia, Brazil and the United States are currently suffering from canker outbreaks.

The disease can be detected in orchards and on fruit by the appearance of lesions. Early detection is critical in quarantine situations. Bacteria are tested for pathogenicity by inoculating multiple citrus species with the bacterium. Simultaneously, other diagnostic tests (antibody detection, fatty-acid profiling, and genetic procedures using PCR) are conducted to identify the particular canker strain. Citrus canker outbreaks are prevented and managed in a number of ways. In countries that do not have canker, the disease is prevented from entering the country by quarantine measures. In countries with new outbreaks, eradication programs that are started soon after the disease has been discovered have been successful; such programs rely on destruction of affected orchards. When eradication has been unsuccessful and the disease has become established, management options include replacing susceptible citrus cultivars with resistant cultivars, applying preventive sprays of copper-based bactericides, and destroying infected trees and all surrounding trees within an appropriate radius.

The citrus industry is the largest fresh-fruit exporting industry in Australia. Australia has had three outbreaks of citrus canker; all three were successfully eradicated. The disease was found twice during the 1900s in the Northern Territory and was eradicated each time. During the first outbreak in 1912, every citrus tree north of latitude 19° south was destroyed, taking 11 years to eradicate the disease. In 2004, Asiatic citrus canker was detected in an orchard in Emerald, Queensland, and was thought to have occurred from the illegal import of infected citrus plants. The state and federal governments have ordered that all commercial orchards, all non-commercial citrus trees, and all native lime trees (*C. glauca*) in the vicinity of Emerald be destroyed rather than trying to isolate infected trees.

Food Security

The United Nations Food and Agriculture Organization (FAO) defines food security as existing when "all people, at all times, have physical and economic access to sufficient safe and nutritious food that meets their dietary needs and food preferences for an active and healthy life". The four qualifications that must be met for a food secure system include physical availability, economic and physical access, appropriate utilization, and stability of the prior three elements over time.

Of the 6.7 billion people on the planet, about 2 billion are food insecure. As the global population grows to 9 billion by 2050, and as diets shift to emphasize higher energy products and greater overall consumption, food systems will be subjected to even greater pressure. Climate change presents additional threats to food security, affecting crop yields, distribution of pests and diseases, weather patterns, and growing seasons around the world.

Food security has thus become an increasingly important topic in agricultural policy as decision makers attempt to reduce poverty and malnutrition while augmenting adaptive capacity to climate change. The Commission on Sustainable Agriculture and Climate Change listed high-priority policy actions to address food security, including integrating food security and sustainable agriculture into global and national policies, significantly raising the level of global investment in food systems, and developing specific programs and policies to support the most vulnerable populations (namely, those that are already subject to food insecurity).

Food Sovereignty

'Food sovereignty', a term coined by members of Via Campesina in 1996, is about the right of peoples to define their own food systems. Advocates of food sovereignty put the people who produce, distribute, and consume food at the centre of decisions on food systems and policies, rather than the demands of markets and corporations that they believe have come to dominate the global food system. This movement is advocated by a number of farmers, peasants, pastoralists, fisherfolk, indigenous peoples, women, rural youth, and environmental organizations.

COMMERCIAL POLICY

A commercial policy is a government's policy governing international trade. Commercial policy is an all encompassing term that is used to cover topics which involve international trade. Trade policy is often described in terms of a scale between the extremes of free trade (no restrictions on trade) on one side and protectionism (high restrictions to protect domestic producers) on the other.

A common commercial policy can sometimes agreed by treaty within a customs union, as with the European Union's common commercial policy and in Mercosur.

A nation's commercial policy will include and take into account the policies adopted by that nation's government while negotiating international trade. There are several factors that can have an impact on a nation's commercial policy, all of which can have an impact on international trade policies.

Theories on International Trade Policy

Trade policy has been controversial since the days of Mercantilism. Economics (or political economy) has developed in major part as an effort to make clear various effects of trade policies. See International trade theory. Hottest topic in economic policy is upgrading in Global Value Chains.

Types and aspects of Commercial Policy

Regionalism

Regionalism, or Regional Trade Agreements (RTA), are trade policies and agreements that are crafted by the nations in a region for the purposes of increasing international trade in the area. RTAs have been described by supporters as a means of increasing free trade with the goal of eventually merging into larger, either bilateral or multilateral, trade deals. The more relatively local area of RTAs are useful in resolving trade issues as well without causing gridlock in other trade agreements. Critics of RTAs say that they are a hindrance to the negotiation of trade because they can be lopsided or unfairly beneficial to one side over the other sides, particularly if some of the participants are nations that are still in development.

As China was rising in economic power and prominence, they turned to regionalism as a strategic method of leveling the playing field with Europe and the United States. In 2000, China signed the Bangkok agreement with the Association of Southeast Asian Nations (ASEAN) to reduce tariffs in the region. The signing of the agreement also began the push for a formal Free Trade Agreement between China and ASEAN. However, strained relations between China and other Asian nations such as Japan have prevented the same level of regional FTAs to be put in place with Northeast Asia.

Bilateral Free Trade Agreements

When two countries enter into a bilateral trade agreement, they are essentially giving one another special deals and favorable treatment in the arrangements. These privileges can include lowering tariffs on each others goods and services. The United States has signed such treaties as the North American Free Trade Agreement in 1994 as well as with Israel in the 1980s. Experts who support such free trade agreements argue that these deals help to increase competition and offers larger markets that businesses can reach out to. Critics of bilateral agreements claim that a larger nation, such as the United States, can use these agreements to unfairly push smaller states into much harsher work loads than the World Trade Organization already requires.

Relations between the European Union and South Korea have led to both parties signing several bilateral agreements regarding trade policy. In 2009, South Korea and the EU signed the EU-Korea Free Trade Agreement. The signing of the agreement created an FTA that is second only to NAFTA in size. The agreement held the benefits of increased free trade between the participants in the FTA as well as increased challenge to the United States.

Preferential Trade Agreements

Preferential agreements are trade deals that involve nations making deals with specific countries that can aid the interests of one another as opposed to the nondiscriminatory deals that are pushed by the WTO. Nations have been increasingly preferring such deals since the 1950s as they are quicker to show gains for the parties involved in the agreements. A common argument that has been made is that it allows businesses to open up markets that would otherwise be considered closed and therefore falls into the free trade idea that most countries will push for. Countries that have similar levels of GDP and a higher scope in their economies as well as their relative position to one another and the rest of the world are more likely to have preferential trade agreements. PTAs can also be applied to regional areas with unions such as NAFTA, the European Union, and ASEAN being examples of regional PTAs.

Those who opposer PTAs argue that these deals have increased the importance of where a product is made so that tariffs can be applied accordingly. The certification of a product's origin also unfairly holds back smaller countries that have less resources to spend. Others argue that PTAs can hinder negotiations of trade disputes and places an emphasis of which country has more power.

Ways in which Commercial Policy is Affected

Tariffs

Trade tariffs are a tax that are placed on the import of foreign goods. Tariffs increase the price of imports and are usually levied onto the country the goods are being imported from. Governments will use tariffs as a way to promote competition within their own country with businesses of the foreign country that wishes to sell their goods or services. In some instances, a country's government will use them as a means of protectionism for their own interests. In modern history, generally starting at the mid-20th century, the use of tariffs has been largely diminished in favor of the rise of international trade. Beginning in 2017, the Trump administration began to impose tariffs on several of nations that were involved in trade deals with the United States. The countries targeted by the Trump Tariffs then retaliated with their own tariffs on American goods.

Import Quotas

Import quotas are the limitations of the amount of goods that can be imported into the country from foreign businesses. Generally, an import quota is set for a specific period of time with one year being the most common metric. Some versions of the quotas limits the quantity of specific goods being imported into a country while other versions place the limit on the value of said goods. The objectives of quotas can include: the protections of a nations interests, ensuring a balance of trade so as not to create deficits, retaliation to restrictive trade policies of other countries that do business on the international playing field.

CULTURAL POLICY

One example of institutions created by governments as part of a country's cultural policy is the creation and ongoing funding of national galleries and museums.

Cultural policy is the government actions, laws and programs that regulate, protect, encourage and financially (or otherwise) support activities related to the arts and creative sectors, such as painting, sculpture, music, dance, literature, and filmmaking, among others and culture, which may involve activities related to language, heritage and diversity. The idea of cultural policy was developed at UNESCO in the 1960s. Generally, this involves governments setting in place processes, legal classifications, regulations, legislation and institutions (e.g. galleries, museums, libraries, opera houses, etc.) which promote and facilitate cultural diversity and creative expressions in a range of art forms and creative activities. Cultural policies vary from one country to another, but generally they aim to improve the accessibility of arts and creative activities to citizens and promote the artistic, musical, ethnic, sociolinguistic, literary and other expressions of all people in a country. In some countries, especially since the 1970s, there is an emphasis on supporting the culture of Indigenous peoples and marginalized communities and ensuring that cultural industries (e.g. filmmaking or TV production) are representative of a country's diverse cultural heritage and ethnic and linguistic demographics.

Cultural policy can be done at a nation-state level, at a sub-national level (e.g. U.S. states or Canadian provinces), at a regional level or at a municipal level (e.g. a city government creating a museum or arts centre). Examples of cultural policy-making at the nation-state level could include anything from funding music education or theatre programs at little to no cost, to hosting corporate-sponsored art exhibitions in a government museum, to establishing legal codes (such as the U.S. Internal Revenue Service's 501(c)(3) tax designation for not-for-profit enterprises) and creating political institutions (such as the various ministries of culture and departments of culture and the National Endowment for the Humanities and the National Endowment for the Arts in the United States), arts granting councils, and cultural institutions such as galleries and museums. Similar significant organisations in the United Kingdom include the Department for Culture, Media and Sport (DCMS), and Arts Council England.

Throughout much of the twentieth century, many of the activities that compose cultural policy in the 2010s were governed under the title of "arts policy". Arts policy includes direct funding to artists, creators and art institutions and indirect funding to artists and arts institutions through the tax system (e.g. by making donations to arts charities tax-deductible). However, as Kevin Mulcahy has observed, "cultural policy encompasses a much broader array of activities than were addressed under arts policy. Whereas arts policy was effectively limited to addressing aesthetic concerns (e.g. funding art galleries and opera houses), the significance of the transformation to cultural policy can be observed in its demonstrable emphases on cultural identity, valorization of indigineity [Indigenous people's culture] and analyses of historical dynamics (such as hegemony and colonialism)." A general trend in Western industrialized nations is a shift, since the 1970s and 1980s, away from solely supporting a small number of relatively elite, professionalized art forms and institutions (e.g. Classical music, painting, sculpture, art galleries) to also supporting amateur and community cultural and creative activities (e.g. community theatre) and cultural forms which were not considered part of the Western canon by previous generations (e.g. traditional music such as blues, World music, and so on).

Theoretical Approaches

A railway museum in Japan displays antique locomotives.

Cultural policy, while a small part of the budgets of even the most generous of governments, governs a sector of immense complexity. It entails "a large, heterogeneous set of individuals and organizations engaged in the creation, production, presentation, distribution, and preservation of and education about aesthetic heritage, and entertainment activities, products and artifacts". A cultural policy necessarily encompasses a broad array of activities and typically involves public support for:

- Heritage, battlefield and historic preservation sites.
- Zoos, botanical gardens, arboretums, aquariums, parks.
- Libraries and museums (fine arts, scientific, historical).
- Visual arts (film, painting, sculpture, pottery, architecture).
- Performing arts (symphonic, chamber and choral music; jazz, hip-hop and folk music; ballet, ballroom and modern dance; opera and musical theatre; circus performances, rodeos and marching bands).
- Public humanities programs (public broadcasting, creative writing, poetry).

Some governments may place policy areas from this list in other ministries or departments. For example, national parks may be assigned to an environment department, or public humanities may be delegated to an education department.

Since culture is a public good (i.e., contributes a public value to society for which it is hard to exclude non-payers, as all of society benefits from arts and culture) and something that is generally viewed as a merit good, governments have pursued programs to promote greater accessibility. In this way of thinking, significant aesthetic works such as paintings and sculptures should be made broadly available to the public. In other words, "high culture" should not be the exclusive preserve of a particular social class or of a metropolitan location. Rather, the benefits of the highest reaches of cultural excellence should be made in an egalitarian manner; national cultural treasures should be accessible without regard to the impediments of class circumstances, educational attainment or place of habitation. A democratic state cannot be seen as simply indulging the aesthetic preferences of a few, however enlightened, or of overtly infusing art with political values. Consequently, a democratic cultural policy must articulate its purposes in ways that demonstrate how the public interest is being served. These purposes have often been expressed as involving either the creation of cultural democracy or the democratization of culture.

The objective of cultural democratization is the aesthetic enlightenment, enhanced dignity, and educational development of the general citizenry. "Dissemination was the key concept with the aim of establishing equal opportunity for all citizens to participate in publicly organized and financed cultural activities". To further this goal, performances and exhibitions are low cost; public art education promotes equality of aesthetic opportunity; national institutions tour and perform in work places, retirement homes and housing complexes.

As indicated earlier, the "democratization of culture" is a top-down approach that promulgates certain forms of cultural programming that are deemed to be a public good. Clearly, such an objective is open to criticism for what is termed cultural elitism; that is, the assumption that some aesthetic expressions are inherently superior - at least as determined by a cognoscenti concerned with the acquisition of cultural capital. "The problem with this policy is that, fundamentally, it intends to create larger audiences for performances whose content is based on the experience of society's privileged groups. In sum, it has taken for granted that the cultural needs of all society's members are alike". The objective of cultural democracy, on the other hand, is to provide for a more participatory (or populist) approach in the definition and provision of cultural opportunities.

The coupling of the concept of democratization of culture to cultural democracy has a pragmatic as well as a philosophical component. Cultural patronage in democratic governments is markedly different from patronage by wealthy individuals or corporations. Private or politically paramount patrons are responsible only to themselves and are free to indulge in their tastes and preferences. Democratic governments, on the other hand, are responsible to the electorate and are held accountable for their policy decisions.

The two objectives just discussed - dissemination of high culture and participation in a broader range of cultural activities - evoke a related debate about the content of public culture: "elitist" or "populist."

Elitism

Proponents of the elitist position argue that cultural policy should emphasize aesthetic quality as the determining criterion for public subvention. This view is typically supported by the major cultural organizations, creative artists in the traditionally defined field of the fine arts, cultural critics, and the well-educated, well-to-do audiences for these art forms. Ronald Dworkin terms this the "lofty approach," which "insists that art and culture must reach a certain degree of sophistication, richness, and excellence in order for human nature to flourish, and that the state must provide this excellence if the people will not or cannot provide it for themselves". Advocates of the elitist position generally focus on supporting the creation, preservation and performance of works of the Western canon, a group of artworks that are viewed as the best artistic and cultural products of Western society.

Populism

By contrast, the populist position advocates defining culture broadly and inclusively and making this culture broadly available. The populist approach emphasizes a less traditional and more pluralist notion of artistic merit and consciously seeks to create a policy of cultural diversity. With a focus on personal enhancement, the populist's position posits very limited boundaries between amateur and professional arts activities. Indeed, the goal is to provide opportunities for those outside the professional mainstream. To give an example, whereas an elite approach advocates support for professional musicians, particularly those from Classical music, a populist approach would advocate support for amateur, community singers and musicians.

"Proponents of populism are frequently advocates of minority arts, folk arts, ethnic arts, or counter-cultural activities" as Kevin V. Mulcahy said. Cultural "elitists," on the other hand, argue in support of excellence over amateurism and favor an emphasis on aesthetic discipline over "culture as everything." There are "two key tensions for national cultural policy between the goals of excellence versus access, and between government roles as facilitator versus architect".

Kevin V. Mulcahy argued that in effect, elitism is cultural democracy as populism is to the democratization of culture. Unfortunately, there has been a tendency to see these positions as mutually exclusive, rather than complementary. "Elitists" are denounced as "high brow snobs" advocating an esoteric culture which focuses on art music and the types of art seen in museums and galleries; populists are dismissed as "pandering philistines" promoting a trivialized and commercialized culture, as they endorse the value of popular music and folk art. However, these mutual stereotypes belie complementariness between two bookends of an artistically autonomous and politically accountable cultural policy. There is a synthesis that can be termed a "latitudinarian approach" to public culture; that is, one that is aesthetically inclusive and broadly accessible.

Glocalization of Arts

Musicologists David Hebert and Mikolaj Rykowski write that when "music is recognized as invaluable cultural heritage, entailing unique artefacts of intellectual property, new developments in this field then become acknowledged as important forms of social *innovation*;" However, they caution policy-makers that with glocalization, the rise of "'big data' offers unprecedentedly powerful tools but also inevitably entails many risks for all kinds of artists (both musicians and their collaborators in other arts) as well as the sustainability of traditional cultural practices."

Such a public-cultural policy would remain faithful to the highest standards of excellence from a broad range of aesthetic expressions while providing the widest possible access to people from different geographic locales, socio-economic strata, and educational background, as Dr. Mulcahy said. In conceiving of public policy as an opportunity to provide alternatives not readily available in the marketplace, public cultural agencies would be better positioned to complement the efforts of the private sector rather than duplicate their activities. Similarly, cultural agencies can promote community development by supporting artistic heritages that are at a competitive disadvantage in a cultural world that is increasingly profit-driven. In sum, excellence should be viewed as the achievements of greatness from a horizontal, rather than a vertical, perspective and a cultural policy as supporting the totality of these varieties of excellence.

These attitudes about a public cultural responsibility stand in marked contrast to much of the rest of the world, where culture is a question of historic patrimony, or the national identities of peoples, whether in independent states or regions within more powerful states. Inevitably, sensitive issues are involved in any discussion of culture as a public policy. However, given the demands in a democratic system that public policies show a return to the taxpayer, cultural policy has frequently argued for support on the basis of utility. It can be argued that there is a parity between the state's responsibility for its citi' social-economic-physical needs and their access to culture and opportunities for artistic self-expression. However, the aesthetic dimension of public policy has never been widely perceived as intuitively obvious or politically imperative. Accordingly, the cultural sector has often argued its case from the secondary, ancillary benefits that result from public support for programs that are seemingly only aesthetic in nature. Cultural policy is not typically justified solely on the grounds that it is a good-in-itself, but rather that it yields other good results.

The future of cultural policy would seem to predict an increasingly inexorable demand that the arts "carry their own weight" rather than rely on a public subsidy to pursue "art for art's sake". Kevin V.

Mulcahy dubbed this "cultural Darwinism" is most pronounced in the United States where public subsidy is limited and publicly supported aesthetic activities are expected to demonstrate a direct public benefit. Non-American cultural institutions are less constrained by the need to maintain diversified revenue streams that demand high levels of earned income and individual and corporate donations to compensate for limited government appropriations.

On the other hand, cultural institutions everywhere are increasingly market-driven in their need for supplementary funds and as a justification for continued public support. The American model of an essentially privatized culture is increasingly attractive to governments seeking to curtail their cultural subsidies. In a system of mixed funding, public culture can nurture the arts groups and cultural activities that contribute to individual self-worth and community definition even if counting for less in the economic bottom-line. At root, a cultural policy is about creating public spheres that are not dependent upon profit motives nor validated by commercial values. As political democracy is dependent upon the existence of civil society and socio-economic pluralism, cultural policy stands as an essential public commitment in realizing these fundamental preconditions.

One of the available and yet underappreciated tools in cultural policy at the national level is the reduction of VAT rates for cultural goods and services. Economic theory can be used to explain how reduced fiscal rates are expected to decrease prices and increase quantities of consumed cultural goods and services. Fiscal policy can be an important part of cultural policy, in particular the VAT rate discounts on cultural consumption, yet it receives less attention than deserved.

DOMESTIC POLICY

The term domestic policy is broadly used to describe a range of issues, including personal rights and freedoms, social welfare, healthcare, education, legislation, law enforcement, natural resources, and energy generation and use. Domestic policy affects how every person in the country lives every day, as it shapes such issues as environmental protection, laws, education, welfare programs, and law enforcement. This is in contrast to foreign policy, which deals with the nation's relationships with other countries, including international trade, and peacekeeping. The two types of policy can be referred to together as public policy.

Types of Domestic Policy

Domestic policies are created in the effort to minimize chaos in the country. This is done on a number of fronts, where there are policies that govern the government, policies that keep law enforcement on the right track, and policies that guide and care for the people. Domestic policy in the United States can be divided into several types, each of which focuses on a different aspect of life in the U.S.

Regulatory Policy – Regulatory Policy seeks to maintain order, outlawing behaviors that pose a danger to society. This is accomplished through policies and laws that restrict people, groups, and companies from doing things that have a detrimental effect on social and political order. Regulatory policy includes such issues as administering voting procedures, enacting traffic ordinances, and creating policies to prevent people from using dangerous drugs. Regulatory policy also controls business markets and regulates industry, protects the environment, and sets policy for the workplace.

Distributive Policy – Distributive policy is concerned with providing goods and services, administered through public agencies, to various organizations. These goods and services are paid for by the citizens' taxes, and include such items as public education, public roadways, public safety, and welfare.

Redistributive Policy – Redistributive policy is a tricky issue, as it involves moving tax dollars from one organization, which received the money through distributive policy, to other organizations. On the face, such redistribution is supposed to be done in an attempt to eliminate adverse social issues, such as poverty. In practice, this is rarely so cut-and-dry. Because the nation's leaders are able to use redistribution to gain advantages in other budget issues, or even to enhance one group's power over another.

Constituent Policy – Constituent policies create agencies with executive power to work as an agent of the government. For instance, at some point, new departments or agencies were created to deal with taxes, and to administer the Social Security plan. Constituent policy is also concerned with laws, and with fiscal policy, and is responsible for development of new departments, distribution of funds internally, and creating rules for public servants.

Other Types of Domestic Policy

Although the above policy types comprise the primary categories, there are many types of policy that are created and used to keep the U.S. operating smoothly. Examples of domestic policy that fall within the purview of the above categories include:

- Public Policy,
- Defense Policy,
- Economic Policy,
- Energy Policy,
- Environmental Policy,
- Public Health Policy,
- Transportation Policy.

Domestic Social Policy Division

A division of the Congressional Research Service, the Domestic Social Policy Division ("DSP") is responsible to analyze issues of domestic policies and social programs. After looking into the policies and programs it is tasked with, reports are provided to Congress, allowing legislators to make appropriate decisions in making future decisions, enacting laws, and overseeing existing agencies.

Policies and social programs examined by the DSP include:

- Public Education,

- Labor Policy and Worker Safety,
- Healthcare Services,
- Health Research,
- Healthcare Insurance,
- Policies and Studies on Aging,
- Social Security, both pensions and disability insurance,
- Immigration,
- Homeland Security,
- Domestic Intelligence,
- Criminal Justice,
- Welfare, Nutrition, and Housing programs.

Responsibility for researching such a broad spectrum of services and agencies in this example of domestic policy responsibility, is a daunting task. To bring order to the undertaking in this example of domestic policy organization, the DSP is broken down into six research subdivisions, each subdivision having its own research manager. Those subdivisions include:

Domestic Security and Immigration

The Domestic Security and Immigration subdivision researches issues of criminal justice, including:

- Criminal Justice – Including drug control, gun control, juvenile justice, crime trends, sentencing guidelines, and the FBI.
- Domestic Intelligence – Including activities of the FBI, the Drug Enforcement Agency ("DEA"), the Alcohol, Tobacco, and Firearms division ("ATF"), and certain components of the Department of Homeland Security ("DHS").
- Border Security – Including Border Patrol, screening for terrorists, and disposition of unauthorized aliens.
- Immigration – Including issues of legal immigration, naturalization, and temporary workers.

Children and Families

The Children and Families subdivision researches issues concerning the health and welfare of children and families, including:

- Child Welfare – Including foster care, adoption, runaway and homeless youth, teen pregnancy.
- Low-Income Families – Including welfare, food stamps, Head Start education programs, and child support.

- Housing – Including public housing subsidies, Section 8 Housing Choice Vouchers Program, housing programs for special populations, home ownership initiatives, and homelessness.

Education and Labor

The Education and Labor subdivision researches issues concerning elementary and secondary education, including:

- Federal Aid to School Districts – Including aid allocation formulas (math formulas to determine how much financial aid each district will receive), accountability, and special education.
- Postsecondary Education and Job Training – Including financial aid for college costs, student aid, and vocational education.
- Labor – Including equal pay, minimum wage and overtime wage standards, and other labor standards.

Health Services and Research

The Health Services and Research subdivision researches issues concerning public health and research, including:

- Medical Research and Healthcare Services – Including research into diseases at the National Institutes of Health ("NIH"), stem cell research, and maintaining of electronic medical records.
- Public Health – Including regulation of prescription drugs and medical devices at the Food and Drug Administration ("FDA"), health preparedness, and emergency response.
- Health Issues for the Aging – Including long-term care, and chronic disease management.
- Veterans' Healthcare – Including accessibility, and other healthcare concerns.

Health Insurance and Financing

The Health Insurance and Financing subdivision researches issues related to the provision of health insurance to all Americans, as well as financing issues related to healthcare and health insurance, including:

- Health Insurance – Including Medicare, Medicaid, and state children's health insurance.
- Health Insurance Access – Including healthcare coverage, and insurance reform.

Income Security

The Income Security subdivision researches issues related to the financial requirements of the elderly, disabled, and unemployed, including:

- Social Security,

- Income for the Disabled,
- Unemployment Compensation,
- Retirement Savings and Pensions.

GOVERNMENT ECONOMIC POLICY

Government economic policy refers to the measures by which a government attempts to influence the economy. The national budget generally reflects the economic policy of a government, and it is partly through the budget that the government exercises its three principal methods of establishing control: the allocative function, the stabilization function, and the distributive function.

Over time, there have been considerable changes in emphasis on these different economic functions of the budget. In the 19th century, government finance was primarily concerned with the allocative function. The job of government was to raise revenue as cheaply and efficiently as possible to perform the limited tasks that it could do better than the private sector. As the 20th century began, the distribution function acquired increased significance. Social welfare benefits became important, and many countries introduced graduated tax systems. In the later interwar period, and more especially in the 1950s and '60s, stabilization was central, although equity was also a major concern in the design of tax systems. In the 1970s and '80s, however, the pendulum swung back. Once more, allocative issues came to the fore, and stabilization and distribution became less significant in government finance.

Allocative Function

The allocative function in budgeting determines on what government revenue will be spent. Because a high proportion of national income is now devoted to public expenditure, allocation decisions become more significant in political and economic terms. At all times and in all countries the calls for expenditure on specific services or activities, or for more generous transfer payments, will always exceed the amount that can reasonably be raised in taxation or by borrowing. The debate about how these scarce resources should be allocated has continued for hundreds of years, and, although numerous methods of deciding on priorities have emerged, it has never been satisfactorily resolved. In practice, most democracies contain a number of different factions that disagree on the proper allocation of resources and indeed the proper level of public sector involvement in the economy; the frequent change of national governments is related to the constant search for the right answers.

Public Goods

Economists have sought to provide objective criteria for public expenditures through the so-called theory of public goods. It is generally recognized that some goods needed by the public cannot be provided through the private market. Lighthouses are a classic example. The costs of a lighthouse are such that no one shipowner will want to finance it; on the other hand, if a lighthouse is provided for one shipowner, it can be made available to all for no additional cost. Indeed it must be available to all, since there is no practical means of excluding ships from using the facility provided by the lighthouse, even if their owners have refused to pay for it. The only practical method of providing such services is by collective action.

If goods are to be provided in this way, rather than through the private market, it is immediately necessary to confront the twin problems of deciding how much to provide and who should pay for that provision. Even if all individuals wanted the service equally—as, perhaps, with lighthouses—their views on the extent of the service would be influenced by the allocation of the costs. Where different households may have different preferences and some may not want the service at all—as, for example, with defense by nuclear weapons—these difficulties are compounded. Economists have tried to devise abstract voting schemes that would reconcile these difficulties, but these appear to have little practical application.

Moreover, others would challenge this whole approach to the problem. It would be absurd to say that the consumer has a taste for national defense and that it is the job of the government to satisfy it. The task of national leaders is to evolve a defense policy and persuade the public to accept it. Similarly, conservationists must attempt to awaken the public to the importance of parks and wildlife. In the context of public policy, the efficient allocation of resources consists not merely of distributing funds in the pursuit of given objectives but also involves determining the objectives themselves.

Genuine public goods pose severe problems for the national budget; it is very difficult to decide how far particular goods—the arts, national parks, even defense—should be supplied, and therefore no formal procedure of determination is likely to evolve. What should be given to each will continue to be the subject of intense political debate, with allocation changing as the government changes.

Merit Goods

The concept of merit goods assists governments in deciding which public or other goods should be supplied. Merit goods are commodities that the public sector provides free or cheaply because the government wishes to encourage their consumption. Goods such as subsidized housing or social services, which predominantly help the poor, or health care services, which help the poor and elderly, are generally regarded as having considerable merit and therefore have a strong claim on government resources. Other examples include the provision of retraining schemes or urban regeneration programs.

Cost-benefit Analysis

Once decisions have been made on how the limited national budget should be divided between different groups of activities, or even before this, public authorities need to decide which specific projects should be undertaken. One method that has been used is cost-benefit analysis. This attempts to do for government programs what the forces of the marketplace do for business programs: to measure, and compare in terms of money, the discounted streams of future benefits and future costs associated with a proposed project. If the ratio of benefits to costs is considered satisfactory, the project should be undertaken. "Satisfactory" means, among other things, that the project is superior to any available public or private alternative. Or, if funds are limited, public investment projects may be assigned priorities according to their cost-benefit ratios.

One difficulty with cost-benefit analysis is that every government agency has an incentive to estimate favourable ratios for its own projects. It must, after all, compete with other agencies for funds. No one can be certain as to the returns to be expected from an irrigation canal or a highway. Private investors have also been known to exaggerate their claims in appealing to stockholders, but they are generally subject to market sanctions that encourage them to err on the side of caution.

In addition to the possibility that cost-benefit analysis may be biased by the preformed views of those commissioning the study, there are other, more fundamental difficulties. Almost all proposals have effects that are difficult to value in monetary terms. The siting of a new airport brings problems of noise and property blight to local people and increases the risk that civilians may die in an accident. Putting a sensible value on human life has been a continuing difficulty for those carrying out cost-benefit analyses, even though every project does in fact affect probabilities of life and death. These problems are, of course, not confined to cost-benefit analysis. Additional expenditure on health service or on road safety or better housing or heating old people's homes in winter all affect the number of people who die prematurely. The failure of cost-benefit analysis to provide answers to the problems of valuing life, or the quality of life, is a reflection of the wider problem confronting all decisions on public expenditure: the influence of subjective judgment.

Public Ownership and Privatization

Until the mid-1970s the proportion of economic activity controlled by the government and the share of taxes in national income tended to increase in most countries. Since then, however, challenges to this growth in the role of government have become increasingly influential, and moves to privatization have been common.

There are several types of privatization. One involves the sale to private owners of state-owned assets, and this is most correctly called privatization. Publicly owned houses may be sold to their occupants. Commodity stockpiles may be reduced or disbanded. Increasingly, however, attention has been turned to the sale of publicly owned industries, thus reversing the move to nationalization that occurred, particularly in western Europe, around and after World War II.

Where the privatized industry operates in a competitive environment, no new problems arise. Singapore has privatized its airline system, for example, which now competes with a mixture of privately and publicly owned international airlines. Where privatization occurs but monopoly continues, however, there are new difficulties. Both Japan and the United Kingdom have privatized their telecommunications networks. Although, in certain limited areas of telecommunications, competition is possible—and has been allowed to develop in both the United States and Britain—technical and legal restrictions inhibit competition in many sectors of the industry.

Regulation is necessary, therefore, to restrict the freedom of privatized monopolies, or near monopolies, to raise prices and to exploit consumers in other ways. In the United States, which has by far the longest history of regulating private utilities, such regulation has normally limited the rate of return that they earn to what is considered a fair level. A disadvantage of this is that it may give the industry no greater incentive to increased efficiency than would exist in public ownership, since higher costs can be passed directly onto consumers. There have been experiments, therefore, with other forms of regulation, which seek to strike a balance between incentives for better performance and the ability to exploit consumers.

A further problem for such regulation is that utilities and similar industries normally operate in both competitive and monopoly markets. They may be inclined to use their monopoly power in some areas to gain unfair competitive advantages in others. Despite these difficulties, an increasingly wide range of industries, ranging from water supply to airports, are now considered candidates for privatization.

Privatization can also mean the dismantling of existing statutory restrictions on competition. State activities are often protected by legal prohibitions on competing private enterprise. German railways, for example, are entirely state-owned, and the law not only prevents competing railroads but severely restricts coach services and limits competitive trucking. The dismantling of such restrictions is seen as one method of improving the efficiency of state concerns.

Another demand of privatization is the contracting out of publicly provided services. U.S. municipalities have often entrusted activities such as refuse collection, and in some cases even fire service, to private contractors, and European countries are increasingly experimenting with similar schemes. These possibilities demonstrate that a service may be government-financed but not necessarily provided by the government; if extended more widely, the concept could yield a different view of the economic role of the state.

While the objective of privatization is often to increase the efficiency of government activities, its implementation may also have important effects on government revenue. Any savings that result from lower costs lead directly to lower tax rates. Where budgeting procedures do not distinguish between capital and current transactions, the proceeds of privatization sales provide a once-and-for-all boost to revenues. The availability of this source of funding for state activity has given an artificial attractiveness to privatization, especially in the United Kingdom. If an industry is sold for the present value of its expected earnings and if these earnings are the same in public and private ownership, privatization should have no net impact on public finances. If it is expected to be more efficient in the private sector, government finance, on balance, gains. If it is sold for less than the maximum revenue that would be obtained—and this is often the case, either because of the difficulty of selling assets as large as nationalized industries or because the government wishes to secure a wide dispersion of share ownership—the impact is likely to be negative.

Other Forms of Government Intervention

Government spending is not the only way in which government allocates resources. Its regional policies will determine whether domestic and overseas investors build factories in particular places, while its taxation policies will determine whether they build them at all. Government competition and merger policies affect the structure of industry and commerce, while regulatory activities—setting the number of hours shops may be open or who may buy cigarettes—have profound effects on commercial activities.

Government also affects allocations by setting the legal and administrative framework within which the economy functions. It may specify minimum wage levels or control the siting of new ventures and the activities of existing ones. Such activities of government profoundly affect the allocation of resources, but they are rarely monitored or subject to serious control.

Stabilization Function

Stabilization of the economy (e.g. full employment, control of inflation, and an equitable balance of payments) is one of the goals that governments attempt to achieve through manipulation of fiscal and monetary policies. Fiscal policy relates to taxes and expenditures, monetary policy to financial markets and the supply of credit, money, and other financial assets.

The use of fiscal and monetary policy as a means of stabilizing the economy is relatively recent, for the most part a development of the period after World War II. During the 19th century the only stabilization policy was that associated with the international gold standard. Under the gold standard, if a deficit occurred in a country's balance of payments, gold tended to flow out of the country. To counteract this process, the monetary authorities would raise interest rates and stiffen credit requirements, causing a fall in prices, income, and employment; this in turn led to a reduction in imports and an expansion of exports, thus improving the balance of payments. If a country had a surplus in its balance of payments, gold tended to flow in; this meant that the interest rate fell and the supply of money and credit was increased. As a consequence, imports were stimulated and exports discouraged so that the surplus in the balance of payments tended to disappear. The adjustment mechanism also included another important element: capital movements between countries. When interest rates fell in surplus countries and rose in deficit countries, mobile international financial capital tended to flow from the former to the latter, contributing to the elimination of deficits and surpluses in the balance of payments. The working of this mechanism was partly automatic and partly the result of deliberate actions by the monetary authorities in each country.

In this form of stabilization policy, external stability was achieved at the cost of stability in the domestic economy: fluctuations in domestic prices, incomes, and employment functioned as the levers for bringing about equilibrium in the balance of payments. Occasionally governments attempted to reduce the impact of this mechanism on the domestic economy, particularly on the price level. In particular, governments in some surplus countries took "sterilization actions" to prevent the gold inflow from increasing the supply of money and credit to the maximum extent. This could be done if the central bank offset its purchases of foreign exchange and gold with sales of government securities on the domestic credit market.

A somewhat more ambitious type of stabilization policy emerged in the period after World War I. During the late 1920s and early 1930s the need to reduce unemployment acquired more urgency. Previously, the exchange rate, the balance of payments, and occasionally the price level had been considered more important than the situation in the labour market. During the 1920s unemployment in Great Britain rose to very high levels (between 20 and 30 percent of the labour force). Consequently, there was much discussion of whether employment could be increased by actions of the public authorities. At first, the discussion in Great Britain centred on the feasibility of public works programs as a means of putting men to work; there was a growing belief that these programs might also be a good means of raising the general level of economic activity through their effect on purchasing power. Some maintained that budget deficits would also raise the level of economic activity. An active part in this discussion was taken by the economist J.M. Keynes, and also by the Liberal Party, which in 1928 published proposals for government intervention entitled Britain's Industrial Future.

The first countries to adopt the new policies were Sweden and Germany. When the Nazi Party took power in Germany in 1933, its rearmament policies helped to reduce unemployment and to stimulate the economy. In Sweden, the new Social Democratic government attempted in more modest ways to expand the economy and ease unemployment through increased government expenditures in 1932–33. In the United States, a very limited attempt was made by the administration of Pres. Herbert Hoover; but Franklin D. Roosevelt made a more aggressive effort with such projects as the Works Progress Administration (WPA), which carried on its payroll an average of more than 2,000,000 workers per year from 1935 to 1941. Unemployment, however, persisted at a high level until World War II, although there was a significant drop from a level of about 25 percent in 1933.

Stabilization Theory

The new stabilization policy needed a theoretical rationale if it was ever to win general acceptance from the leaders of public opinion. The main credit for providing this belongs to Keynes. In his General Theory of Employment, Interest and Money he endeavoured to show that a capitalist economy with its decentralized market system does not automatically generate full employment and stable prices and that governments should pursue deliberate stabilization policies. There has been much controversy among economists over the substance and meaning of Keynes's theoretical contribution. Essentially, he argued that high levels of unemployment might persist indefinitely unless governments took monetary and fiscal action. At that time he believed that fiscal action was likely to be more effective than monetary measures. In the deep depression of the 1930s, interest rates had ceased to exert much influence on the ways in which owners of wealth disposed of their funds; they might choose to hold larger cash balances instead of spending more money as the traditional theory had suggested. Nor were investors inclined to take advantage of low interest rates if they could not find profitable uses for borrowed funds, particularly if their firms were already suffering from excess capacity. Keynes's pessimistic view of monetary policy had a strong influence on economists and governments during and immediately after World War II, with the result that monetary policy was not tried very much during the 1940s. It was often forgotten during the policy discussions of the time that Keynes's views on the efficacy of monetary policy were related to the particular situation of the 1930s.

Another influential idea embodied in Keynes's writing was that of economic stagnation. He suggested that in the advanced industrial countries people tended to save more as their incomes grew larger and that private consumption tended to be a smaller and smaller part of the national income. This implied that investment would have to take a continually larger share of the national income in order to maintain full employment. Since he doubted that investment would rise sufficiently to do this, Keynes was rather pessimistic about the possibility of achieving full employment in the long run. He thus suggested that there might be some permanent tendency to high levels of unemployment. This also had considerable influence on economic policy during the early postwar period; it was some time before those in decision-making positions realized that inflation, rather than stagnation and unemployment, was to be the main problem confronting them.

The desirability of pursuing policies to maintain high levels of employment was generally accepted in most industrial countries after the war. In 1944 the British government stated in its White Paper on Employment Policy that "the government accept as one of their primary aims and responsibilities the maintenance of a high and stable level of employment after the war." One of the most influential British economists at this time was Sir William Beveridge, whose book Full Employment in a Free Society had a strong impact on general thinking. Similar ideas were expressed in the United States in the Employment Act of 1946, which stated: "The Congress hereby declares that it is the continuing policy and responsibility of the Federal Government to promote maximum employment, production and purchasing power." The Employment Act was less specific as to policy than the British government's White Paper, but it established a council of economic advisers to assist the president and called upon him to present to every regular session of Congress a report on the state of the economy. The president was also required to present a program showing "ways and means of promoting a high level of employment and production." Similar programs were adopted in other countries. In Sweden in 1944 the Social Democrats published a document somewhat similar to the British White Paper, and other such declarations were made in Canada and Australia.

Fiscal Policy

Fiscal policy attempts to control the actions of individuals and companies by means of spending and taxation decisions. On the expenditure side, it can achieve this by spending money in ways—for example, on construction projects—that stimulate other activity, while on the taxation side it can affect work, investment, or production decisions by changing tax rates and levels. Fiscal policy thus has two major components: an overall effect generated by the balance between the resources the government puts into the economy through expenditures and the resources it takes out through taxation, charges, or borrowing; and a microeconomic effect generated by the specific policies it adopts. Both are important in stabilizing the economy.

Overall fiscal policy involves the government in deciding whether it should spend more than it receives or less. The development of countercyclical fiscal policies in the post-World War II period reflected the explicit attempt by some governments to protect their population from world recessions by deliberately spending additional money at appropriate times. Experience with countercyclical fiscal policy has been disappointing; in many cases, the lag between identifying the problem and fiscal response has been too long, with the result that a fiscal boost coincided with the next boom, while a contraction might coincide with the next recession. Fiscal policies that were intended to be countercyclical could end up exacerbating the original problems.

Another facet to fiscal policy is a government's attempt to guide the development of the economy by more specifically targeted policies. Thus most countries have from time to time attempted to cushion particular areas from the effects of a decline in their dominant industry by regional policies, to affect labour supply and demand by taxation, and to change the pattern of consumer purchases by changes to indirect taxes. These policies sometimes backfire as unforeseen consequences and interactions occur.

The simple notion of budget balance, although widespread, can be seriously misleading to one who attempts to decide whether a government is being expansionary or contractionary at a particular time. If nothing else were happening, and there were no inflation, no changes in unemployment or exchange rates, and the country were to have a constant population of all ages, then the government's fiscal position, or stance, might be said to be neutral (neither expansionary nor contractionary) if spending were an exact match of taxation, charges, and profits on public sector activities. (Even in such a case, however, if it were pursuing specific microeconomic policies, its neutrality might hide significant effects on the behaviour of the economy.) This notion has led many countries to believe that fiscal position is appropriately measured by the size of public borrowing, because this measures the difference between the amount government spends and the amount it receives.

The recognition that simple budget balance (not accounting for inflation) may not in fact be neutral when other things are changing has led to a number of suggestions for more sophisticated measures of fiscal position. The full-employment budget surplus suggested by the Council of Economic Advisers in the United States, for instance, attempts to adjust the simple measure of budget deficit or surplus in reaction to the effects of deviations from a level of unemployment that it regards as "normal" or "full." The argument for this kind of adjustment is that high levels of unemployment cause increased benefit payments and reduced tax receipts that are abnormal, and if the government were to try to maintain a simple budget balance at times of high employment, this would require a large contraction in the other activities it supports. A simple deficit, then, may be a surplus on a full-employment basis, and government action may be severely contractionary despite positive levels of borrowing.

Another type of suggested adjustment recognizes that inflation erodes the real value of public debt. The neutral simple budget balance, it is argued, only requires that the government maintain its real asset position. If inflation is eroding the real value of existing debt, then the government may borrow to an adjusted, or revised, level before its actions actually reduce public assets.

Although it has come to be recognized that a simple budget deficit or surplus does not adequately reflect a government's fiscal position, no country directly employs measures revised for unemployment and inflation in deciding on countercyclical policies. This is partly because they are more difficult for politicians to understand and partly because it is genuinely difficult to decide on the precise form they should take. Whatever the reason, many countries, even at times of high inflation and unemployment, continue to focus on the simple budget balance measures. The United Kingdom, for example, continued in 1980–81 to attempt to reduce public borrowing during a serious world recession and ran an adjusted surplus. This procyclical policy is blamed by many as a cause of the high levels of unemployment that subsequently prevailed in that country.

The heyday of fiscal stabilization policies was, however, the 1950s and '60s. In the 1970s governments became increasingly concerned about inflationary pressures, and important disturbances, particularly the oil crisis, disrupted world economies. Stabilization became a less important policy goal and one that governments were increasingly unable to achieve. Monetarist economic theories acquired increased influence. The primary economic issues determining fiscal policies once again became the more traditional concerns of allocation and distribution.

Monetary Policy

Although the governmental budget is primarily concerned with fiscal policy (defining what resources it will raise and what it will spend), the government also has a number of tools that it can use to affect the economy through monetary control. By managing its portfolio of debt, it can affect interest rates, and by deciding on the amount of new money injected into the economy, it can affect the amount of cash in circulation and, therefore, indirectly affect prices and other economic variables. In recent years, governments, discouraged by past failures with fiscal manipulation, have turned to monetarist policies to attempt control of the economy.

At its simplest, monetarist theory postulates that in the economy there is a fixed amount of money, which circulates at a given velocity. This money is then available to finance the various transactions carried out in the economy at the prevailing prices. Under these circumstances, according to the theory, control of the price level can be maintained by controlling the amount of available money.

Although a desire to control inflation has been at the heart of the recent rise to prominence of monetary policies in many countries, monetary policy can be used to affect a number of different facets of economic behaviour. In time of unemployment the central bank may stimulate private investment expenditure, and possibly also household spending on consumer goods, by reducing interest rates and taking measures to increase the supply of credit, liquid assets, and money. The customary tools for doing this are open market operations, the discount rate of the central bank, and cash reserve requirements for commercial banks.

In open market operations the central bank buys government securities—bonds and treasury bills—from the private sector. The effect is to reduce interest rates by bidding up bond prices. The sellers of the government securities obtain cash that they deposit in the banks, thus increasing the cash reserves of the banks and enabling them to expand credit to private borrowers; this in turn causes interest rates in the private sector to fall and the terms of credit to become easier. In response, firms are likely to increase their investment expenditures, and households are likely to spend more on consumer goods.

The second tool of monetary policy, the discount rate of the central banks, is often used together with open market operations. This is the interest rate at which commercial banks can borrow funds from the central bank. If the discount rate is reduced, banks become more willing to extend credit to private borrowers because they can obtain funds themselves on easier terms. In many countries, changes in the discount rate tend to be followed by similar changes in the interest rates charged by banks to their borrowers.

The third tool of monetary policy, that of the cash reserve requirements (and, in some countries, certain types of government securities) for commercial banks, provides that banks must maintain money balances (in the form of deposits in the central bank) at a certain proportion of their liabilities. This means that the banks cannot expand their earning assets such as government securities and private loans, beyond that point. If the government reduces the reserve requirements, the banks can expand their loans further, thus increasing the total volume of credit outstanding.

Monetary policy, like fiscal policy, may also be used to combat inflationary tendencies by reversing the above measures; the central bank will then sell government securities (thereby increasing interest rates and reducing the supply of private credit and money), raise the discount rate, or increase reserve requirements.

Stabilization Policy Problems

A broad distinction may be made between two types of stabilization policies: discretionary and automatic. Discretionary policies involve deliberate actions taken by the authorities, such as open market operations, changes in discount rates and reserve requirements, and changes in tax rates or government expenditures. Automatic policies put reliance on built-in stabilizers that function without any deliberate intervention by the authorities. In the monetary field, for example, an increase in commodity prices tends to reduce the real value of financial assets, and if the government does nothing to offset this by increasing the volume of financial assets in the system, private spending will tend to decline. On the fiscal side, the main automatic stabilizer is the relation between tax revenues and cyclical changes in the economy. During booms, tax revenues rise and the need for expenditures on unemployment compensation decreases, channeling a larger proportion of the national income into government coffers; these effects are accentuated if the tax system is progressive because tax revenues rise more rapidly than money incomes. Provided that the government does not raise its expenditures along with the increased revenues, the budget tends to have a braking effect on private expenditure in boom times and an expansionary effect in times of recession.

Problem of Time Lags

There has been much discussion over the merits of discretionary policies as against automatic stabilizers. One advantage of automatic stabilizers is that the effects occur without the necessity of government action, which means that there is no delay, or lag, because of political controversies, administrative problems, or difficulties in determining whether the time has come to act. There are three types of lag in economic policy: the recognition lag, the decision lag, and the effect lag.

The recognition lag is the time it takes for the authorities to discover the need to make a change in economic policy. The reasons for this type of lag are that statistical information is often somewhat behind the event and that it is sometimes difficult to distinguish between random fluctuations and fundamental shifts in economic trends. Governments prefer to wait until there is certainty that, say, an increase in unemployment is not a passing thing.

The decision lag is the period between the time when the need for action is recognized and the time when action is taken. Although the recognition lag is presumably of about the same duration for both monetary and fiscal policies, the decision lag is usually considerably shorter for monetary policy than for fiscal policy. The central bank can change monetary policy almost overnight, whereas a change in fiscal policy is more complex, both politically and administratively. In many countries changes in income taxes, for example, can be made only at the beginning of a calendar year; such changes are often complicated by political discussions in the legislative body.

The effect lag is the amount of time between the time action is taken and an effect is realized. Monetary policy involves longer delays than fiscal policy; the time between a change in monetary policy and its ultimate effect on private investment may be between one and two years.

Some economists argue that the sum of all the lags is so long and uncertain that the best strategy is not to take any action; by the time the effects occur the economic situation may be radically different. Some countries have tried to shorten the lags in fiscal and monetary policy. One way to reduce the recognition lag is to improve the forecasting techniques, for example, by using sophisticated questionnaires or computerized econometric models.

In order to reduce the decision lag in fiscal policy, some countries have given the authorities power to take limited action without the prior consent of the legislature. In the United Kingdom the government introduced a regulation that allowed it to make immediate changes in tax policy. In

Belgium and West Germany the governments also have some discretionary powers to change tax rates without first asking the legislature. In most countries, however, the legislative bodies have been reluctant to give up control of the budget, and increasing skepticism about the effectiveness of stabilization policy has led to a retreat from frequent small adjustments to fiscal policy.

Attempts to shorten the effect lag of fiscal policy have produced new policy tools. Some countries now use systems of taxes or subsidies to influence business investment within a relatively short time. Attempts have also been made to reduce the effect lag in monetary policy. Some countries have tried using various tools of credit rationing rather than relying on traditional measures such as open market operations. But the effect lag is still a serious problem for monetary policy.

Conflicts among Goals

Perhaps the most serious unsolved problem of stabilization policy is the multiplicity of goals that policymakers must consider. Every government has aims other than stabilizing the economy. First, it must stay in power—a need that is likely to limit the alternatives open to stabilization policy, particularly in periods of prosperity immediately before elections. Second, some monetary and fiscal actions impinge on particular groups in society, and governments may wish to avoid what appear to be discriminatory policies. Third, a policy designed to achieve one element of stabilization, such as full employment, may prevent the achievement of another.

The conflict between full employment and price stability seems to arise in two different sets of circumstances. Often wage increases that are made in the normal collective bargaining process are greater than the increases in labour productivity (or output per man-hour); such wage increases tend to increase the cost of production and to force prices upward. The government is then confronted with a choice between two unpleasant alternatives. One is to allow the general price level to rise approximately in proportion to the increase in production costs; the other alternative is to try to hold prices down by taking measures to restrict aggregate demand, thus making it difficult for firms to shift their increased costs to the consumer through higher prices. The latter alternative means increased unemployment. Many governments have been confronted with exactly this choice of alternatives. Wage gains made in collective bargaining have forced them to choose between allowing prices to move upward or attempting to hold prices stable at the cost of greater unemployment.

Another reason for the conflict between full employment and price stability is the tendency of wage increases to accelerate when the level of employment rises and the number of job vacancies increases. In other words, as the economy approaches full employment wages tend to rise at an increasing speed. As prices begin to rise, the conflict between full employment and price stability may be further exacerbated by the expectation that they will rise still further; this may, for example, induce employees and their organizations to press for greater wage increases than they otherwise would in order to compensate for the expected price increases.

Another conflict in policy may arise with respect to the balance of payments. When the economy is in a period of boom, there is a tendency for imports to increase, and sometimes for exports to decrease as well, with obvious difficulties for the balance of payments. The crisis may be heightened by short-term capital movements if buyers and sellers of foreign exchange expect that there may be a devaluation of the country's currency. This has caused much difficulty for many countries in the period since World War II. In Britain and Denmark, notably, periods of boom have usually been accompanied by balance-of-payments problems. When that occurs, the government must sooner or later take restrictive actions that slow the economy down and increase unemployment; if speculation in the currency is already under way, it may be necessary to pursue the restrictive policy far into the next recession. The problem is accentuated if there have been substantial price increases during the boom that have reduced the country's ability to compete with other countries. It is ironic that a temporary improvement in the employment situation may, if it leads to an accelerated increase in the price level, serve to create greater unemployment in the future, when restrictive actions become necessary for balance-of-payments reasons.

Attempts have been made to eliminate these conflicts of policy. One remedy is "incomes policy," direct efforts by the government to prevent employers and unions from raising prices and wages. Various methods have been tried. The most moderate is the so-called guideposts system, under which the government announces the need for restraints on wage increases and perhaps also sets targets to guide unions and management; this was attempted in the United States in the early 1960s. In Sweden, responsibility for limiting wage increases has been assigned to labour-management organizations where bargaining takes place in a centralized fashion. A more interventionist approach is for the government to enter the bargaining process and try to persuade unions to limit their wage demands. The government may go still further and announce a wage freeze, or even a system of wage and price control. In the Netherlands, the courts have occasionally been empowered to set wages, but the resulting decisions have often been uncoordinated with the rest of stabilization policy.

Incomes policies have sometimes succeeded for short periods. Generally, however, public refusal to accept the restraints has eventually led to their collapse. In the United States, the guideposts broke down during the boom of the mid-1960s, and attempts at incomes policy in Sweden and Britain have not been notable for their success. Even in the Netherlands later attempts to impose the system have failed to limit the rate of wage increase.

Governmental Competence

Governments have displayed serious deficiencies in their ability to handle stabilization policy. Political leaders often lack economic information and understanding, and their economic advisers find it difficult to explain the economic situation to them and to apprise them of the relevant tools. There are also a variety of political inhibitions against taking action. One consequence is that what is designed to be a countercyclical policy becomes a procyclical one; instead of stabilizing the economy it tends to destabilize it. The postwar experience in Britain is held by some to demonstrate the deficiencies of government in handling monetary and fiscal policy. In time of boom the government often followed an expansionary course; when a balance-of-payments crisis developed it then took restrictive action—too late—and pushed the economy into deeper recession than would otherwise have occurred. On the basis of this experience, some economists have argued that a policy that did not attempt to counter the short-run swings in the economy would have been more successful in achieving stabilization. They maintain that the authorities should concentrate on letting the volume of money and credit increase steadily at a rate dictated by the long-term growth trend of the economy. Those who hold this view believe that capitalist economies are inherently stable, that crises are usually the result of bad policies on the part of the public authorities. Most economists do not share their optimism as to the stability of the economy if left alone; they continue to believe that governments must seek better tools for the purpose of short-run stabilization.

Experience in Selected Countries

The application of full-employment policies after World War II was made more difficult by the fact that the postwar situation was radically different from that of the 1930s, when much of the policy thinking had been done. Most governments and their advisers expected a depression after the war, but it never materialized. One explanation is that the reallocation of resources from military to civilian uses proceeded more smoothly than expected. Another explanation is that the consumers spent a larger part of their disposable income than they had been observed to do in the 1930s, upsetting some of the statistical projections based on empirical data from those years. A third explanation, which applies perhaps to the years after 1948, was the Cold War between the United States and the Soviet Union, which raised defense spending in many countries.

The period of the late 1940s and early 1950s proved to be characterized by tendencies to inflation rather than to unemployment. Governments were slow to realize this and to shift their emphasis from employment-creating policies to anti-inflationary policies. The fact that governments had accepted, to a large extent, the belief that monetary policy was not very important made it difficult for them to combat the tendencies to inflation. In most countries a passive, even expansionary, monetary policy was in effect; interest rates were kept down and the supply of money was allowed to grow faster than would have been consistent with stable prices. Inflationary tendencies were further stimulated by the Korean War and the great increases in raw material prices that accompanied it.

During the 1950s several important developments influenced the attitudes of governments toward stabilization policy. Most of the economic controls engendered by the war were removed, particularly in international trade and finance. The western European countries were in a period of rapid economic growth. With the removal of direct controls on prices, imports, and building investment, governments began to develop and refine the tools of monetary and fiscal policy. In most countries the passive attitude toward monetary policy disappeared during the early 1950s; there was increased interest in more flexible monetary management. Interest also grew in developing a systematic fiscal policy that would offset the cyclical swings in production and employment. The most energetic attempts to devise a countercyclical fiscal policy were made in Britain and Sweden. Other European countries and the United States placed more reliance on monetary policy.

In the United States, a contributing factor in the revival of monetary policy was a theoretical reformulation that took place among monetary and banking experts. This was the so-called availability theory of credit; it held that monetary policy had its effect on spending not only directly through interest rates but also by restricting the general availability of credit and liquid funds. It was argued that even rather small changes in the rate of interest for government securities could have a considerable impact on the supply of private credit; if the supply diminished, this would induce banks and other financial institutions to stiffen their credit standards and ration credit to their customers; this in turn, it was argued, would tend to curb investment and thus have a braking effect on the economy. Similar ideas were at work in other countries, but with more emphasis on limiting the availability of credit through credit rationing, loan ceilings, control of private bond issues, regulation of installment credit for the purchase of durable consumer goods, and so on.

Serious attempts have been made to put a countercyclical monetary policy into practice in most advanced industrialized countries since the middle of the 1950s. In some, such as the United States, the emphasis has been, as suggested above, on changes in the interest rate and in the supply of money and credit; in others, such as France, Italy, and Japan, the emphasis has been on the rationing of credit by the central bank.

Fiscal policy has found less use than monetary policy in efforts to control cyclical fluctuations in the economy. It has been most favoured in Britain, the Scandinavian countries, and the Netherlands. There are specific situations in which fiscal measures have been used to stimulate the economy in other countries, as in Belgium and West Germany during the recessions of 1958 and 1962. Another example is the postponement of certain military expenditures in the United States as an anti-inflationary measure during the boom of the mid-1950s, and, most notably, the tax cuts passed by Congress in 1964 and 1981 as a stimulus to economic expansion. Several countries have taken restrictive fiscal actions to overcome balance-of-payments crises, including France and Finland on various occasions. During the later 20th century there was an increasing tendency to employ fiscal policies in the short run, partly in order to assist monetary policy in solving cyclical problems.

Distributive Function

Virtually everything that a government does has some effect on the distribution of income or wealth at the various levels of society. Improvements in health care facilities benefit the sick, the old, and those about to have children. An increase in taxes on tobacco and beer affects the poor disproportionately, while an increase in capital taxes similarly affects the rich. Even regulatory and legislative activity benefits one group out of proportion to another. The redistributive consequences of the governmental budget can be reflected in a variety of ways; sometimes they are explicit and sometimes they are cited in the debate that follows the presentation of a budget. Usually, however, these consequences are hidden, unintended, and imperfectly understood.

Incidence of Taxation and Expenditure

The incidence of taxes is a subject that has generated much academic debate. It is usual to distinguish between the legal incidence of a tax and its effective, or final, incidence. The legal incidence is on the person or company who is legally obliged to pay the tax. Effective, or final, incidence refers to who actually ends up paying the tax; if, for example, the whole of a sales tax can be passed on in higher prices to the consumer, then consumers bear the final incidence of the tax.

Whether the final incidence of the tax is on those who actually pay it depends on their market power relative to the people with whom they trade. A payroll tax, for example, is likely to be reflected in lower wages if labour is mobile and in plentiful supply, but may be borne, at least in part, by the employer if there are labour shortages. Similarly, if a manufacturer is facing intense international competition, his ability to pass on any increase in a sales tax is limited; on the other hand, his ability to do so is much greater if he is the sole supplier of a good.

Arguments for Income Redistribution

Although governments do affect the distribution of resources in numerous ways, this is often a by-product of the other things they are trying to do. It has been long debated whether or not governments should seek explicitly to redistribute income from the rich to the poor and, if so, to what extent. More generosity to the poor, whether through higher benefits or through a more progressive tax system, means a higher tax burden on richer people, with, it is argued, consequent effects on work effort and on other behaviour. The appropriate degree of redistribution has been the subject of an extensive literature on optimal taxes, but economists generally agree that the final determination must be through the political process.

Economists point to a number of arguments favouring explicit as opposed to indirect methods of redistribution. The primary argument is that these would provide a more efficient means of eradicating severe hardship, suffering, or starvation. Left to itself, the market economy creates casualties among those who lack the skills to participate fully or those who have failed to generate sufficient resources to tide them over into old age. Countries have evolved programs for the prevention of severe need, although the definition of an acceptable minimum standard of living is typically more generous in European countries than in, for example, the United States, and this is reflected in the higher share of public expenditure in those countries. In most countries the definition of poverty, as measured by the level to which the state benefit system brings everyone's income, has moved from being "absolute" (determined by the minimum requirement of food, clothing, and shelter) to a more relative concept, which allows the poor to share in real rises in living standards.

The second argument for redistribution is that overall social welfare is thereby increased. An additional dollar makes more difference to the standard of living of someone earning $100 per week than to that of someone earning $1,000. Even if everyone has income above an agreed minimum level, there is a case for redistribution from the rich to the not-so-rich. The extent to which this should be pursued depends partly on the perceived distortions the redistribution would cause and partly on how much more value the far more numerous not-so-rich can squeeze out of each additional dollar.

Other arguments for redistribution occur where the market fails to allow individuals to redistribute between periods in their own lives. The classic example is that people tend to have their periods of highest expenditure (while bringing up children) at the points of minimum income (early in life). Those families with little or no access to credit markets can do very little about this, which has been used as one argument for redistribution toward those bringing up children. A second argument contends that children convey benefits to society as a whole, so that parents should be rewarded for creating a public good. This argument would, of course, have little strength in countries with serious problems of overpopulation.

A final group of arguments also concerns market failure. If particular areas or occupations have declined and the work force has not adjusted to this decline by moving to other areas or through retraining, then some subsidy to cushion the recessive effects might be considered appropriate. Most countries redistribute from better-off regions to those that have declined, or they allocate funds for specific programs designed to help particular groups.

FOREIGN POLICY

A state's foreign policy consists of the strategies it uses to protect its international and domestic interests and determines the way it interacts with other state and non-state actors. The primary purpose of foreign policy is to defend a nation's national interests, which can be in nonviolent or violent ways.

- Foreign policy encompasses the tactics and process by which a nation interacts with other nations in order to further its own interests.
- Foreign policy may make use of diplomacy or other more direct means such as aggression rooted in military power.
- International bodies such as the United Nations and its predecessor, the League of Nations, help smooth relations between countries via diplomatic means.
- Major foreign policy theories are Realism, Liberalism, Economic Structuralism, Psychological Theory, and Constructivism.

Examples of Foreign Policy

In 2013 China developed a foreign policy known as the Belt and Road Initiative, the nation's strategy to develop stronger economic ties in Africa, Europe, and North America. In the United States, many presidents are known for their landmark foreign policy decisions such as the Monroe Doctrine which opposed the imperialist takeover of an independent state. A foreign policy can also be the decision to not participate in international organizations and conversations, such as the more isolationist policies of North Korea.

Diplomacy and Foreign Policy

When foreign policy relies on diplomacy, heads of state negotiate and collaborate with other world leaders to prevent conflict. Usually, diplomats are sent to represent a nation's foreign policy interests at international events. While an emphasis on diplomacy is a cornerstone of many states' foreign policy, there are others that rely on military pressure or other less diplomatic means.

Diplomacy has played a crucial role in the de-escalation of international crises, and the Cuban Missile Crisis of 1962 is a prime example of this. During the Cold War, intelligence informed President John F. Kennedy that the Soviet Union was sending weapons to Cuba, possibly preparing for a strike against the United States. President Kennedy was forced to choose between a foreign policy solution that was purely diplomatic, speaking to the Soviet Union President Nikita Khrushchev or one that was more militaristic. The former president decided to enact a blockade around Cuba and threaten further military action if Soviet ships carrying missiles attempted to break through.

In order to prevent further escalation, Khrushchev agreed to remove all missiles from Cuba, and in return, Kennedy agreed not to invade Cuba and to remove U.S. missiles from Turkey (which was within striking distance of the Soviet Union). This moment in time is significant because the two governments negotiated a solution that ended the current conflict, the blockade, as well as de-escalated the larger tension, the missiles near each other's borders.

Foreign Policy and Diplomatic Organizations

Foreign policy has existed as long as people have organized themselves into varying factions. However, the study of foreign policy and the creation of international organizations to promote diplomacy is fairly recent.

One of the first established international bodies for discussing foreign policy was the Concert of Europe in 1814 after the Napoleonic wars. This gave the major European powers (Austria, France, Great Britain, Prussia, and Russia) a forum to solve issues diplomatically instead of resorting to military threats or wars.

In the 20th Century, World War I and II once again exposed the need for an international forum to de-escalate conflict and keep the peace. The League of Nations (which was formed by former U.S. President Woodrow Wilson but ultimately did not include the U.S.) was created in 1920 with the primary purpose of maintaining world peace. After the League of Nations dissolved, it was replaced by the United Nations in 1954 after World War II, an organization to promote international cooperation and now includes 193 countries as members.

It is important to note that many of these organizations are concentrated around Europe and the Western Hemisphere as a whole. Because of European countries' history of imperialism and colonization, they often wielded the greatest international political and economic powers and subsequently created these global systems. However, there are continental diplomatic bodies such as the African Union, Asia Cooperation Dialogue, and Union of South American Countries which facilitate multilateral cooperation in their respective regions as well.

Foreign Policy Theories

The study of foreign policy reveals several theories as to why states act the way they do. The prevailing theories are Realism, Liberalism, Economic Structuralism, Psychological Theory, and Constructivism.

Realism

Realism states that interests are always determined in terms of power and states will always act according to their best interest. Classical Realism follows 16th-century political theorist Niccolò Machiavelli's famous quote from his foreign policy book "The Prince": "It is much safer to be feared than loved."

It follows that the world is full of chaos because humans are egoistic and will do anything to have power. The structural reading of realism, however, focuses more on the state than the individual: All governments will react to pressures in the same way because they are more concerned about national security than power.

Liberalism

The theory of liberalism emphasizes liberty and equality in all aspects and believes that the rights of the individual are superior to the needs of the state. It also follows that the chaos of the world can be pacified with international cooperation and global citizenship. Economically, liberalism values free trade above all and believes the state should rarely intervene in economic issues, as this is where problems arise. The market has a long-term trajectory towards stability, and nothing should interfere with that.

Economic Structuralism

Economic structuralism, or Marxism, was pioneered by Karl Marx, who believed that capitalism was immoral because it is the immoral exploitation of the many by the few. However, theorist

Vladimir Lenin brought the analysis to an international level by explaining that imperialist capitalist nations succeed by dumping their excess products in economically weaker nations, which drives down the prices and further weakens the economy in those areas. Essentially, issues arise in international relations because of this concentration of capital, and change can only occur through the action of the proletariat.

Psychological Theories

Psychological theories explain international politics on a more individual level and seek to understand how an individual's psychology can affect their foreign policy decisions. This follows that diplomacy is deeply affected by the individual ability to judge, which is often colored by how solutions are presented, the time available for the decision, and level of risk. This explains why political decision making is often inconsistent or may not follow a specific ideology.

Constructivism

Constructivism believes that ideas influence identities and drive interests. The current structures only exist because years of social practice have made it so. If a situation needs to be resolved or a system must be changed, social and ideological movements have the power to bring about reforms. A core example of constructivism is human rights, which are observed by some nations, but not others. Over the past few centuries, as social ideas and norms around human rights, gender, age, and racial equality have evolved, laws have changed to reflect these new societal norms.

POLICY MONITORING

Monitoring is the process of observing. It is not controlling. Policy monitoring has come to mean the process of observing the progress of policy implementation and resource utilisation, and anticipating deviations from policy expectations. Its implications are that management takes steps to ensure that all activities related to policy implementation are completed within the given time and budget. Monitoring can be defined as "the process of inducing action for adherence to schedule". If monitoring shows that a particular policy activity is deviating from planned parameters then the management may take required measures to replan that particular activity. But if there is a significant variation from planned parameters, it is important to analyse the source of deviation before deciding upon the remedial measures.

Policy monitoring in brief is based on the following five assumptions:

1. Policy/programme is measurable in terms of certain indicators or desired objectives.
2. Personnel responsibility for the programme performance exists at all levels in the organisation.
3. Adequacy of time for monitoring is ensured.
4. There are proper tools for identifying deviations from programme performance.
5. Provision exists for adjustments, which correct the deviations from planned expectations outcomes.

The significance of the monitoring of public policy lies in seeing that intended results are achieved through the efficient use of resources. Monitoring helps in designing and implementing systems for the processes, which provide just the right mount of detail for adequate control of policy execution. Experience has shown that effective monitoring can ensure the proper execution of policy with desired results in the shortest amount of time.

An effective monitoring of public policies aids in cost reduction, time saving, and effective resource utilisation. The key issue in monitoring is to create an information system that gives policy makers and policy iinplementers the information they need to make timely decisions and policies that will keep policy programme performance as close as possible to the objectives of the policy. Therefore, it is important that monitoring and control processes should be given due importance and be designed properly.

Approaches to Policy Monitoring

Various policy monitoring models and approaches have been advanced for the purpose of securing effective monitoring of policy implementation. These models may perform differently according to the evaluation criteria employed. Model evaluation then becomes the task of listing the pros and cons of different approaches. A few approaches in relation to monitoring of public policies are discussed here.

Managerial Approaches

Managerial approaches to monitoring have come to form the operational paradigm in the implementation of public policies. The management of the public sector has now adopted more or less business-like style, the techniques of which were once thought of as private-sector methods.

CPM and PERT

In this context, two approaches, namely, i) Critical Path Method (CPM), and ii) Programme Evaluation and Review Technique (PERT) have gained wide recognition not only in the private sector but also in the public sector. Both CPM and PERT approaches employ the idea of managing large-scale policy programmes. As a means of addressing the issues of material and resource use in the most efficient manner, the concepts of CPM and PERT have proved quite useful. These refer to the planning of a particular programme, aIlocating people and other resources, and monitoring progress. The aim of CPM and PERT is to control the execution of a policy programme by controlling the network of activities and events which compose the stages of policy implementation. The CPM is a technique, which aims to identify those activities that are critical to the successful implementation of a policy programme on time.

A network is drawn to show the starting period of the policy programme, and the estimated time period involved in moving from one critical activity to another. On the other hand, PERT is a technique, which predicates that the duration of critical activities are uncertain. It involves a graphic estimation of the time and resources necessary for policy execution. This can be applied to a number of efforts, ranging from a housing project to the scheduling and deployment of personnel. The PERT systems are programmed on the basis of three types of calculation of this uncertainty: the most probable duration, the shortest forecast of direction, and the longest forecast of duration.

The PERT analysis is often used in the implementation of large scale policy programmes (such as, rural development) where there is a high level of uncertainty surrounding the completion of a policy programme. In this way policy programme is monitored and controlled through PERT and CPM approaches.

PPBS

In addition to CPM and PERT approaches, Planning - Programming - Budgeting System (PPBS) has been regarded as an impostant technique associated with policy analysis. The PPBS approach seeks to set clear goals, outputs, and values in the budgetary process, and to create a system of analysis and review in which the costs and benefits of a policy programme could be calculated over several years. This approach is based on' the idea that an organisation's activity can be viewed as the production of defined products or outputs. Costs and benefits of each product can be determined. The PPBS aims at locating decisions about pasts of the budget in the context of the whole of the government spending strategy. The model is derived from the classical rational approach, beginning with the identification of goals, objectives, needs and problems, and culminating in monitoring, review, and feedback.

Charles Schultz, who is associated with the advancement of this model, observes that PPBS subjects programmes to competition from alternative and more effective or efficient programmes. Thus, the PPBS approach aims at establishing goals and strategies, analysing their cause and benefits, focusing on objectives to be achieved, and monitoring through an on going review of results.

As an approach, it also aims at exercising control on budget expenditures. However, it is argued by some that the PPBS is somewhat ill-suited for monitoring; the PPBS simply failed to live up to its promise. Although the PPBS was largely a failure, its introduction brought into policy management a more comprehensive approach to Cost-Benefit Analysis (CBA).

Activity Bar Chart

For monitoring technical performance of a policy, the Activity Bar Chart can be mapped. It is an important device for monitoring policy performance as it projects expectations for policy results. The Activity Bar' Chart plans each technical activity by time and deliverables. It shows the dates by which those deliverables should be completed. For example, an Activity Bar Chart can be cleveloped for a housing policy designed to replace urban slums with low-cost housing.

Systems Approach

Monitoring is an operational activity, which occurs ill the process of implementing aiven policy. programme. The main objective of monitoring is to ensure that resource inputs are used in such ways as to generate the highest quality of policy outputs. An effective monitoring, therefore, requires proper thrilling. Here, structuring in policy work can involve both the simulating of the organisation and structuring the policy programme itself, and the combining of these two structures to provide a framework for integration. The structuring tools at implementation gaps as something that should be analysed in the context of a 'system', which as a whole is involved in the delivery of policy programme and services. The systems analyst is concerned in knowing how a total sequence of programme activities, and inputs and outputs contribute to the success or failure of a policy delivery programme.

Caster and his associates suggest that a successful implementation system involves four types of control, that is, i) coordination over time; ii) coordination at particular time; iii) detailed logistics and scheduling; and iv) defending and maintaining structural boundaries. It may be emphasised that systems approach lays stress on attaining adequate levels of cooperation and coordination within the policy programme by focusing on the importance of real world for effective monitoring.

Effective implementation and its subset monitoring depend on certain elements, such as, formulating strategy for the monitoring of the policy, and analysing what has happened in terms of what should have happened according to the plan and implementing change so as to make up for the order to realise an objective or goal.

Formative Approach

According to this approach, monitoring starts with a schedule and works for the success of a policy programme when it is being implemented. It involves an analysis of the extent to which a programme is being implemented and the conditions that note its successful implementation. The implementation stage, therefore, requires formative evaluation, which monitors the way in which a programme is being administration manage so as to provide feedback that may help to improve the implementation process.

Monitoring of the process of implementation provides techniques for evaluating the way in which a programme is being managed or delivered, Thus, this information is utilised to correct or improve the policy delivery process more effectively. This takes the form of various kinds of centralised Management Information Systems (MIS) that can routine the collection of information. The MIS has been greatly improved by the use of computers. It helps an ongoing accumulation and organisation of information, which can feed into the managerial decision-making process. A cbre technique of the MIS approach to evaluation and monitoring is that of using performance measurement lt as a primary source of information about the effectiveness and efficiency of policy delivery. This is a form of monitoring, which has come to a pre-eminent position since the late 1970s, when there was a growing demand for efficiency measured by inputs and outputs, due to pressures on public finances.

Performance Measurement Approach

Performance Measurement Approach is applied to know about the effectiveness and efficiency of policy delivery. Measurement is akin to monitoring. It means watching Performance Indicators (PIS) all parameters with a view to detecting the earliest available signs of any deviation: from desired results or performance. Once it is found that some aspect of the policy is deviating too far from expected parameters then it is the job of the policy implementing manager to exert some influence on that aspect or change the parameters.

Generally, some adjustment can be made in resource utilisation or scheduling. Sometimes, anew technical activity may be taken in hand. In this approach, Performance Indicators (PIS) can be developed and used. Peter Jackson argues that measures of performance can provide an effective substitute for profits so as to improve the management of schools, hospitals, local government, and other services. Jackson identifies a number of roles PIS can play in making for better implementation, such as, increasing accountability; providing a basis for policy planning and control; supplying important information to monitor organisational activities; and identifying the basis of a staff appraisal system. Jackson believes that well designed and implemented measures can enhance the value for money (economy, efficiency, and effectiveness) and have apart to play in the delivery of public goods and services. The case for PIs would maintain that they have a number of advantages: they determine progress in moving towards goals; identify problem areas; and contribute to improving personnel management overall. Thus, on the whole, PIS help to improve the capacity of the bureaucracy to control organisations and people.

Monitoring and Control Compliance

The delivery of public policy is unlikely and uncertain without monitoring compliance. A good policy, if it is to be carried out, therefore, must have effective means of enforcement. Kenneth Building distinguishes between three kinds of power, that is, threat, explore range, and love. Enforcement through threats can have productive and integrative consequences (exercise of power by income tax authorities). The use of exchange power may involve bargaining to settle terms of trade. The power of love may involve an appeal to a moral sense or a sense of citizenship. It calls for compliance on the basis of social and personal responsibility. As a model for a delivery strategy, Buildings' classification points towards the mix of enforcements: threat, exchange and love.

For proper implementation and effective functioning, Hood examines and identifies four modes of administrative enforcement and their effectiveness.

- Set aside/modify rules (government may choose either to set the rules aside or to modify the rules), Spread the word (government may choose to use publicity and persuasion),
- Pursue and punish violators (government may choose to use legal and police action),
- Make it difficult and impossible to break rules (in this case the enforcement method involves making the grass physically difficult or in-convinent to get at in the first place).

According to Etzioni, there are three kinds of power that provide a link between the enforcement of public policy and the problems of compliance within the organisations responsible for implementing it. He believes that there are three basic reasons, which compel people in the organisations to play with rules, orders, discipline or policies. Firstly, people do so out of a sense of agreement, love or morality. Secondly, security, they do so because of fear. Thirdly, they may do so because it is in their monetory or remunerative interest. Enforcement may, therefore, be the consequence of:

- Normative (moral).
- Coercive (alienative).
- Remunerative (calculative) power.
- Individual Responsibility.

A policy may rely on monetary rewards or it may ask people to exercise a moral choice. Keeping the western context in view, Etziorii argues that effective organisations are those, which achieve a balanced mix between low levels of fear (corosion and alienation); and high levels of money (remuneration and calculation), and love (non-native and moral) involvements. In seeking to make sure that a policy is carried out effectively, implementation will require a mix of different enforcement modes.

With the rise of mass communications and the use of campaigns based on technology information in areas of social (health and education, women's empowerment, and development) and environmental policies, an increasing emphasis is placed on individual responsibility for problems. For example, campaigns on forest conservation urge that we take individual responsibility for forest conservation.

Constraints in Policy Monitoring

Effective policy implementation requires adequate. monitoring. Policy programmes or activities have to be properly monitored in order to produce the maximum efficiency in resource utilisation. But quite often monitoring is constrained by many factors and forces operating at the internal and external levels. First of all, problems in monitoring relates to poor design of the implementing system with regard of all details to enable good monitoring.

Second, time is a constraint for policy monitoring. Too often the implementing staff feel so pressed to achieve results that they take shortcuts and try to avoid monitoring and control. Experience has shown that monitoring and control when adequately designed and executed can generate the highest quality results in the shortest possible time. A common constraint for the policy implementation authority is the availability of limited corrective actions for application whenever a programme is found to be deviating in some respect from projected performance. For example, cost overruns owing to fluctuations in financial markets often leave the implementing authority with the feeling that their implementation task is becoming difficult.

Fourth, a pervasive obstacle to policy monitoring is ignorance on the part of the monitoring officials about its role and methods. It is often observed that the monitoring staff and key personnel associated with implementation of policies lack the requisite knowledge and skills to monitor and control policy programme performance.

Remedial Measures for Effective Monitoring

Designing the Monitoring System

The emphasis in monitoring is on completion of the policy programme or policy activities (technical performance) on schedule (time performance), and within the section budget (cost performance). To enable this, it is necessary to define precisely the specific characteristics of technical, cost and time on the basis of which performance should be controlled. It is equally important to remain sensitive to deviations in all three elements -technical, time and cost performance. It is not enough to watch cost performance or scheduling alone. Activity Bar Chart, Resource Bar Chart, and Cash Flow Projection tools can be properly designed and developed for monitoring policy performance. These charts and tools can be used to assist considerations, when a noted deviation is worthy of correction and when it is not. It is not enough to watch cost performance or scheduling alone. It is possible for a policy delivery to be on schedule and within budget and still fumble on goal fullfilment.

Communicating about Performance

The role of routine communications for policy performance is invaluable. Policy progression, deviations from planned progress, corrections and plans for completion are key components of policy communications. Every person involved in the policy programme requires ongoing communications at various levels of detail. Higher level management (Secretary Director of the Department concerned or Planning agencies) requires summary reports with a frequency on the status of policy implementation. Operational members of the programme also require detailed information. The objective of communications is to keep people informed so that they are on the sight track, and provide feedback to those involved in the policy. Further, regular meetings to review policy progression must be held at all levels in the organisation.

Monitoring Progress

The objective of monitoring and control is to ensure, through the policy implementation process, that resource inputs are used as efficiently as possible to produce the high quality of policy outputs. Policy managers must compare the time, cost, and technical performance of the policy to the budget, schedule, and tasks defined in the policy programme. This should be done in a systematic manner at regular intervals and not in a haphazard way. Any significant deviations from the planned performance (technical, cost, and time) must be reported immediately, as these anomalies affect the viability and success of the whole policy programme. Further, based on the information below, it is necessary to update the policy regularly. It must also reflect the current status of the policy and any changes that become necessary because of new information, on budgetary or time constraints or other unexpected contingencies.

Improving Capacity of the Monitoring Staff

Effective monitoring largely depends upon the ability, commitment, and attitude of the monitoring staff. The process of monitoring requires some level of effort on the part of people who are particularly skilled in the process. It requires skills in planning and accounting as well as general. management. The monitoring staff need to be delegated the requisite authority to monitor and control. Key functionaries should be made responsible for meaningful contributions to monitor and control decisions.

Taking Corrective Actions

Policy monitoring and control system, through its reports and meetings, should help in taking or recommending corrective actions when there are any deviations from the planned results. There are generally three types of actions, which can be initiated or taken:

- Correction and Improvement: When the policy programme continues to signal merit, a corrective action usually entails a reallocation of resources (staff, money or time).
- Replanning: Replanning of the policy programme may be undertaken to reduce or increase the size of the policy programme in terms of staff, budget or time schedule. Replanting means changing peoples' expectations about the policy results.
- Cancellation: Cancellation is the last resort of action. It means the cancellation of the whole, policy programme. Sometimes this is advisable, particularly in instances of major crises.

POLICY ALIENATION

Policy alienation refers to a framework which examines the experiences of governmental employees with new policies they have to implement. It has been used to describe the experiences of front-line public professionals with new policies. It is defined "as a general cognitive state of psychological disconnection from the policy programme being implemented."

A number of examples can clarify the concept of policy alienation. For example, Bottery, examining the pressures on professionals stemming from new policies in education and health care in Great Britain, cites a teacher arguing that: "The changes have been outrageous, and have produced a culture of meritocracy and high flyers. There's massive paperwork because the politicians don't believe teachers are to be trusted." This indicates that professionals had difficulties identifying with the policies they had to implement. A second example refers to the introduction of a new reimbursement policy in mental healthcare in the Netherlands. In one large-scale survey, as many as nine out of ten professionals wanted to abandon this new policy. Psychologists even went as far as to openly demonstrate on the street against this policy. A major reason for this was that many could not align their professional values with the content of the policy. As one professional noted:

"Within the new healthcare system economic values are dominant. Too little attention is being paid to the content: professionals helping patients. The result is that professionals become more aware of the costs and revenues of their behavior. This comes at the expense of acting according to professional standards."

Overall, a number of studies show an increasing discontent among public professionals toward public policies, although more positive experiences can also be found. The policy alienation framework was developed to better understand the experiences of front-line public professionals with new policies.

Effects of Policy Alienation

Currently, there is an intense debate concerning professionals in the public sector. Many of the pressures that professionals face are related to the difficulties they have with the policies they have to implement. When implementers are unable to identify with a policy, this can negatively influence policy effectiveness. Furthermore, a high degree of policy alienation can affect the quality of interactions between professionals and citizens, which may eventually influence the output legitimacy of government. The policy alienation framework is used to analyze this topic. It has been shown that policy alienation increases resistance to a new policy, lowers behavioral support for the policy and decreases job satisfaction of public professionals. Hence, it has both influences on the individual professional, as well as on policy effectiveness.

Conceptualization

Alienation broadly refers to a sense of social estrangement, an absence of social support or meaningful social connection. Sociologists, public administration scholars, and other social scientists have used the alienation concept in various studies. As a result, a number of meanings have been attributed to the term. In an attempt to provide clarity, Seeman broke these meanings down into five alienation dimensions: powerlessness, meaninglessness, normlessness, social isolation, and self-estrangement.

Many scholars have used these dimensions to devise operational measures for alienation so that they can examine the concept in a range of settings. Mau, for example, used four dimensions in examining student alienation. Rayce et al., when investigating adolescent alienation, used three of the five dimensions. Further, many other researchers have used Seeman's classification in examining the concept of work alienation. Blauner devised operational measures for three of the dimensions: powerlessness, meaninglessness, and social isolation.

The policy alienation framework was conceptualized based on the works of sociologists such as Hegel, Marx, Seeman, and Blauner. Furthermore, works of public administration scholars were used, particularly on Lipsky (street-level bureaucracy). Like work alienation, policy alienation is multidimensional, consisting of policy powerlessness and policy meaninglessness dimensions. In the work alienation literature, the dimensions of powerlessness and meaninglessness are also considered very important.

In essence, powerlessness is a person's lack of control over events in their life. In the realm of policy formulation and implementation, policy powerlessness relates to the degree of influence public professionals have over shaping a policy program. Powerlessness can occur when a new policy is drafted without the help of the professionals, by for example not consulting their professionals associations or labor unions. Furthermore, on an operational level professionals can feel powerless when they have to adhere to tight procedures and rules when implementing a policy. This kind of powerlessness may be particularly pronounced in professionals whose expectations of discretion and autonomy contradict notions of bureaucratic control

The second dimension of policy alienation is meaninglessness. In the realm of policy making and implementation, policy meaninglessness refers to a professional's perception of the contribution that the policy makes to a greater purpose, most notably to society or to their own clients. For instance, a professional can feel that implementing a policy is meaningless, if it does not deliver any apparent beneficial outcomes for society, such as more safety on the streets.

References

- What-is-public-policy: publicpolicyonline.com, Retrieved 22 June, 2019
- Peppard, Christiana Z. "Fresh water scarcity: An introduction to the problem". TED Ed: Lessons Worth Sharing. TED.com. Retrieved 28 August 2015
- Public-policy-and-its-features, government-policies-for-business-growth, commercial-knowledge, guides: toppr.com, Retrieved 23 May, 2019
- Wan, Ming (2010-05-01). "The Great Recession and China's Policy Toward Asian Regionalism". Asian Survey. 50 (3): 520–538. Doi:10.1525/as.2010.50.3.520. ISSN 0004-4687
- Domestic-polic: legaldictionary.net, Retrieved 24 June, 2019
- Duyvendak, W. G. J., Knijn, T., & Kremer, M., eds. (2006). Policy, people, and the new professional. De-professionalisation and re-professionalisation in care and welfare. Amsterdam: Amsterdam University Press. ISBN 978-90-5356-885-9
- Government-economic-policy, topic: britannica.com, Retrieved 25 July, 2019
- Foreign-policy-definition-examples-4178057: thoughtco.com, Retrieved 26 August, 2019

4

Sub-fields of Public Administration

Public administration can be divided into diverse sub-fields such as public-sector ethics, policy analysis, public budgeting, organizational theory and human resource management. The topics elaborated in this chapter will help in gaining a better perspective about these sub-fields of public administration.

ORGANIZATIONAL THEORY

Organizational Theory refers to the set of interrelated concepts, definitions that explain the behavior of individuals or groups or subgroups, who interacts with each other to perform the activities intended towards the accomplishment of a common goal.

In other words, the organizational theory studies the effect of social relationships between the individuals within the organization along with their actions on the organization as a whole. Also, it studies the effects of internal and external business environment such as political, legal, cultural, etc. on the organization.

The term organization refers to the group of individuals who come together to perform a set of tasks with the intent to accomplish the common objectives. The organization is based on the concept of synergy, which means, a group can do more work than an individual working alone.

Thus, in order to study the relationships between the individuals working together and their overall effect on the performance of the organization is well explained through the organizational theories. Some important organizational theories are:

1. Classical Theory,
2. Scientific Management Theory,
3. Administrative Theory,
4. Bureaucratic Theory,
5. Neo-Classical Theory,
6. Modern Theory.

An organizational structure plays a vital role in the success of any enterprise. Thus, the organizational theories help in identifying the suitable structure for an organization, efficient enough to deal with the specific problems.

Contingency Theory of Decision Making

The basis of contingency theory in management is that there is no one best way to handle any task or process. Whether organizing an entire company or planning a production work flow, the best solution is influenced more by internal and external constraints than by a predetermined method or management style.

Organizational Decisions

Contingency theory maintains there is no universal way to set up a business or company successfully. The design of the corporate structure and culture must be in line with its various environments: economic, social and physical. The subsystems of a business also influence successful organizational planning. For example, an information technology business will have different upper-management structure because of the need for a collaborative, cooperative work force that may not thrive under traditional, hierarchical structures.

Leadership Decisions

Applying contingency theory to leadership, management style changes with different organizational situations. A leader's behavior is dependent on three factors that define a favorable leadership situation. Leader-member relations describe the dynamic with staff. Task structure refers to how rigid work assignments are. Position power dictates how able a leader is to exercise authority on a group. In a small business, this could mean an owner's style may need to be fluid with even a single change to her staff.

Task Decisions

When applied to decision-making, the effectiveness of the decision in question depends on a balance of how important the decision is, how complete the decision maker's and the subordinates' information is on the subject, and the likelihood of acceptance of the decision by subordinates. Changing the nature of any one factor alters the relationship with the other two. This may require the small business owner to share more information about an unpopular decision to increase the chances her staff will accept the changes.

Other Constraints

Factors that alter balances in contingency theory relationships are widespread. Any influence on a business or process may change the way a decision is made, or even the need for a decision at all. Some common constraints include: The size of an organization, differences between senior and operational management styles, socioeconomic conditions, government regulations, technologies, attitudes between workers and managers, inherited corporate cultures. Your small business will have its own unique constraints based on type of business, your community, staff and the current economic climate in general.

Contingency Theory of Leadership

The Contingency Theory of Leadership states that a leader's effectiveness is contingent upon with how his or her leadership style matches to the situation. That is, the leader must find out what kind of leadership style and situation he or she thrives in. The Contingency Theory is concerned with the following:

- There is no one best style of leadership.
- A leader is effective when his or her style of leadership fits with the situation.

The Contingency Theory of leadership was developed by Fred Fiedler in 1958 during his research of leader effectiveness in group situations. Fiedler believed that one's effectiveness to lead depended on their control of the situation and the style of leadership. Unlike the Situational Theory of leadership, leader effectiveness is contingent on the leader's style matching the situation, not adapting to it. This theory assumes that styles are fixed, and that they cannot be adapted or modified. A leader is most effective when his or her attributes and style of leadership is matched with the situation and environment around them.

Working of Fiedler's Contingency Theory

The Contingency theory is not concerned with having the leader adapt to a situation, rather the goal is to match the leader's style with a compatible situation. To make best use of this theory, it is important to find what style a leader has. This is done through the Least Preferred Coworker Scale (LPC).

The LPC is a list of questions designed to find out what kind of employee a leader would most like to work with, and in turn shows the leaders style. Fiedler's Contingency Model attempts to match the leader's style using LPC to the situation in which they would thrive.

- High LPC Score– leader with good personal skills and relies on relationships with others to accomplish tasks; people-oriented.
- Low LPC Score– leader that accomplishes goals through focus on the task and positional power; task-oriented.

Task-oriented leaders are most effective when their positional power is high, as well as the task structure. People or relation-oriented leaders perform their best when the relationship levels between themselves and followers are at their greatest. After finding the style of the leader, Fiedler's Model states that finding the best situation for the leader, also known as "situational favorableness".

A situation is defined by three factors in the contingency theory:

- Leader-Member Relation- how the leader interacts with employees.
- Task Structure- how tasks are set up by the leader.
- Positional Power- the amount of power a leader has over followers.

These three factors combine to form the situation in which a leader's style is effective or ineffective. If the three factors match up to the style of the leader, success is projected. It is important to remember that the opposite can happen as well. If a leader is put into a situation opposite of his or her favored task structure, member relation, and level of power, then failure is to ensue. The three factors of contingency situation have less of an impact on leaders who are task-oriented, or score low LPC's, than leaders who are people-oriented and score high LPC's. By using the results from the LPC to find a person's leadership style, and analyzing their preferred leader-member relation, task structure, and positional power, finding the right job or position for someone can be more accurately accomplished.

Comparisons to other Leadership Theories

Comparing Fiedler's Contingency Theory to other theories, we see that the contingency theory incorporates some parts of other theories. In many ways, the contingency theory derives from the trait theory. A leader's traits are directly related to the most effective style and situation in which they lead. The factor of relations with followers related to the transactional and transformational theories. The Contingency Theory states that a leader's relations impact their effectiveness, which is the basis of these two theories. In transactional leadership, a leader's ability to influence followers with rewards and punishments for behavior to ensure member goals is the basis of the style (Leadership, n.d). In Transformational Theory, the leader relies on building relationships between themselves and followers. Leaders who are people-oriented rely on these relationships to be effective and have influence over his or her followers.

Strengths of Contingency Theory

- Used to create leadership profiles for organizations;
- Puts emphasis on combination of leaders style and the situation;
- "It is predictive; there is a well-defined method to evaluate LPC and Situations".

The Contingency Theory can be used to create leadership profiles for organizations, in which certain styles can be matched with situations that have proven to be successful. Companies can know what type of person would fit in each position of the organization whenever there is an opening. This theory also helps to reduce what is expected from leaders, and instead puts emphasis on finding a match to the situation. This theory, although complex, is very useful in matching professionals to the right situations and determining the best person for a job.

PUBLIC SECTOR ETHICS

Public administration is viewed as a part of the executive branch of government. Following Charles de Montesquieu ideas we may recognize executive as an element of the state power and this element consists of agencies, ministries and other structures jointly referred to as "Public Administration". This view of public administration combines in general all activities concerning public good and public interest. Within the administrative state machinery we may find public administration officials, special administrative procedures and many other mechanisms, which are characteristic to all bureaucratic organizations.

Public administration is a part of our daily life and to a large extent governs it. The administrative apparatus consist of people who are also members of the local community (communities). Citizens and public officials, who have access to power, have to coexist together in one area, one space. The difference between them is that public administration officials have to provide services in aid of community. Because of this work, based on public monies and property the possibility of betraying public trust is probable. There is no simplest thing, than spending someone's money, even if we do not get direct profits. Ethical behavior and decisions maintaining citizens' trust, ensure effective and efficient use of resources, and allow government to preserve individual rights while assisting those who will benefit the most. Ethics is one of the vital components that allow democracy to thrive in any country. Ethics in government is critical to realizing the promises of democracy. In a democracy, government has an obligation to treat everyone equally and to provide the greatest good to most of citizens. The effective operation of democratic government requires that public officials and employees be independent, impartial, and responsible to the people. Government decisions and policies should be made within the proper structure of government; public office shall not be used for personal gain; and the public has to have confidence in the integrity of its government. When ethical wrongdoings and scandals occur in government, they pose a threat to the democratic principles of the rule of law, equity, and individual rights. Fraud, bribery, and other abuses in government take the power from people and give it to a few in position of control, which distorts the concept of the equality of all participants of public life.

The definition of social ethics embraces a set of norms, assessments and opinions, which are characteristic of a group of people. This very simple definition of ethics points to society, citizens, groups of people as creators of norms and standards of behavior. Ethics are standards of conduct. These standards can be applied to personal behavior. Ethics distinguish between the right and wrong ways directing behavior in our personal and professional life. Following this way of thinking we may establish a definition of "administrative ethics" using the words: norms, legal regulations, assessments of public administration officials, public service. Public service ethics are a prerequisite to, and underpinning of public trust, and are a keystone of good governance. Public service is a public trust. Citizens expect public servants to serve the public interest with fairness and to manage public resources properly on a daily basis. Fair and reliable public services inspire public trust and create a favorable environment for businesses, thus contributing to well–functioning markets and economic growth.

Public servants operate in a changing environment. They are presently subject to greater public scrutiny and increased demands from citizens; they also face stricter limits on resources. They have to assume new functions and responsibilities as a result of: devolution and greater managerial discretion; increased commercialization of the public sector; a changing public/private sector interface and changing accountability arrangements. In short they have to adopt new ways of carrying out the business of government. While public management reforms have realized important returns in terms of efficiency and effectiveness, some of the adjustments may have had unintended impact on ethics and standards of conduct. This is not to suggest that changes have caused an increase in misconduct or unethical behavior. But they may place public servants in situations involving conflicts of interests or objectives where there are few guidelines as to how they should act. There may indeed be a growing mismatch between traditional values and systems governing the behaviour of public servants and the roles they are expected to fulfill in a changing public sector environment. Public service has its own values and the most important of them is: the integrity.

It can be interpreted to cover a broad range of bureaucratic behavior, but it is used also to refer to administrative or public service ethics, to principles and standards of right conduct for public servants. Certain principles and standards of ethical behavior (e.g. honesty, promise keeping) are of such enduring importance in all walks of life that they can be described as ethical values. These ethical values can be used to resolve conflicts between such public service as responsiveness and efficiency; they can also be applied to clashes between public service values on one hand, and social values like liberty and equality on the second.

Governments and international agencies draw their attention to developing and maintaining high standards and values, ethics and conduct in public administration as a mean of combating corruption. All these factors are essential components of ethical infrastructure of public life. The term ethics infrastructure as defined by the Organization for Economic Cooperation and Development (OECD), refers to a range of tools and processes for regulating against undesirable behavior and/or providing incentives to encourage good conduct of public officials. The OECD identifies eight key components of an ethics infrastructure as follows:

- Political commitment,
- Effective legal framework,
- Efficient accountability mechanisms,
- Workable codes of conduct,
- Professional socialization mechanisms (including training),
- Supportive public service conditions,
- Existence of central ethics coordinating body,
- An active civil society able to act as a watchdog over the actions of officials.

Each of the components of the ethics infrastructure performs one or more of three overlapping roles in controlling behavior, providing guidance to behavior or managing other elements of the infrastructure. The importance of each of these elements and the relative synergy between them will depend on the institutional and governance conditions and traditions of each country.

Political leadership and commitment are one of the most significant elements of ethical infrastructure of public life. There is no doubt that for the successful implementation of reforms it is crucial to secure the certain level of bureaucratic commitment to fight corruption and other unethical practices.

Every country has certain legal framework with provisions to cover various unethical and corrupt practices such as the breath of official trust and duties, abuse of power, misappropriation, and extortion, corrupt practices, acceptance of undue advantage and abuse of officials influence. The key problem is, therefore, not corruption, but weak enforcement. Without effective enforcement mechanisms, legal and administrative provisions on ethics and corruption are in themselves ineffective. Weak enforcement capacity may be blamed partly on the fact that several document, which makes access to them difficult, especially where enforcement officers lack experience.

Accountability system is determined by the strengths and weakness of the existing organizational arrangements and procedures to detect and punish corruption and other unethical practices. The weaknesses of the administrative system with implication for ethics are structural hierarchies, cumbersome procedures and weak control over administrative action. Individual senior officials seem to wield too much power and discretion without effective accountability. Administrative procedures are such that routine decisions by front line staff often have to be cleared through the hierarchy. The consequences of that are resulting delays and frustrations in obtaining decisions and services on time, which partly encourages bribery and petty corruption at the point of service delivery. There is need to simplify systems and procedures in order to remove the unnecessary blockages in organizational systems that create opportunities for bribes to be extorted from the public. Ethics reforms and anti-corruption strategies would not be useful if they left in place the restrictive laws and cumbersome processes that produced incentive for bribery and other unethical practices in the first place.

Enforcing accountability for the exercise of bureaucratic power has become more difficult as public service has continued to grow in size and as there responsibilities have grown in complexity. The decision-making process in government is often so lengthy and complicated that it is difficult to single out those public servants who should be held responsible for specific recommendations and decisions. Another obstacle on the road to accountability is the wide range of authorities to which public servants are deemed to be accountable.

Code of ethics play a guiding role in the ethics infrastructure, but they also take on a controlling function since they establish and publicize boundaries of behavior and set standards for public servants. Whatever level they apply to, the development and implementation of workable codes of ethics require sound management strategy that secures genuine employee acceptance of underlying values and ethics being promoted. The creation of Codes of Ethics or other forms of policies will be counter productive if such instruments remain as no more than a collection of slogans or nice, good-looking principles. In such a case, politicians seeking to verify their intentions or proposals as "good" or "ethical" will make use of them. In reality such instruments can serve as means of "covering" illegal activities and lead to not only legal but also to a cynical form of moral corruption. Opposition politicians might use such standards as tools in their partisan fights with governing parties without any real concern for the principles involved. On the other hand, governing parties can use them as a form of "cover-up" and as a means of defense against valid criticism. Such practices will work a short time only and will them lead top the loss of public trust, which, once lost, is difficult to regain or rebuild.

As Rose-Ackerman has pointed out "if public sector pay is very low, corruption tends to be a survival strategy". Public service conditions, particularly human resource policies, directly influence conduct. The conditions may be more or less conductive to ethical behavior by public servants. For example, low payments in public sector are partly blamed for the prevalence of petty corruption and other unethical practices in low-income countries. Insofar as these conditions can affect morale and productivity in the public services and influence ethical behavior, they cannot be ignored by any reform of ethics. Public service conditions are also directly related to the ability to attract and retain qualified and experienced staff. Human resource management capacity within the various line including institutions, is also weak. Systems and procedures for recruitment, promotions and transfer, training opportunities have critical roles to play in managing ethics and checking corruption in the public sector. To improve performance and encourage ethical behavior in the public services, promotion and pay incensement need to be linked more strictly to performance with an effort to create awareness among public servants on how they will be assessed and promoted.

Bodies that coordinate the overall ethics framework range from parliamentary committees, central agencies, and departments or specially created independent agencies mandated to oversee ethics in the public service. They serve a management function by coordinating and supporting all the other infrastructure elements. They operate either through directly implementing ethics initiatives or by delegating these tasks to the other departments or agencies.

The role of civil society institutions in ethical infrastructure of public life is very often compared with position of the watchdogs on the behavior of public officials. Their effectiveness is determined by the level of public criticism of government tolerated in the particular society and the position of free and independent media as an important factor of exposing corruption and other unethical actions. Government oversight and external mechanisms for accountability are not adequate for combating corruption and other unethical behavior unless they are supplemented by strong civic institutions, which are able to question government decisions and official actions to ensure that they abide by the rule of law and ethical standards in the public service.

POLICY ANALYSIS

Policy analysis refers to the evaluation and study of the formulation, adoption, and implementation of a principle or course of action intended to ameliorate economic, social, or other public issues. Policy analysis is concerned primarily with policy alternatives that are expected to produce novel solutions. Policy analysis requires careful systematic and empirical study.

The complexities of policy analysis have contributed to the development and growth of policy science, which applies a variety of theories and tools from the hard sciences (e.g. biology and chemistry), social sciences (e.g. sociology, psychology, and anthropology), and humanities (e.g. history and philosophy) in an effort to better understand aspects of human society, its problems, and the solutions to those problems. Policy analysis is important in modern complex societies, which typically have vast numbers of public policies and sophisticated and often interconnected challenges, such that public policies have tremendous social, economic, and political implications. Moreover, public policy is a dynamic process, operating under changing social, political, and economic conditions. Policy analysis helps public officials understand how social, economic, and political conditions change and how public policies must evolve in order to meet the changing needs of a changing society.

Formulating Effective Policies

Policy analysis plays an important role in helping to define and outline the goals of a proposed policy and in identifying similarities and differences in expected outcomes and estimated costs with competing alternative policies. Many public policies are designed to solve both current and future problems, and thus policy analysis attempts to forecast future needs based on past and present conditions. Policy outcomes can be found in a variety of different forms—tangible outputs and less-tangible outputs for which the impacts are more difficult to measure. In many cases, it is difficult to determine if the policy itself resulted in desired change or if other exogenous or external factors were the most direct cause. Nevertheless, it is important to determine if policy is responsible for the desired change; otherwise, there would be no need for the policy. Policy analysts often use theoretically grounded statistical models to determine if the policy will have the desired impact. In a final stage of policy analysis, analysts collate the information gathered to determine which policy alternative will best meet present and future needs.

Methods of Analysis

There are two types of empirical analysis: qualitative studies and quantitative studies. Qualitative studies involve a variety of different tools. For example, some qualitative studies involve archival analysis, studying policy history and determining what has been done in the past to solve certain policy problems. Qualitative studies might also involve personal interviews, asking individuals to describe in words a variety of issues surrounding the policy process—from policy agendas to formulation, implementation, and evaluation. Interviews with policy makers and with the clientele being served by a particular policy may provide valuable information about policy goals, processes, and outcomes.

Archival analysis is particularly important in public policy analysis. Through studies of policy history, policy analysts can learn important lessons from earlier times and apply those lessons to current or future problems and goals. A new policy goal may sound highly innovative and cost-effective and promise to meet worthy goals, but archival research may illustrate the hidden costs and pitfalls that might result in policy failure.

Personal interviews are also an important method of improving public policy. Public policy is formulated and implemented by professionals working in government, oftentimes for an entire career. Through their individual experiences in particular policy areas, the experiences of elected and appointed officials become key policy artifacts. When these individuals leave government service, their experience and wisdom are often lost. One way to prevent this is to document the informal lessons or experiences of senior elected and appointed officials. Personal interviews are perhaps the most effective method of accomplishing this goal, largely because a personal interview technique will allow for a high degree of flexibility in information collection.

Quantitative studies are of tremendous value to policy analysts in their continual efforts to address important policy issues. Cost-benefit analysis is one of the most common forms of quantitative policy analysis. It is primarily concerned with comparing the amount of expected or known benefits produced from a particular policy choice with the expected or known costs associated with that choice. Of the two elements of the equation, the determination of costs is often more easily computed. Costs are most often measured in monetary terms; labour and supplies are easily converted to dollar costs. While there are always hidden costs associated with any policy decision, those costs can be estimated given previous experiences in prior public policy endeavours. Opportunity costs—the costs associated with choosing a particular policy over an alternative policy—can also be estimated.

Benefit calculation is oftentimes a difficult endeavour. In order to complete the cost-benefit calculation, benefits must be assigned a numeric value, and most frequently the numeric value is made in monetary terms. Yet, most aspects of public policy benefit are not easily measured in monetary terms. Individual clientele of a policy and individual officials fulfilling policy goals have a tremendous influence on the quality of a policy outcome or output, but the calculation of a benefit is often measured and aggregated in a manner that fails to capture those nuances.

Despite limitations in estimation, benefits must be measured in monetary or unit output terms for a cost-benefit calculation to proceed. Policy makers may determine benefit estimates through survey research by asking clientele of a policy to indicate how the public policy has impacted their lives. Policy makers also view the benefit in terms of the output of a policy—that is, the number of individuals who were served. In higher education policy, for instance, policy makers may conduct surveys of alumni to determine the impact of their higher education experience on their salary level and to also inquire about their positive and negative experiences at the university or college. Additionally, policy makers may conduct a head count of the number of student credit hours generated and the number of university or college graduates to measure policy output and equate it to a benefit.

Complexities of Policy Analysis

Public policy is dynamic and requires that policy makers adjust policy to changing conditions and needs. When a change of policy direction or emphasis occurs, it usually requires increased resource expenditures. For example, if a public school's administrators determine that students' reading disabilities are impeding their general progress in school, it might be necessary to increase resources devoted to reading programs. The goal would be to increase benefit as a result of increased expenditure on a particular facet of a public policy. The increased benefit is called a marginal benefit, while the increased cost is known as a marginal cost. In cost-benefit analysis, important marginal increases in cost are justifiable in terms of increased benefits. If a benefit does not increase at a rate greater than cost increases, then the marginal policy changes are economically inefficient.

The dynamic quality of public policy is also considered in a procedure known as discounting. The value of a particular resource (e.g. money) does not remain the same over time. For example, money that is not spent may grow in value, simply by gaining interest or investment value. Once money is spent for a particular policy, that interest or investment value potential is lost. The longer the money remains invested, the greater the potential value that can be generated. Therefore, current resources frequently have greater potential value than resources collected or retained in future years; not all money is equal once time is factored into analysis. The discounting procedure allows policy makers to compare monetary values on an equal basis, thereby making the cost-benefit analyses more accurate in terms of both present and future costs associated with a policy.

The ability to conduct accurate and complete cost-benefit analyses is often hampered by a variety of other factors that play a role in public policy. When one chooses to move or not to move in a particular policy direction, there is the risk of policy failures. Those risks might mean that resources that were spent with good intentions never produced an expected benefit. Oftentimes the risks of failure are so great that policy makers avoid potential political ire by simply not choosing to take on high-risk (yet potentially valuable) policy goals.

Existing public policy often carries with it a lower level of risk than newer public policies. Frequently, there are unforeseen indirect start-up costs associated with new policies. Additionally, public policies are often vague and require the establishment of rules and procedures for day-to-day operations. The costs of implementation cannot always be determined before a public policy is put into place. However, they must be factored into cursory cost-benefit analysis to determine the feasibility of a particular prospective public policy.

Whether government is considering a new direction for public policy or simply implementing existing policy, the changing nature of society's needs must be continually monitored. People migrate, economic and social conditions change, and the nature of public problems continually evolves. Demographic data helps policy analysts determine if social and economic change is occurring in an equitable manner. Demographic analysis played an important part in documenting the rise of economic and social inequality that arose in the post-World War II era. While the analyses were interpreted by political conservatives and liberals in different ways, the findings themselves played an important role in developing public policies intended to remedy the inequities, the impacts of which could be studied in future demographic analysis.

Policy analysts use decision theory to plan for contingencies that arise in policy formulation and implementation. Decision theory is an attempt to explore all possible contingencies extant in a particular policy. The approach is especially useful after a particular policy has been adopted by government. Following policy adoption, the details of policy practice must be explored in full. For the most part, policy adoption means that a particular set of general policy goals has been recognized as being a function of government. Government agencies in charge of meeting those goals frequently must determine how to deal with a variety of alternative decisions that will have to be made and what outcomes (and the value of those outcomes) are likely from each of those decisions. Decision theory involves determining the probability that various events will occur and factoring that probability into decision analysis.

Policy analysts may use experimentation to cost-effectively "test" public policy alternatives. Experiments are one the most effective methods of determining a causal connection between the presence of a public policy and particular outcomes. Policy experiments, however, may face ethical challenges. For example, denying a policy benefit to those outside of the experiment may be harmful. Conversely, ethical challenges arise when individuals are subjected to a poor policy.

Outcomes of Policy Analysis

The outcomes of public policy analysis are highly varied. In one sense, policy analysis provides elected and nonelected government decision makers the opportunity to develop a greater understanding of a policy problem and possible solutions. Through policy analysis, it is possible to gain a greater understanding of the projected costs and possible benefits that will emerge from the adoption of a particular policy alternative. Decision makers often seek the most economical alternative possible—the alternative that offers the most in the way of benefit and the least in the way of cost. Government is asked to deal with a number of policy goals with limited resources; therefore, it is wise to stretch tax dollars. Policy analysis can help decision makers make rational decisions.

PUBLIC BUDGETING

The budget in its elementary form had been part of almost all monarchies of the history. There have been written documents regarding the existence of the state treasury, accountants and auditors who were employed by the monarchs to protect the royal treasury. The modern democracies have the legislatures playing an important role in the managing of public finances. The taxes that are collected and the revenues that are generated by the government through several means are to be used for the development and welfare of the society. The emergence of the Welfare State made it important that the government money is being judiciously used to better the living conditions of society in general and the marginalized sections in particular.

The process of budgets fulfills important functions in the economy of the nation. They act as a means to carry out several objectives of the public organization. Some of the important roles of budget in the national economy are:

- Prioritization of the allocation of the public resources.
- Achieving policy goals through prudent financial planning.
- Establishing accountability regarding the usage of the tax payers money.
- Financial controls also ensure compliance to rules and increase in efficiency.

In some countries, the executive part of the government also plays an important part regarding the revenues and expenditures of the government and the legislative is reduced to just an approving and reviewing authority, e.g. in UK where the budget process is primarily dominated by the executive (the House of Commons). A more balanced approach of distributing power is practiced in the USA where the legislature can review and make changes to the budget presented by the President and the President finally approves it after satisfactory checks and balances are concluded.

The dominance of executive or legislature in the budgeting process is a matter of debate as many consider the legislative to be an obstacle in the fast paced globalized economy where foreign direct investment and monetary funding from organizations like IMF and World Bank is of crucial importance to several democracies. There are several measures suggested to expedite the decision making process from fixing the term of the legislatures, introducing citizen panels, attaching funding power at local levels to bringing in two year budgetary cycle and special legislation regarding expenditure management.

The government expenditure is funded by a common pool of tax payer's money and the policies that are formed with this money are further used to fund projects. The catch here lies in the fact that the people who actually are paying for these policies are the larger group while the people who benefit from these policies might be a much smaller group, which translates that one might not be enjoying the benefits for which one is paying money. Such scenario leads to an excessive spending of public money on policies which are not beneficial to the society as a whole. Such situations are prevalent in democracies which are multi-lingual, multi-ethnic and divided on the basis of regions, religions and other factors.

HUMAN RESOURCE MANAGEMENT IN PUBLIC ADMINISTRATION

Human resource management in public administration concerns human resource management as it applies specifically to the field of public administration. It is considered to be an in-house structure that ensures unbiased treatment, ethical standards, and promotes a value-based system.

Function

The function of human resources management is to provide the employees with the capability to manage: healthcare, record keeping, promotion and advancement, benefits, compensation, etc. The function, in terms of the employers benefit, is to create a management system to achieve long-term goals and plans. The management allows companies to study, target, and execute long-term employment goals. For any company to have an efficient ability to grow and advance human resource management is a key.

Human resources are designed to manage the following:

- Employee Benefits: Include various types of non-wage compensation provided to employees in addition to their normal wages or salaries.
- Employee health care: The identification of recognition of a disease by a physician/ physician's assistant/nurse practitioner.
- Compensation: Something, typically money, awarded to someone as a recompense for loss, injury, or suffering.
- Annual, sick, and personal leave: Excused (and generally unpaid) leave for unexpected (such as accident or sickness) or expected (anniversaries, birthdays, marriage) events important to the individual.
- Sick banks: A fund accumulated to pay off a corporate or public debt.
- Discipline: The practice of training people to obey rules or a code of behavior, using punishment to correct disobedience.
- Records (tax information, personnel files, etc.): Also known as records and information management or RIM, is the professional practice of managing the records of an organization throughout their life cycle, from the time they are created to their eventual disposal.
- Recruitment and employee retention strategies: Refers to the ability of an organization to retain its employees.
- Salary and Wages Administrations: Process of compensating an organization's employees in accordance with accepted policy and procedures.

Leading Contributors

Historically, when a new president came into power, political leaders would appoint their supporters to political offices in thanks for the campaign assistance. This became known as the spoils system and became popular in the United States during the presidency of Andrew Jackson. In his first address to Congress, Jackson defended the system; he believed that public offices should be rotated among supporters to help the nation achieve its ideals. Jackson maintained that to perform well in public office, did not require special intelligence or training and rotating the office would ensure that the government did not develop corrupt civil servants. The system was viewed as a reward to supporters of the party and a way to build a stronger government. During the first 18 months of Jackson's presidency he replaced fewer than 1,000 of the 10,000 civil servants due to politics, and fewer than 20 percent of officeholders were removed. Many of the men Jackson appointed to offices came from backgrounds of wealth and high social status. The system continued after Jackson's presidency and opposition against the system began to grow. During the presidency of Ulysses S. Grant corruption and inefficiency began to reach staggering proportion. This led to a larger outcry against the system and helped bring about change in 1883.

George H. Pendleton: Senator from Ohio sponsored the Civil Service Reform Act in 1883, which sought to implement a merit-based program in the federal government. Its principal tenets include:

- Hiring employees by merit.
- Receiving pay according to position, not personal characteristics.
- Protection from political interference and dismissal via regime changes.
- Government workers have an obligation to accountability (transparency).

Chester Barnard: taught an organization was the cooperation of human activity and to survive an organization needed to have efficiency and effectiveness. His definition of effectiveness: being able to accomplish the goals that were set and efficiency – if the goals are reached by the individuals of the organization then cooperation among them will continue.

Paul C. Light: discusses the Shadow Government and how it is used to make the Federal government appear smaller, even as the Federal government grows. The Shadow Government is made up of those entities that produce goods or services for the government under contracts, grants, or mandates.

Volcker Commission: also known as the National Commission on Public Service was established in 1989, to rebuild the federal civil service. The commission was established by the United States Chairman of the Federal Reserve Paul A. Volcker. The main concern of the commission was morale because it was beginning to fall as were recruitment and retention among civil service employees and would soon become a crisis. This possible crisis was believed to be hindering the ability of the government to function effectively as the demand on the government began to grow.

The commission identified three main threats:

- Public attitudes and political leadership: The public did not trust or respect the government and the leaders. This also included federal agencies.
- Internal management systems: The federal agencies were losing experienced personnel due to problems with the leadership in the federal agencies. Mid-level workers were leaving the departments and entry level recruits were rethinking the commitments they made to the government.

The commission made some recommendations to address the problems. These included:

- Strengthening the relationship between presidential appointees and career civil servants by building a spirit of partnership between the two.
- Reducing the number of presidential appointees so that there is more room at the top for civil servants.
- Providing competitive pay to aid in recruiting and retaining excellent people while demanding competitive performance of them.

Pertinent Legislating

Pendleton Civil Service Reform Act 1883: Designed to end to the spoils system and provide federal government jobs based on merit and be selected through competitive exams. The act also made firing and demoting employees for political reasons unlawful. It also made requiring employees to give political service or contributions unlawful. The act also established the Civil Service Commission to enforce these rules. It was used to reinforce the efficiency of government.

Civil Service Reform Act of 1978: Encompassed a wide variety of reforms including the creation of the Office of Personnel Management (OPM), the Merit Systems Protection Board (MSPB), The Federal Labor Relations Authority, and abolished the Civil Service Commission. The act seeks greater accountability of federal employees for their performance. The act also provides protection for "whistleblowers" and employees calling attention to any government malpractices.

Hatch Act of 1939: Was passed into legislation to prohibit federal government employees from participating in certain political activities both on and off duty. The employee could not support or oppose a political party, partisan political group, or a candidate for a partisan political party.

In 1993, Congress passed legislation that amended the act as it applies to federal employees. Under the amendment most federal employees are now able to take part in political management and political campaigns. The act also applies to local and state employees who are employed with programs financed by loan or grants from the government or a federal agency. If the employee works for a research or educational institutions supported by a state, the employee is not under the restrictions of the act. The government employees that are covered by the new amendment are in executive agencies or in positions in the U.S. Postal Service and Postal Rate Commission.

Classification Act of 1949: Established the classification standards program, this law states that positions are to be classified based on the duties and responsibilities assigned and the qualifications required to do the work. The position classifications standards are built on the foundation of the grade levels.

Title VII from Civil Rights Act of 1964: Founded the Equal Employment Opportunity Commission (EEOC) and forbade discrimination in hiring, firing, and compensation based on race, color, religion, gender, or national origin. It is also unlawful for an employer to segregate, limit, or classify employees in any way that will deprive them of employment opportunities or affect their employment status. In addition, it is unlawful to discriminate on these five bases in an apprenticeship, training, or retraining programs.

Enhancement of Health Department Capacity for Health Care- Associated Infection Prevention Through Recovery Act-Funded Programs 2009: This program resulted in increases capacity for HAI surveillance and prevention across all 51 state and territorial health departments that received funding.

Human Resource Management Focus in Equal Employment Opportunity (EEO)

Equal Employment Opportunity is continually in the spotlight of human resource (HR) management even after over 40 years of progress. The number of EEO complaints and lawsuits remains significant, indicating that ongoing progress is needed to decrease employment discrimination. EEO issues in HR Management are so prevalent that it has become one of the biggest concerns for HR professionals.

While HR professionals agree that equal employment opportunities are a legitimate focus, there is considerable controversy over best way to achieve equality. One way is to use the "blind to differences" approach, which argues that differences among people should be ignored and everyone should be treated equally. The second common approach is affirmative action, through which employers are urged to employ people based on their race, age, gender, or national origin. The idea is to make up for historical discrimination by giving groups who have been affected enhanced opportunities for employment." The former approach emphasizes equal treatment regardless of individual differences; the latter emphasizes fairness based on individual circumstances.

Thus, it is important for HR professionals to understand Equal Employment Opportunity (EEO) discrimination process because of the significant complaints and lawsuits that will undoubtedly be encountered throughout HR Management. "This discussion is to enhance the reader's understanding of the EEO process; the parts in each section of this discussion track the EEO process as chronologically as possible. However, the goal of this discussion is not to provide an exhaustive study of complex legal subjects. Digest summaries and articles themselves do not have the force of law and the reader is advised to look to the actual decisions and other sources discussed for a more precise understanding of applicable EEO law."

Initiating and Navigating the EEO Process

Part 1: The Pre-Complaint Process: The EEO process is initiated when an individual contacts an EEO counselor concerning a suspected violation of one or more of the laws that the Equal Employment Opportunity Commission (EEOC) enforces. "The Commission's regulations, promulgated under applicable statutory law, can be found in relevant parts in Title 29 of the Code of Federal Regulations ("Labor"). The federal sector process itself is detailed in 29 C.F.R. Part 1614; and further amplified in Management Directive 110 (hereinafter, Maryland-110). MD-110 has often been referred to as the EEO counselor's "bible" for the wealth of information, appendices, and forms contained therein regarding the EEO process.

Under the EEOC-enforced statutes currently in force, there are 8 bases of employment discrimination that may be alleged regarding an agency action, policy, or practice in the EEO process. "The U.S. Equal Employment Opportunity Commission (EEOC) is responsible for enforcing federal laws that make it illegal to discriminate against a job applicant or an employee because of the person's race, color, religion, sex (including pregnancy), national origin, age (40 or older), disability or genetic information. It is also illegal to discriminate against a person because the person complained about discrimination, filed a charge of discrimination, or participated in an employment discrimination investigation or lawsuit."

"Most employers with at least 15 employees are covered by EEOC laws (20 employees in age discrimination cases). Most labor unions and employment agencies are also covered. The laws apply to all types of work situations, including hiring, firing, promotions, harassment, training, wages, and benefits."

Once an individual has filed a charge of discrimination, it is important that the individual must adhere to certain time frames and follow specified procedures in order to avoid dismissal of their complaints. For example, an EEO complaint may possibly be dismissed for failure to begin EEO counseling within 45 days of the suspected discriminatory incident or effective date of alleged discriminatory personnel action.

However, an "aggrieved person" or "counselee" must consult with an EEO counselor prior to filing a complaint in order to resolve the disputed matter informally. The counselor's role is to provide a solution of the alleged discrimination before the complaint is formally filed. After which, during the 30-day period the Counselor is to complete counseling, provide for the counselee (i.e., the aggrieved person) a written list of the counselee's rights and responsibilities. These include the following:

- The right to request a hearing or an immediate final decision after an investigation by the agency.
- The responsibility to exercise certain election rights.
- The right to file a civil action in federal court after filing with EEOC a notice of intent to sue under the ADEA instead of pursuing a complaint of age discrimination in the administrative EEO process.
- The need to be aware of administrative EEO and federal court time frames.
- An understanding that only the claims raised in pre-complaint counseling (or issues and claims like or related to issues or claims raised in pre-complaint counseling) may be alleged in a subsequent complaint filed with the agency.

"Such EEO contact must occur within 45 days of when the aggrieved person knew or should have known of the alleged discriminatory matter, or, in the case of a personnel action, within 45 days of the effective date of the personnel action. At the time of initiating EEO counseling and throughout the EEO process, the counselee is permitted to have a representative who may be, but is not required to be, an attorney. The counselor, who may be an agency employee and work either full-time in EEO or in a collateral duty role, is required to be neutral and favor neither the counselee nor the agency."

"Failure of the aggrieved person to raise a matter in counseling may result in subsequent dismissal of the formal EEO complaint. Through the counseling process claims are set forth and clarified, and the counselor conducts a limited inquiry (not an investigation) for the purpose of achieving resolution."

During the counselor's inquiry, the counselor may utilize certain procedures common to mediation but does not engage in actual mediation, even if that counselor is also a certified mediator. Throughout this counseling, or pre-complaint stage, the Counselor will also notify the counselee of pertinent legal choices that are available. Also, during this process the EEO counselor must inform the counselee that, where the agency offers ADR, the counselee must elect to choose between engaging in ADR or continuing informal counseling, but not both. Despite the choice of ADR or continuing the process of informal counseling, if resolution is not achieved, the counselee will have the opportunity to file a formal EEO complaint. "The ADR process in the pre-complaint phase is limited to a maximum of 90 days. However, the EEOC encourages the parties to engage in ADR to attempt to resolve their dispute at any subsequent time up to and including the appellate process."

Further, "Counselors must advise individuals of their duty to keep the agency and Commission informed of their current address and to serve copies of appeal papers on the agency. The notice [of the right to file a formal complaint within 15 days of the counselee's receipt of the notice] shall include notice of the right to file a class complaint. If the aggrieved person informs the Counselor that he or she wishes to file a class complaint, the counselor shall explain the class complaint procedures and the responsibilities of a class agent."

The Counselor must also notify the counselee of his or her right to remain anonymous until the grievance is officially filed, where and with whom the formal complaint is to be filed, "and of the complainant's duty to assure that the agency is informed immediately if the complainant retains counsel or a representative" In addition, "the Counselor shall not attempt in any way to hinder the aggrieved person from filing a complaint."

Before a formal complaint may go to federal court as a civil action to pursue the aggrieved individual's discrimination claims, the EEO administrative process reviews the claim. This is known as [exhaustion of administrative remedies]. "In complaints concerning Title VII, the Rehabilitation Act, and the ADEA—where the complainant chooses to go through the EEO process--the "exhaustion" requirement is satisfied after 180 days from the filing of the individual complaint or the class complaint if an appeal has not been filed and final action has not been taken by the agency." Equal Pay Act claims, on the other hand, must be filed within two years (or three years for willful violations) of the alleged discrimination, despite their standing in the administrative process.

There are exceptions to the above requirement. An EEO complaint filed under the ADEA may exempt a complaint from the above requirement. If the complaint gives the commission at least 30 days written notice of the intent to file an action, it may bypass the EEO process and go directly to a U.S. District Court and file a civil action naming the head of an allegedly discriminating agency. "A complainant who is asserting a claim under the EPA, however, may bypass the EEO administrative process completely and go directly to court. The filing of a civil action by the complainant will terminate the processing of an administrative complaint or appeal filed with the EEOC, and, therefore, the complainant should notify the agency and Commission when s/he has filed a civil action."

In addition to the claim processes discussed, a counselee may have to choose between continuing his or her claims in the negotiated grievance process or the EEO process. "When an aggrieved person is employed by an agency that is subject to 5 U.S.C. 7121(d), and is covered by a collective bargaining agreement that permits claims of discrimination to be raised in a negotiated grievance procedure, that employee must elect to proceed either through the EEO process or the negotiated grievance procedure, but not both." However, a complainant should be aware that, if he or she chooses to pursue a negotiated grievance before filing an EEO complaint, the time limitations in the EEO process will not be extended unless the agency consents to an extension in writing.

Another important election that an EEO Counselor must inform the counselee of is mixed cases.

Essentially, a mixed case is a claim of discrimination that is appealable to the Merit Systems Protection Board (MSPB). Regulations related to mixed cases can be found at 29 C.F.R. § 1614.302. To determine if MSPB may have jurisdiction there are two important questions that must be answered. First, does the employee have standing to appear before the MSPB? "For example, a probationary employee does not have standing to go to MSPB on an EEO-based claim. Employees of certain agencies, e.g., the FBI, CIA, TVA, the U.S. Postal Service, and certain non-appropriated fund activities (such as the Army and Air Force Exchange) do not have standing. Those employees may, however, pursue their claims through the regular EEO process with their agency." Secondly, does the claim occur from an action appealable to MSPB? Commonly, the more severe the personnel action at hand, the more likely it will be appealable to MSPB, e.g., removal, suspension for more than 14 days, and reduction in grade.

In short, an aggrieved individual can file a mixed case complaint with the agency or a mixed case appeal with the MSPB but not both at the same time. The aggrieved person must choose one or the other. In the initial case of a mixed case complaint being filed, the complaint proceeds through the EEO process as with any EEO complaint, with these exceptions:

- There is no right to a hearing before an EEOC administrative judge (AJ) after an investigation.
- The investigation is limited to 120 days (not 180).
- The agency must issue a final agency decision (FAD) within 45 days following the investigation.
- If dissatisfied with the FAD, complainant must appeal the FAD, within 30 days of receipt of the FAD, to the MSPB (not to the EEOC).

If the aggrieved individual chooses to file a mixed case "appeal" instead of a mixed case "complaint", then this individual may request a hearing before an MSPB administrative judge (AJ) but not an EEOC administrative judge (AJ). Afterwards, if the aggrieved individual is dissatisfied with the MSPB's verdict on his or her claims of discrimination under the statutes the EEOC enforces, they may choose to file a petition with the EEOC from the MSPB decision.

Part 2: Filing the Individual Complaint: Once the counseling is over and if there has been no resolution to the claim or claims, the EEO counselor must provide the counselee with a Notice of Final Interview and the Right to File a Formal Complaint with the appropriate agency official. The counselee then is required to file the formal complaint within a time period of 15 days once the Notice of Final Interview has been received. This complaint must be signed by either the complainant or the individual's attorney. The complaint is also required to contain a phone number and address where the complainant or his or her attorney can be reached. The complainant is responsible for proceeding with the complaint with or without a designated representative.

The formal complaint must contain a precise statement that identifies the aggrieved individual and the agency and the actions or practices that form the basis of the complaint. The agency in turn, must provide the complainant with written acknowledgement of the complaint and the date of filing. The agency's acknowledgement letter will include the following information:

- The address of the EEOC office where a request for a hearing is to be sent.

- The right to appeal the final action on or dismissal of a complaint.
- The requirement that the agency conduct an impartial and appropriate investigation within 180 days of the filing of the complaint unless the parties agree in writing to extend the time period.

Part 3: Amending and Consolidating Complaints: A complainant may amend a pending complaint to add claims that are related or similar to those raised in the pending complaint, prior to the agency's mailing of the notice required by 29 C.F.R. 1614.108(f) at the conclusion of the investigation. If the complainant needs to add or amend a new incident of alleged discrimination during the processing of an EEO complaint, the complainant will be instructed by the investigator or other EEO staff person to submit a letter to the agency's EEO Director or Complaints Manager at that time. The letter submitted must describe the new incident or amendments added by the complainant. Once the EEO officials review this request and determine the proper handling of the amendment they will decide if new EEO counseling is required. No new counseling is required when:

- Additional evidence is offered in support of the existing claim, but does not raise a new claim.
- The incident raises a new claim that is like or related to the claims(s) raised in the pending complaint.

"Additional evidence becomes part of the investigation of the pending claim and the complainant is so notified. The complaint must be amended where a new claim is like or related to the claim(s) raised in the pending complaint, and the EEO official must notify both the complainant and the investigator, in writing, acknowledging receipt of the amendment and the date it was filed. The EEO official will also instruct the investigator to investigate the new claim. New counseling will be required if the new claim is not like or related to the claim(s) in the pending complaint. The new claim will be the subject of a separate complaint and be subject to all of the regulatory case processing requirements."

Part 4: The Investigation: EEO investigations are covered in 29 C.F.R. 1614.108 and the instructions are contained in the Commission's Management Directives. An efficient investigation is one that is conducted impartially with and contains an appropriate factual record. A correct factual record is one that allows a reasonable fact finder to draw conclusions as to whether discrimination occurred. "All agency employees, including the complainant, are required to cooperate with the investigation and "witness testimony is given under oath or affirmation and without a promise that the agency will keep the testimony or information provided confidential."

During this process the investigators must thoroughly investigate the complaint and are authorized to administer oaths and require witness testimony and documentation. An investigator cannot make or suggest findings of discrimination and must be free of conflicts or the appearance of conflicts of interest throughout the investigation of complaints. The evidence gathered by the investigator should only be relevant to the case in order to determine whether discrimination has occurred and if so, create the "appropriate remedy." Generally, investigations should be completed within 180 days of the filing of the individual complaint, unless the parties agree in writing to extend the period an additional 90 days.

At the end of the investigation, the agency must present the complainant with a copy of the complaint file, including the report of investigation, and the notice of the right to request either an immediate final decision from the agency or a hearing before an EEOC AJ. A complainant also may request an AJ hearing after 180 days from the filing of the complaint even if the investigation has not been completed. The complainant must receive a copy of the complaint file, plus the report of investigation (ROI), and a copy of the hearing transcript if a hearing was held.

This discussion has provided the detailed EEO process with regard to the processing of individual EEO complaints of discrimination, in accordance with 29 C.F.R. Part 1614. "The principles reflected in those procedures are also intended to guide the processing of class complaints of discrimination under 29 C.F.R. § 1614.204." The overall purpose of this discussion is to enhance the reader's understanding of the EEO process; the parts in each section of this discussion track the EEO process as chronologically as possible. However, the goal of this discussion is not to provide an exhaustive study of complex legal subjects. Digest summaries and articles themselves do not have the force of law and the reader is advised to look to the actual decisions and other sources discussed for a more precise understanding of applicable EEO law".

HR Structure

Federal Level**:** The Federal classification system is not a pay plan, but is vital to the structure and administrations of employee compensation. The pay system is influenced by the grade level and by quality of performance, length of service, and recruitment and retention considerations. The law requires the Office of Personnel Management (OPM) to define Federal occupations, establish official position titles, and describe the grades of various levels of work. OPM approves and issues position classification standards that must be used by federal agencies to determine the title, series, and grade of positions.

The classification standards help assure that the Federal personnel management program runs soundly because agencies are now becoming more decentralized and now have more authority to classify positions. Agencies are required to classify positions according to the criteria and the guidance that OPM has issued. The official titles that are published in classification standards have to be used for personnel, budget, and fiscal purposes. The occupations in federal agencies may change over time, but the duties, responsibilities, and qualifications remain the same so careful application of appropriate classification of the standards needs to be related to the kind of work for the position. When classifying a position the first decision to be made is the pay system. There is the General Schedule (GS) and the Federal Wage System (FWS), which covers trade, craft, or laboring experience.

General Schedule Covers positions from grades GS–1 to GS–15 and consists of twenty two occupational groups and is divided into five categories:

- Professional – Requires knowledge either acquired through training or education equivalent to a bachelor's degree or higher. It also requires the exercise of judgment, discretion and personal responsibility. Examples can be attorneys, medical officers, and biologists. Usually a person who is in the field of HR, and has gone through the education required, stays in the field for long-term career goals. People of this category are seen in the upper management of HR departments.

- Administrative – Requires the exercise of analytical ability, judgment, discretion, and personal responsibility, and the application of a substantial body of knowledge of principles, concepts, and practices applicable to one or more fields of administration or management. These positions do not require specialized education, but do require skills usually gained while attaining a college level education. Examples can be budget analysts and general supply specialists. These positions will most likely be filed by career employees that act in a managerial function.
- Technical – Requires extensive practical knowledge, gained through experience and specific training and these occupations may involve substantial elements of the work of the professional or administrative field. Technical employees usually carry out tasks, methods, procedures, and computations that are laid out either in published or oral instructions. Depending upon the level of difficulty of work, these procedures often require a high degree of technical skill, care, and precision. Examples of the technical category would be forestry technician, accounting technician, and pharmacy technicians.
- Clerical – Involves work in support of office, business, or fiscal operations. Typically involves general office or program support duties such as preparing, receiving, reviewing, and verifying documents; processing transactions; maintaining office records; locating and compiling data or information from files. Examples can be secretaries, data transcribers, and mail clerks.
- Other – There are some occupations in the General Schedule which do not clearly fit into one of the groups. Some firefighter and various law enforcement agencies have specialized positions that manage HR duties within the organization.

References

- Organizational-theory: businessjargons.com, Retrieved 27 January, 2019
- Stewart Liff, Improving the Performance of Government Employees: A Manager's Guide, AMACOM, New York, (2011), ISBN 978-0-8144-1622-8
- Contingency-theory-decision-making-44645: smallbusiness.chron.com, Retrieved 28 February, 2019
- Mathis, L., Jackson, H., (2006). Human Resource Management 12th ed. Managing Equal Employment and Diversity., pg. 105. Retrieved, February 11, 2010
- Contingency-theory-of-leadership, chapter, rsm424: missouriwestern.edu, Retrieved 29 March, 2019
- Policy-analysis, topic: britannica.com, Retrieved 30 April, 2019
- Budget-in-public-administration: managementstudyguide.com, Retrieved 1 May, 2019

5

Decision-making Models

The cognitive process which results in the selection of a belief or a course of action among various alternative possibilities is referred to as decision making. Some of the important decision-making models are Simon's rational decision-making process and rationalist model. This chapter discusses in detail these types of decision-making models.

There is a difference between administration and administrative processes and if we fail to understand it confusion is bound to arise. By administration we mean the execution of governments or authority's policies or decisions whereas administrative process implies the methods or procedures that are applied for running the administration. In every form of administration certain policies or decisions are adopted for the management of organisation or various departments of government.

Decision-making is one of the various administrative processes. Let us briefly define it. Simon's definition runs as: "Decisions are something more than factual propositions. they are descriptive of a future state of affairs and this description can be true or false in a strictly empirical sense, but they possess an imperative quality, they select one future of state of affairs in preference to another and direct behaviour towards the chosen alternative. In short, they have an ethical as well as factual content."

In this definition Simon has briefly stated the nature of decision. In his opinion decisions are both factual and ethical. The aim of decision is to take steps for the future development of an organisation or better management of the department under a government. So we can say that a decision deals with both the present and future of organisation.

Stephen Wasby has defined the idea from a different background (Conflict Theory). He says: "Decision-making is usually defined as a process or sequence of activities involving stages of problem recognition, search for information, definition of alternatives, and the selection by an actor(s) of one from two or more alternatives consistent with the ranked preferences."

In every form of public administration there generally arises certain problems which require solution. But the methods of techniques of solution must follow definite principles. There shall exist clear- cut principles or procedures which will guide the administrators in running the administration of the organisation, or state department. The decisions will be taken such a way as to maximise the benefits or satisfy the actor's goal. This is called "satisficing".

Briefly stated, decision-making is a part of the management of both private and public organization or department. Herbert Simon "declared" that a theory of administration should be concerned with the processes of decision as well as the processes of action. That is public administration is concerned with both action and decision. Simon says that without decision there can hardly be any action.

Compromise and Composite

An executive or concerned authority cannot take a decision at one sitting or quickly. He will have to bring a number of alternatives or possibilities under consideration before arriving at the final decision. This process can be stated as a form of compromise.

Talking about compromise a critic observes: "Modifications of organisational objectives usually represented compromises between several groups of potential participants in order to secure their joint cooperation". An organisation is never a one-man body. Different persons and groups are directly or indirectly involved in every organisation and because of this no single man can take a decision. Before arriving at a decision he will have to consult various groups or persons and number of aspects. Naturally, the decision or approach of a single man cannot be final. A compromise is always an inevitability.

According to Simon, administration is a group activity. In any administrative system or organisation information and advice flow in all directions. In an open system (an organisation always acts in such a system) an administrative department cannot keep itself aloof from others. For the better future of the organisation the authority must keep lively contact with all. This is the premise of compromise.

Before taking final decision the authority must collect all information and test them because the news or information may not be relevant for the organisation. Simon has said that it is the duty of the administrator to judge or test the value of every information. Naturally the decision-making is not an easy task. Let us quote Simon: "The ablest administrators are the first to admit that their decisions are, in general, the sheerest guess-work, that any confidence they evidence is the protective shield with which the practical man armours himself and his subordinates from his doubts." What Simon wants to say is that decision-making is a very important part of organisation.

Simon next says that every decision is a composite decision-which means that behind every decision there are clear contributions of a number of persons and tor that reason it is called a composite decision. It has been said by Herbert Simon that no decision in an organisation is made by any single person. He writes, "Even though the final responsibility for taking a particular action rests with some definite person in studying the manner in which this decision was reached that is various components can be traced' through the formal and informal channels of communicating to many individuals".

When all the aspects of a decision are properly considered or scanned it will be found that behind every decision there is contribution of many individuals or bodies —of course, everyone's contribution may not be very important, but the importance of a contribution cannot be ignored.

We have earlier noted that for the proper management of public administration it is essential that behind every decision there must be rationality. Sometimes the term rationality cannot be defined or explained properly. But the persons associated with the making of decision know, at least partially, what is rational. However, the term rationality is subject to change with the change of time and circumstances, yet this notion has good deal of importance in public administration.

Models of Decision-making

Incremental Change

There are several approaches to or models of decision-making process of public administration. One such model or approach is incrementalism whose author is C.E. Lindblom. Lindblom suggests two alternative approaches which a policymaker may adopt. One such approach (or model) is that the policy-maker simply tries to use all related values or alternatives in order of importance.

He compares all these values or the results of methods and tries to find out which method or approach will ensure to him maximum benefit. This is no doubt a very complicated method and time-consuming. It is generally called incremental change through successive limited comparisons. In short, it is called incrementalism.

Lindblom has said that the policy-maker may not attempt a long-drawn and comparatively complex process. Rather, he may set or prepare a very simple goal and disregard the other values or goals. The policy-maker starts his activities and tries to achieve the goal. He also compares the results or consequences of the limited goal and after that he tries to reach the final decision. In other words, the policy-maker does not try to embark on an ambitious project.

He confines himself within limited choices, compares the results of those choices and, finally, decides one. It has been pointed out by a critic that "according to Lindblom the second process is much commoner and is the fact inevitable. The former assumes intellectual capacities and sources of information than men in fact do not possess and would make unrealistic demands on time and money in complex-problems".

C.E. Lindblom's approach or model is also called a bargaining approach. It is so called because the policy-maker makes one type of comparisons among different methods or processes for the purpose of getting maximum benefits or favourable results for his organisation. According to Lindblom, the decision-making is primarily a value-related or value-laden matter and his objective is to harvest maximum benefits for his organisation. He suggests changes in an incremental way and for that reason it is called incrementalism. He, again, makes attempt to compare different results derived from different policies.

The incrementalism or bargaining approach is generally used in the case of internal public administration, but in foreign policies its use is not rare. A decision-maker does not jump upon a decision without bargaining or comparing the pros and cons of every policy and, after comparing, he generally settles at one. Explaining Lindblom's incrementalism, it has been said that in any branch of public administration a policy is never made permanently, it is once made and remade again and again and the process continues until the policy-maker is fully satisfied.

One critic makes the following observation: "Policy-making is a process of successive approximation of some desired objective". Lindblom claims that his 'incrementalism' or limited comparison approach is superior to many other approaches or methods because it is practical and is based on scientific reasoning. Generally, a policy-maker endeavours to arrive at a final decision after comparing the consequences and the results of policy. The adoption of policy depends upon his satisfaction.

Rational and Extra-rational Model

Y.Dror has suggested an alternative model or approach for policy-making and it is called Rational and Extra-rational model. It may better be called combination of rational and extra-rational models. Dror says that Lindblom's incrementalism—though blessed with some plus points—has certain limitations. Dror says that Lindblom's approach is closer to reality. Every policy-maker tries to make a comparison among various values or policies.

He investigates the advantages and drawbacks of every approach and finally decides one. Talking about the limitations of Lindblom's model it has been pointed out by a critic that the incremental change by successive limited comparison is only adequate if the results of present policies are reasonably satisfactory if there is continuity in the nature of the problems and if there is continuity in the available means for dealing with it.

But Dror says that, in public administration or in the activities of an organisation, the same problem does persist for long time and if the problem changes and situation also changes the Lindblom model may not work with full satisfaction or may not work at all. Dror further observes that in modern society both knowledge and techniques change and when this happens Lindblom's model will be unworkable.

Dror has said that a scanning of modern situation reveals the following: one is, rapid changes in the aspirations and desires of people are always taking place. He again says that, once an issue is defined, that definition does not last along. The issue is being redefined persistently and this creates problem for the policy-maker. Finally, the consumers may be dissatisfied with the activities or policies of that policy-maker. Lindblom's model fails to solve these issues.

After pointing out the limitations of Lindblom's incrementalism, Dror has suggested an alternative model which is known as "normative optimum model" which combines "muddling through" and rational comprehensive model. The central idea of this model is the foundation of every model should be and ought to be the maximum amount of rationality and this could be achieved through continuous search and research of alternatives. Dror has suggested that every organisation must decide .its own goals and these goals must be periodically revised reformulated and estimated to cope with change of time and physical circumstances. For the enhancement of rationality the authority must study the situation from time to time and bring the situation in its new form under active consideration.

The central aspect of Dror's model is rationality and muddling through in the vehicle which will ensure rationality. Dror has said that since rationality is the main aspect of his model the authority must focus its attention to it. The idea of rationality is a highly complex concept and it is to some extent puzzling. While determining objectives the policy-maker must bring the resource under his consideration; without resources the objectives shall never be achieved.

In explaining Dror's model one critic has said: "We should allow a place for interactive judgment and holistic impressions". There is another suggestion in Dror's model. The policy-maker must consider the fruitful application of new techniques and other methods. He has further pointed out that opinions of experts must be duly considered and if it is not done the rationality concept will be seriously affected.

Administrative Rationality

J. M. Pfiffner has suggested another model for policy-making. It is known as Administrative rationality. Pfiffner claims that his administrative rationality is basically different from Lindblom's model. Let us explain the administrative rationality model.

"The orthodox concepts of rationality conform to those usually attributed to economic man, the scientific method and engineering man. Rational decision making is thought of as the gathering of all pertinent facts, canvassing the alternatives for action and selecting the one which will produce maximum results through a thought process our principal thesis is that administrative rationality differs from orthodox concepts of rationality because it does take into account an additional spectrum of facts. These are the facts relative to emotions, politics, power, group dynamics, personality and mental health." According to, Pfiffner policy-making, considering all aspects, is a highly complicated issue and it is not determined by any single factor even if the factor is important.

The policy is not always made from the above but is the resultant of many forces-both seen and unseen. There are number of issues and forces in the lower echelons which, in one way or other, influences the policy-making. If the policy is determined at the topmost level and the opinions of lower echelons are not properly considered the policy may not be able to serve the purpose of the policymaker. According to Pfiffner, policy is as much a result of an agreement as command. In other words, a real or practical policy must include the views of all.

Pfiffner has said that personal values have an important part to play in the decision-making process.

He concludes that among the "standards of validity" that if a decision has to be made there may have to be included:

1. Some degree of conformance with the personal interests, and values of the decision-maker,
2. Conformance with the values of superiors,
3. Acceptability to those who would be affected by the decision and those who will have to implement it,
4. Face validity in the sense that it looks reasonable m its content, and
5. A built in justification.

Which will furnish excuses and justifications in case the results are not as hoped". This implies that in the field of policy-making personal values and estimations have special importance and crucial role to play.

Every executive or a man holding key position has his own estimation about the working and future of organisation. He proceeds according to his own reasons and value-judgement. This he tries to apply to making of decisions. He injects his reason and values into the substance of decision-making. In large number of organisations personal values, knowledge, reason inject new concepts into the body of decision-making.

The experts are of opinion that the personal values play very important role. "Our research indicates that the organisations are in general pluralistic in nature. They are not unitary and monocratic, rather federative and cooperative." The implication is that large number of persons of various ranks and status play important role in the decision-making process.

Committee Decisions

R. F. Bales has introduced a "New" element or concept in the decision-making process —it is called Committee decisions. According to Bales, in practice, decisions are generally taken at various conferences attended by number of executives and important persons having thorough knowledge about organisations. Bales further claims that very often the decisions are not made in any particular organisation's meeting. A number of meetings are held and thread-bare discussions take place. After a lot of discussion dealing with all the possible aspects the final decision is adopted.

In the conference the participants express their personal views and experiences regarding the policy matters and, finally, a decision is adopted. The interesting aspect is that the decision is the product of cross-current of views; it is not a one-man activity. Sometimes discussions proceed on dialectically— which means that the opinion of one man does not always prevail.

The argument or reason of one is followed by a counter-argument and in this way discussion proceeds. Finally, a decision is taken which contains the important major views of the participants. It has been said that generally a decision takes several conferences. Bales himself has admitted that though the committee system is regarded as a factor of decisions yet it may not be a reliable method. In various cases it has been found that, in the conference, serious disagreements surface and these stand on the way of arriving at a decision. Bales says 'that the emergence of disagreement is a serious aspect of the decision-making process. Sometimes the decision-making is held up due to the disagreements but this is unavoidable.

General Assessment

Flerbert Simon was the first man who brought the importance of decision-making in public administration and functioning of organisation to our notice. Subsequently, a good number of experts threw light on it. It is now held by all that decision-making is a vital aspect of public administration and organisation. Without proper or real decision no organisation can achieve success.

Simon has further observed that mere decision cannot make administration successful. It must be realistic. A large number of administrationists have painstakingly thrown light on the realistic character of decision. Major contributions have their places in our analysis. Simon has pointed out that all the organisations are in one way or other goal-oriented. Naturally, every organisation or public administration must (while making policy) see that the decision must be able to achieve the goal.

Organisation is not something which will grow and work automatically like natural phenomena. These are human organisations and behind their origin, growth and functioning there are human efforts and definite human thought. Barnard has elaborated this aspect in a number of ways. Barnard's main plank of thought and argument is cooperation and application of thought and reason and continuous research are the main aspects of policy-making function. Interpreting his viewpoint a critic makes the following observation: "Decisions, he says, tend to be made on a basis relating to organisational purposes, rather than to individual motives or aspirations".

Generally an executive is called the chief architect of an organisation. But the fact is that he alone can never help the realisation of the major aims of the organisation.

The activities of organisation are a continuous process. The experience of the past guide the future. A policy-maker formulated new policy or revises the present policy on the basis of past experience. The policy-maker tries to get idea from the past and this is very important. How past works is quite explicit in the following comment: "In an established organisation, scope for decision is constrained by prior decisions, explicit or implicit, expressed in earlier investments, previously approved budget, moral commitments to individuals and departments, contracts of employments".

The influences of politics or political ideas and decisions, national and international events cannot be underestimated. Particularly in this age of globalisation and liberalisation the international events influence the policymaking affairs of an organisation or public administration. An organisation cannot ignore the international events and phenomena. An export-oriented organisation must carefully study the situation of international market and trade while making important decisions regarding the export of commodities manufactured by it. It is quite logical and realistic.

Personal liking and disliking have very little to do with the working of international market. In the second half of the last century and even before that major decision-making theories were built- up and in those years globalisation had practically no existence. Today this has gained an important status of international event and its influence on many major national and international events is quite perceptible.

A balanced analysis of decision-making must take this into account. It may naively be stated that on the decision-making process of all developing countries there is clear influence of the capitalist countries. It is because few multinational corporations practically control the world economy, particularly trade, commerce and commercial activities. Naturally, the organisation of the Third World states cannot go beyond this orbit.

Decision-making and Rationality

Rationality vs Non-rationality

In the last few pages we have discussed the importance of rationality in the decision-making process. In this topic we intend to throw light on the reverse side of the issue. That is, few eminent experts in public administration are of the view that rationality does not always play the most vital role. Rather, the role has been exaggerated.

"The one finding unearthed by social scientists about how decisions are made in organisations that seems irrefutable is that the process is only minimally rational. The principal reason for this non-rationality is that the decisions are made by people, and people are less than logical. Herbert Simon, perhaps more than any other social scientist, enlightened the world about this darker side of decision-making".

Simon has said that decision-makers give less importance to rationality and more importance to on-going of the world and the opinions of the decision-maker about the numerous incidents that take place. According to Simon, the decision- makers do not always attach importance to real phenomena or realities at hand.

Henry interprets Simon's judgement in the following words: "Simon held that all human beings make decisions on the basis of worldview that reflects past experiences and perceptions, but not necessarily the realities at hand. Simon called this phenomenon the decision premise." Simon has said that individual values may have importance to particular persons but these do not claim equal importance in the field of decision-making arena.

Bounds of Individual Rationality

We have already noted that there is a certain amount of individual rationality in the making of policy for public administration or the management of organisation. But Simon, in a number of places, emphasises that the contribution of rationality has been exaggerated. He calls this bounded rationality.

Simon's arguments are:

1. An organisation is quite large.
2. Decision- making is a complex matter.
3. Decision of an organisation is subject to change with the change of time and circumstances.
4. Human mind and rationality cannot comprehend all possible situations.
5. One psychologist has said that a mind can distinguish maximum seven categories of phenomena at a time.
6. Human mind is guided by emotion and in the field of policy-making the emotions have no place.
7. Many men are guided by self-love, heuristic feeling, and also nepotism. One cannot force an individual to be free from all these. But all these create obstacles on the way of an impartial policy.

A bold and comprehensive policy requires a good amount of intelligence, experience, farsightedness, and many other qualities. The advocates of bounded rationality emphatically assert that there is doubt how many people possess these qualities. There are various aspects of public administration and organisation. For this reason a comprehensive policy is to be made. But the practical situation teaches us that even persons of exceptional qualities cannot make a policy which will cover all the aspects of public administrates and organisation. It is said that policy-making is a group product. Several persons meet together and-after elaborate discussion-policy is formulated. But this is highly oversimplified. Differences of opinion must crop up and that will create hindrances on the way of making a policy. This is not an imaginary situation.

Bounded Organisational Rationality

Nicholas Henry also points out that there are also bounds of organisational rationality. It means that an organisation cannot take decisions in accordance with its own principle or objective. Nicholas Henry writes: "The decision-maker's own organisation constitutes most of his or her decision-making environment, and this organisational environment can itself exude bounded rationality, and even irrationality" In other words, in several cases, an organisation cannot enjoy enough freedom to make policy by applying its own rationality. We have already pointed out that in the present day world no particular organisation can be treated as a solitary institution.

The globalisation has to a large extent obliterated the geographical barriers and because of this the interdependence among the organisations has considerably increased. In this situation the executives or bureaucrats quite naturally differ among themselves on the assessment of the global situation. This situation may create problems for the formulation of a comprehensive policy for the organisation.

In an earlier analysis we have pointed out that politics and administration are not completely separate from each other and because of this very often politics plays an important part in policy-making affairs, and the nature of politics in it creates divisions among the top policy-makers. There is also another limitation. An aggrieved officer may accept the majority decision. But, in practice, he may not extend his helping hand for the execution of the policy. Our point is the policy is rational, the decision was quite practical. But if a main actor does not cooperate wholeheartedly the implementation of the policy will receive a serious setback and this is unavoidable.

Simon's Rational Decision-making Process

Rationality in Decision-making

Herbert Simon's celebrated work-Administrative Behaviour; A Decision-Making Processes was published in 1945. His first task was to expose the contradictions and some inaccuracies of the scientific administration theory and then to propound a new theory which would be most suitable for a scientific public administration. Let us put it in Simon's own words; "A theory of administration should be concerned with the processes of decision as well as the processes of action." Mere setting up of a theory and no relation to reality is of no value.

Simon wanted to build up the fabric of a theory which would equally be suitable for practical purpose. Simon claims that his theory will be applicable in practice. He believed that making of decision is a very difficult task because, in an organisation, there are several complex and contradictory situations and in the midst of these situations an administrator will have to arrive at a decision which will be most suitable.

Talking about decision, Simon has said that decision is a matter of compromise because there are several alternatives and the decision-maker will have to select one or few alternatives from them. He will have to judge the most suitable alternative because his chief objective is to make a practical and most suitable decision.

The acceptance of one alternative and the rejection of others does not indicate that they are absolutely unsuitable. The mere fact is that at a particular moment the decision-maker selected a particular method. Simon calls this a type of compromise. If in the next time situation changes he may adopt a new course of action. Naturally there is always a scope of compromise.

Behind the acceptance and the concept, rationality always plays the most crucial role. If the decision is not rational it is not expected that it will produce desired results. But in his opinion the concept of rationality is associated with problems. To get rid of this Simon has suggested that a decision may be "subjectively" rational and also "objectively" rational. Let us say what he means by these two words. A decision is supposed to be "objectively" rational if it maximises given values in a given situation.

Again, a decision will be subjectively rational if it maximises attainment relative to the actual knowledge of the subject. A decision would be organisationally rational if it were oriented to the organisation's goals. In this way Simon has explained the various aspects of the decision-making process of an organisation.

Simon's theory of rationality of decision-making differs from his predecessors, particularly the concept of POSDCORB. Simon claims that in all the earlier theories of public administration the value or importance of rationality had no place. But only a rational approach can make an organisation successful. His theory of rational decision-making has inflicted an attack upon the scientific administration theory.

He indirectly castigates that what is called scientific theory—it is not at all rational. It is based on certain personal experiences. But personal experience cannot claim universal application. He thought that the so- called scientific theory or approach to public administration cannot produce desired results. That is why he wanted to find out a rational theory of public administration. Simon demands that his rational decision-making is "an adequate framework for the expensive use of applied behavioural research".

Limits of Rationality

Rationality is the central part of Simon's theory of decision-making. When an administrator is faced with a number of alternatives, he will accept one or two alternatives or the ones he requires. In his Models of Man he has analysed possible aspects of rationality. Taking of rational decision depends upon several factors. For example, when an economic man goes to take a decision he will have to consider a number of factors such as economic conditions that prevail around him, the international economic situation, and his clear knowledge about the economic situation.

In the same ways an administrationist very often is faced with complicated situations and other factors over which he has hardly any control. It has also been stated that the rationality of one person is not detached from rational behaviour of other persons. But the problem is one rational person has no control over the rationality of others. In the administrative world it is not an easy task for a rational man to take a rational decision unilaterally.

Simon was fully aware of it. Not only this, an administrator cannot take a rational decision without considering the environment that prevails around him but reality teaches us that an administrative officer has hardly any control over the environment. Simon has said that the supply of information is also an important factor that has clear impact upon rationality.

If the physical environment changes the choice will also suffer and in that situation the administrator may have very little choice. In spite of all these limitations the rationality of decision-making is an important concept in public administration. After the World War II the book was published and it created ripples in the world of public administration He suggested that few principles cannot set the public' administration in right order Behind everything there must be rationality.

Rationalist Model

Based on the distinction between objectives (background rationality) and means (functional rationality), this approach assumes that all public decisions must first be based on background rationality. Thus, society must establish through the government, the social goals and social values (such as equality, economic development or public order). Clearly, these goals and these values will be different depending on times and the countries that are being analyzed.

We may discuss about the rationalist model, only when it was determined that these values or social goals can operate in functional rationality; it is a mean of seeking ways to maximize these goals. Goal setting and values of the society can often take the form of a concept of "general interest", which then helps to determine the importance and urgency of the problems to be solved. The basis for this rational model, are rationalist theories and those are being rooted in the illuminist rationalism and positivism, current which promoted ways of neutral and objective knowledge on human society. At the basis of these problems lies the idea that human society can and should be resolved in a rational and scientific manner, by gathering all of the information that can be found in the problem, followed by processing them, and obtaining, by applying the most efficient answer, from the cost point of view.

Decisional Process – Rationalist Model

In Professor Marius Profiroiu's opinion, "it is about the approach on decision making, developed by classical economy, in which man is taking rational decisions. The decision is assimilated to a single actor reasoning that seeks to maximize the purposes depending on means at its disposal. He has preferences, he establishes its goals, set's some values and choose their utility. Then searches for available alternatives to solve the problem, alternatives that exhaustively inventoried and whose effects can also worth trying to identify them. In the next phase, it adopts a criteria of choice as objectively as possible, to allow him to identify the best balance between the advantages and disadvantages of each possible alternative. The set of alternatives will then be sorted using these criteria, yielding the solution considered most appropriate to resolve the matter".

The decisional process presented by the rationalist model, comprises the following distinct and sequential stages:

1. Identifying the values and objectives achieved.
2. Analyzing all possible alternatives for achieving the objectives.
3. Researching and selecting information based on the efficiency or effectiveness of various alternatives.
4. Making a comparison between alternatives and their consequences.
5. Choosing the alternative that maximizes the values and objectives.
6. Implementation.
7. Feedback.

The rational actor model has many qualities as decision maker should focus essentially on the problem, the contents of alternatives and preferences, as well as choosing good criteria suitable to the content. Several analysts have adhered to this model and tried to improve it by examining all possible options and their costs. The improved model is called the rational – comprehensive model.

In Professor Lucica Matei's opinion, according to the "rational understanding model" the decision-making process includes the following steps:

1. Determining the objectives: In the process of decision-making, public administrators must first determine which the public policy objectives are. These objectives must be identified in operational terms, so they can be observed and measured. Must be noted that the public administrator does not have the freedom to set goals, being constrained by authority, specialization, hierarchy and so on.
2. Establishing the means: Once you have established public policy objectives should be considered the different means to achieve them. At this stage should as far as possible, that all means that can be identified to be examined. Note that it is unlikely that all possible means were at one time tested and evaluated in practice. The public administrator must try to estimate the consequences of each means in all areas of public interest.
3. Choosing the best alternative: Once all means potential have been identified to reach an end point, it is necessary to choose between them. In accordance with the present model, this choice must be such as to cause maximum efficiency, economy and effectiveness. In situations where these three values are in perfect harmony, shall create an appropriate balance between them.

According to Réjean Landry, the rationalist model of decision-making process involves the following phases:

1. Identifying the context – In this stage are identified the issues to be investigated and the objectives of the involved actors.
2. Determining the possibilities of action – In this stage is seeking actions that may be undertaken for the settlement of the problem.
3. Estimating the consequences – Shall be determined the implications of each possibility action on the issue taken into consideration.
4. Comparison of consequences – At this stage are being calculated the relative costs and benefits of the various possibilities for action.

Choosing a possibility of action: This phase involves choosing the variant that produces the highest net benefits.

A group of American specialists, Charles Lindblom, in "The Science of Muddling through" - Public Administration Review, Herbert Simon in Administrative Behavior, Alan Altshuler and Norman Thomas, in "The Politics of the Federal Bureaucracy" described model and the three stages to be completed in public decision making.

Proceedings of decision making process in three distinct phases:

1. Determination of objectives.

2. Formulation of decision alternatives.
3. Choosing the best alternative:
    - Emphasis should be placed on maximizing efficiency and effectiveness.
    - Elaboration of a program with practical nature, according to the three criteria: effectiveness, efficiency and rationality.
    - Accentuated specialization of the public servants involved.
    - Taking into account the total cost.
    - Specifying clearly decision objectives that should be concise and non-contradictory, etc.

So it must be stressed that the rationalist model of decision-making is not a simple sequence of actions. It is assumed from the beginning, that there is an order between the values established, and public decision-maker is aware of the values on which it intends to be concentrated. Also it is assumed that decision-making stages of the process must always be presented in the order that was established above. It is also assumed that the decision maker is able to obtain all information related to the subject of the decision, and therefore he may actually take into account, all possible alternatives. In conclusion it can be said that the rational model has a large number of requirements.

The rationalist model of decision making process in five steps illustrated in figure.

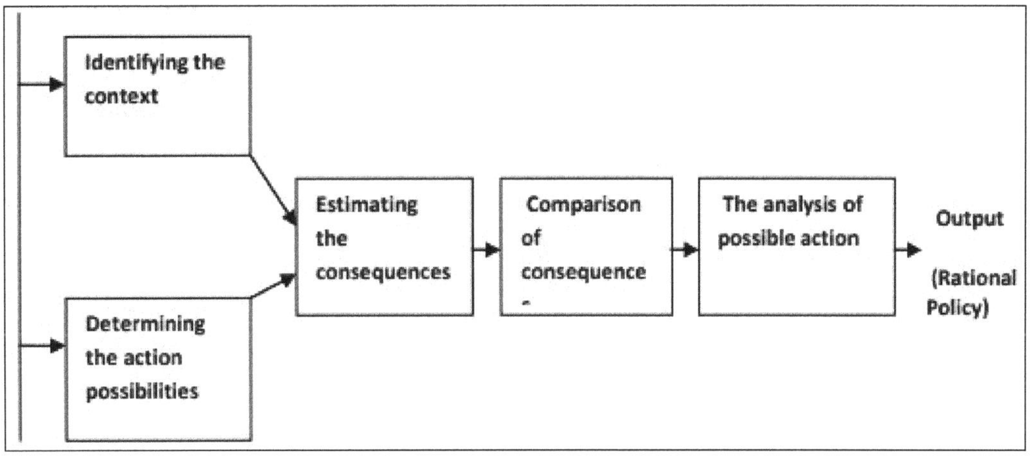

According to Gournay, for the rationalist model, are not taking into account many factors that influence the decision. The first of these factors relates to the number of decision-makers in government. It should be noted that in the rationalist model we do not have to deal with a single decision maker. In public administration there are several decision makers, so more rationalities and values that are involved in the competition. Basically in the rationalist model, the decision maker must take the decision at the right time. In reality, the decision-maker works with several dossiers in parallel and cannot fully concentrate on a single decision. Gournay insists that, for adopting a decision, decision makers do not possess the right tools for them, to make future projections of all the effects of a decision. He mentioned that the relevance of a decision is based on the underlying value of the information to, cases in which all information is available are rare and therefore it is difficult to have an objective decision that takes into account all the important aspects. In addition to lack of time, resources and intellectual routine often prevents public decision-maker to consider all possible alternatives of a decision. This questions the rationality of certain decisions of the public administration. The author reminds us that despite all the efforts made in the sense of rationality, it is impossible to foresee all the consequences that would result from such a decision or another. He believes that a rational process of taking a decision demands from the decision makers, objectivity which cannot be achieved, especially in political decisions.

Barriers and Criticisms of the Rationalist Model

The rational model is very important for analytical purposes, due to the fact that, in practice, faces a multitude of obstacles, derived primarily from the difficulty of assuming a pure rational decisions. Further on shall be presented several of these barriers:

- Benefits for the whole society cannot be determined, but only for certain social groups or individuals, even in the latter case, this leaves to conflicts and contradictions;
- The conflictual benefits and costs, can not be measured accurately (eg: you can not buy the dignity of the individual with an increase of taxes);
- The decision makers are motivated not only by maximizing the social gain, but also by factors such as power, status, financial rewards, reelection, and so on;
- Searching for perfect rational alternative is very difficult, generally it stops when the chosen alternatives are working;
- Investment in major government programs and the adoption of decisions required, are timed by responsible factors, before the elections;
- Collecting the necessary information for choosing the best alternative encounter many difficulties: the cost of information, the time required to collect the most necessary one;
- Segmented nature of the process of public policy making in large bureaucracies makes difficult, accounting and the coordination of all inputs, provided by various categories of specialists and their incorporation into - the ideal decision.

In the literature are also encountered criticisms of this model. Herbert Simon has demonstrated that the theory of absolute rationality is unrealistic.

He tried to apply the theory of decision-making in large undertakings but also realized that its postulates are wrong. Herbert Simon questioned the idea of optimal decision making and demonstrated through empirical research, that the decision is frequently triggered by organizational problems. Simon has also shown that the process of problem solving leads to satisfactory solutions, and under no case to optimal solutions. The rational decision maker acts as if they act in a world of absolute rationality. No constraint (both cognitive and political) presses upon him or on his situation, but they exert a strong influence on the process. There is a certain rationality, but it is limited. Herbert Simon was joined in 1958, James March, together showing that organizations actors, act according to a limited logic rationality, choices made and decisions being subject to constraints originating from human nature itself.

In the reality of action the decision maker encounters major constraints related to several factors:

- Firstly, efficiency, effectiveness and economy are not prevailing values in the public sector. Public sector is reasoning, first, in terms of expenditure, means, budget, and not by income, results, operational account, as they do in undertakings operating in the market. He is also reasoning in terms of "maximum" and not "optimum". Information is missing and that is costly.
- There are few situations in which public decision-maker acts in advance (so called proactive action) before trying to identify the problems and the means of solving them.
- Selection criteria are rare. The available methods to define any approximation of an arbitration between the advantages and disadvantages, there are very few. Are always evoked the same examples regarding public choices that can be based on a scientific set of criteria, allowing comparison of the various alternatives among themselves: decisions regarding major infrastructure of transport (location of roadworks, expanding rail networks, etc.)
- The ability to generate a state of exhaustive alternatives varies rational decision maker inventories all alternatives and all related merits. But here there are limitations related to the nature of behavior in a cognitive situation. Some individuals may not act unless they have at their disposal a considerable amount of information. Others cannot decide unless alternatives were reduced to a smaller number.
- Choice situation triggers a psychological tension. The decision process is often expressed through moments of uncertainty, pressure and tension. The decision maker capacity to support psychological the situation of choice varies from one person to another.

A second problem of understanding rational model is that it assumes that policymakers have time to address the challenges in a rational way, to identify all the detailed and comprehensive potential means of achieving the objectives established and evaluate all these means based on efficiency, economy and effectiveness.

Another difficulty in approaching this model is that specialization which was used so powerfully can also become a burden. "We are all familiar with the image of the right hand of the Government, without knowing what it's doing with the left." This is because the hands operate in different spheres, under the limitations of different times and with different objectives envisaged. But modern government, of course, has more than two hands, he has rather countless tentacles. Public decision-maker that operates in one of these areas is determined from time to time, to disagree with ones another's actions. Often, specialization makes it difficult to analyze the costs of any particular course of government action. An institution that makes decisions in a complex policy area, may create new problems for other institutions. In terms of the rational understanding model, the problem lies in the fact that these costs are difficult to be assessed and analyzed, because they tend to get lost in the system of specialized jurisdictions. The problem is worsened by the fact that, as the administrative status increases, costs that are passed from government to society tend to become a public policy concern. Such things gets even more complicated in situations of economic - financial crisis.

Finally, we can say that, because it is based on theory and abstract professionalism, decisions may be adopted that are inappropriate in practice and these do not match with the nature of contemporary administrative operations, calling for public policy makers to exercise a degree of rationality and competency (professionalism) comprehensive, which exceeds their ability.

Public Decision through the Rational Choice Theory

When making a decision must be find the answer to three questions: What is the problem? What are the possibilities (variants) for solving? Which is the better choice?

Concerning the public administration, because the decision takes different aspects and forms, depending on the author making the request, the field or object to which it refers, stretching sphere, content and nature of provisions that are esthablished, the decision making process itself, presents some particularities which, given the theme, is needed to be taken into account.

9. NINEth STAGE: formulating the conclusions after applying the decision.

⇧

8. EIGHTh STAGE: observing the implementation of the decision;

⇧

7. SEVENTh STAGE: decision application

⇧

6. SIXth STAGE: decision adoption;

⇧

5. FIFth STAGE: outlining and analyzing decision alternatives;

⇧

4. FOURth STAGE: selection and analysis of collected information;

⇧

3. THIRD STAGE: documentation in order to formulate the decision;

⇧

2. SECOND STAGE: defining objective decision and the means of achieving it;

⇧

1. FIRST STAGE: decision initiation

Logical scheme of the rational type of decision-making process.

Stages of decisional process in public administration may be presented as a logical scheme, as follows:

- Initiating decision adoption;
- Establishing the objective and the means of achieving it;
- Data collection, respectively, documentation, in order to formulate the decision;

- Selection and interpretation of data;
- Decision making;
- Implementation of the decision;
- The control execution of the decision.

To explain why in a situation has been taken a certain decision and no other should we appeal to rational choice theory.

In the traditional sense (general, logical) rationality, refers to the property of enunciations or judgments of being able to be deduced (derived) logically from other enunciations or judgments. The truth value of the succeeding statement is dependent on the truth of other statements accepted as true based on various grounds (observation, experiment, practice) and inferential derived trough reasoning. Therefore to emphasize the reasons or the rationality of a proposition shall mean to determine the set of possible antecedents or the possible implications, to determine the multitude of possible consequences.

The term "rational" has very different meanings, some of which relates to knowledge, other human action:

- Rationality consists in conformity with the rules of deductive logic. Let us take the syllogism. Whether we have the premises: All the mayors are elected, and Ion is mayor, then it is reasonable to conclude from this situation, that Ion is elected - but it is unreasonable to conclude that Ion is a Romanian peasant who was concerned about local community issues.
- To be rational means to make accurate mathematical calculations. Indeed, it is reasonable to infer that the number x is bigger than 10 if they know that a) x> 6, and b) x is multiple of 5.
- Rationality consists in reaching to proper conclusions on the meaning of the words we use. If we know someone is a bachelor, then - because we know that "bachelor" means unmarried man - we can conclude that there is no person to be father in law.
- To be rational means to call for amplificative induction. If a student was very well prepared for all exams in the first two years of college, it will be reasonable to conclude that at the exam for today she came back very well prepared.
- Rationality consists in making use correctly of the probability that some event will occur. At the elections for mayor of Bucharest in 2005, polls showed that the difference between DA Alliance candidate, Adrian Videanu, and the SDP Vanghelie, was huge in favor of the first candidate. Therefore, it was reasonable to conclude that the probability that my vote could change the voting results was very small.
- To be rational means to make inferences based on empirical generalizations generally accepted as valid. If it rained yesterday and last night was cold, then it can be concluded that the streets and sidewalks will be slippery in the morning today.

In all six cases, the term "rational" was applied in some of its premises mechanism by which conclusions were inferred; rational is its arguments tautologically speaking, "reasoning" used to extract new knowledge. There are also some very different ways of using the term "rational", which does not applies this time to knowledge, but to our action. The term "rational" is not applicable how we make judgments, but how we act and behave. To be rational means to act to achieve our best purposes; and rational means to treat any other man as a goal in it, not as a means to achieve our goals.

The first meaning of the term "rational" has to do with the means we use to achieve your goals. The second meaning aims the goals rather than means. In the Weberian tradition, it is said that in the first case we are dealing with an instrumental rationality and in the second with value rationality (or axiological).

Instrumental rationality: If you want to talk about a rational choice, then of course that it assumes the reason is, in one way or another related to action. But perhaps we do not want just to assert that reason can judge the actions that we did or that we intend to do, and we can say they are good or not. Rather we want to support something more: that reason somehow influences our choice and, therefore, that reason influences human action.

Very generally speaking, instrumental rationality requires that people should in their choices to respect certain principles and J. Rawls, indicates the following three:

- The principle of effective means: Due to a specific objective and more alternatives (means of achieving that objective) the principle requires adopting the alternative that best meets the purpose. "As a goal you must achieve the lowest expense of means (whatever it may be), or, given the need to fulfill the objective means as broad as it could be."
- The principle of comprehensiveness: An alternative is preferable to another if its application would result in the application of all the goals we attain the other application and other purposes, in other words it is the preferable alternative that has the required comprehensive consequences. If we chose to rehabilitate the sewerage system of a city by the classical method (breaking the road) or robotic (nonintervention on the road), and we know that if we use the second method do whatever we wanted in the first method, and saving funds for aftercare of road destroyed, then it is rational to prefer to use the method of robots.
- Higher probability principle: If the goals we can achieve by two alternatives are generally the same, but it's a greater chance to achieve those goals by applying one of the two alternatives, then it is rational to choose this one. According to Rawls, the three principles (with a wide applicability in decisionmaking in public administration) define the idea of rational choice, which therefore could simply be replaced by invoking them. In other words, when we asked if a choice is rational, our response will be to verify that it meets the three principles.
- Valoric rationality: Most of the times, the conception of rationality is derived from the human tradition and is contrasted with the one, which may be found in I. Kant's work. It should be noted that there are attempts to connect the two traditions. The Rawls one, particularly in later works -1993, 1999, 2001 - his first book A Theory of Justice, is well known.

Relevant to this paper is the notion of the categorical imperative, which represents a moral rule that allows us to judge our actions.

Kant gives three famous formulations of the categorical imperative:

1. Acting under that maximum that you would also like it to become a universal law;
2. Act so that you use humanity both in person and in the person of anyone else, always in the same scope and never as a mean;
3. Act according to the maxims which can also be subject to themselves as universal laws of nature. Starting from the idea that administrative action represents a kind of human action this is itself influenced negatively or positively.

It is relevant that when we deal with an administrative decision that the entire decision making process must be rational, i.e. each stage thereof is logically derived from the previous step. If this is not achieved then the decision is not effective.

For better understanding the above stated it must be made an appeal, to what logician GH Von Wright says, that if an agent engages into an action or final state as scope, and for its realization, another action (mean-action), an absolutely necessary one, then the agent must engage in the achievement of mean-action. Hence the appearance of rationality of logical derivation of the conclusion, that employment renders mediator agent, is to commit the action absolutely necessary to achieve the stated purpose.

Let us suppose that in an emergency (flood, earthquake, etc.), public administration namely its authority or authorities who manage this situation make a decision but do not compliance with the logical order of the stages of decision making, leading ultimately to extension or initial worsening.

To remember is that always results concludes to two or more premises of practical reasoning. The major premise through which is formulated the purpose (mission) to fulfill the minor (minor) premise (or the premises) which shows the action (or actions) intercessory absolutely necessary to the purpose described in the major premise.

Conclusion specificity in such practical reasoning is that, it is a statement of intent, a engagement of the agent, regarding his future attitudes and behavior, often transmitted through an order (order) in situations where to accomplish the mission (purpose) requires the coordination of the subordinate agencies (means).

Here is an example of practical reasoning for an emergency:

1. Major premise: It rained a lot and the Danube overfished its quota of damage. The mission of the public administration is to limit the effect of losses.
2. Minor premise: Danube dams can break certain dike defense in the south of the country.
3. Conclusion: So the public administration decided to strengthen dikes in areas where they are weaker. In a generalized formula, practical reasoning can be played as follows:
   - Agent X plans to achieve goal S;
   - Without X taking M action, he will not reach S;
   - So if X will do necessarily M.

Finally if the decision and conduct of other agents (subordinate), judgment will have the following form:

- X has the mission to achieve S;
- In order to X achieve S, Y must accomplish M1, and Z must accomplish M2;

So X must determine Y, to accomplish state M1, and Z, to accomplish state M2.

It should be noted that practical reasoning has the opportunity to be enriched and improved by introducing chronological dimension structure. This has a great importance for the public action as introduces in its structure and the need for framing within certain intercessory actions and an order of their succession.

Without ordering specified time, practical rationality loses partially or totally the meaning, as if an intervention is being made in the target range or at t time, when it is appropriate, it has no functional effect established. With reference to the above emergency situation (flooding) if the time factor is not taken into account this can lead to inefficiency of the decision.

The act of cognitive control of the situation ongoing constitutes the bases for an uninterrupted coordination of interventions which sets out whom to intervene in what place, at what point exactly and in what sequence, with what means to act to achieve partial goals, that contributes to the execution of the mission.

From highlighting these coordinates appears more clearly the importance of relationships and systematic ordering of the involvement of a gear acting on analytical and deductive operations forming practical rationality. Through it are being conducted the means and instruments transformers so that at certain points or intervals to be obtained certain values of accomplished action (achievement of goals).

6

Understanding E-Governance

The use of information and communication technologies, particularly the internet, for delivering government services is referred to as e-Governance. Some of the major components of e-Governance are e-Rulemaking, e-Participation and e-Services. These diverse components of e-Governance have been thoroughly discussed in this chapter.

E-GOVERNMENT

E-government, in full electronic government, the use of information and communication technologies, particularly the Internet, in government.

A popular way of conceptualizing e-government is to distinguish between three spheres of technologically mediated interactions. Government-to-government interactions are concerned with the use of technologies to enhance the internal efficiency of public bureaucracies, through, for example, the automation of routine tasks and the rapid sharing of information between departments and agencies. Government-to-business interactions typically involve the use of the Internet to reduce the costs to government of buying and selling goods and services from firms. Government-to-citizen interactions involve using the Internet to provide public services and transactions online and to improve the design and delivery of services by incorporating rapid electronic feedback mechanisms, such as instant polls, Web surveys, and e-mail.

Beyond this simple approach, defining e-government is more difficult; it is in a constant state of evolution, and an enormous "gray literature" of white papers, consultation documents, consultancy reports, corporate brochures, and league tables has emerged. There are also different national interpretations of the term, though it undoubtedly crosses borders with remarkable ease, making it arguably one of the fastest-spreading public-sector reform ideas in history.

Use of information and communication technology in government first expanded during the 1950s and '60s, the heyday of ideas of scientific administration. However, e-government as it is most commonly understood today emerged as an agenda for general reform of the public sectors of liberal democratic political systems during the early 1990s. U.S. President Bill Clinton's administration led the way with the 1993 National Performance Review of the federal bureaucracy. The explosion of Internet use in the mid-1990s gave impetus to the idea, and countries such as the United Kingdom, Canada, Australia, and New Zealand soon followed with their own versions. In the United Kingdom the Labour Party, elected in 1997, put electronic service delivery at the centre of its program of Modernizing Government.

In common with other programs of organizational reform, the claims made about e-government differ quite substantially. They can, however, be divided into two main schools of thought.

In one far-reaching perspective, the principal aim is to use digital network technologies to open the state to citizen involvement. The ubiquity of computer networks offers the potential to increase political participation and reshape the state into an open, interactive network form, as an alternative to both traditional, hierarchical, bureaucratic organizations and more recent, marketlike forms of service delivery based on the contracting out of public-sector activities (usually termed the new public management). Proponents of this perspective argue that widespread use of the Internet means that the traditional application of information and communication technologies in public bureaucracies, based on inward-facing mainframe computer systems that originated in the 1960s, should now be superseded by outward-facing networks in which the division between an organization's internal information processing and its external users effectively becomes redundant. Government becomes a learning organization, able to respond to the needs of citizens, who are in turn able to influence public bureaucracies by rapid, aggregative feedback mechanisms such as e-mail, online discussion forums, and interactive Web sites.

A second, less radical school of thought suggests that e-government does not necessarily require greater public involvement in shaping how services are delivered but instead indirectly benefits citizens through the efficiency gains and cost savings produced by the reduction of internal organizational friction, chiefly via the automation of routine tasks. Networks are also at the core of this perspective, but it is essentially concerned with the potential of the Internet and intranets (internal organizational computer networks) to join and coordinate the activities of previously disparate government departments and services that is seen as its most attractive feature. In this view, citizens are perceived mainly as the consumers of public services such as health care information, benefits payments, passport applications, tax returns, and so on. This has been the dominant model in those countries that have taken the lead in introducing e-government reforms.

E-government is not without its critics. Some suggest that changes are limited to a managerial agenda of service delivery more consistent with the new public management and that the opportunities offered by the Internet for invigorating democracy and citizenship might be missed. Other criticisms are that the conservatism of existing administrative elites will scupper any prospects of decisive change, that issues of unequal access (both within and between states) to online services are being neglected, that large corporate information technology interests are exercising an undue influence on the shape of e-government, that traditional face-to-face contacts with public servants, especially those associated with welfare systems, cannot be satisfactorily replaced by Internet communication, that the cost savings promised by reforms have been difficult to demonstrate, and that disintermediation (bypassing) of traditional representative bodies (parliaments, local councils) may occur, to the detriment of democracy.

Early government responses to the Internet often went little further than placing information on the Web in a simple electronic version of traditional paper-based means of dissemination. The arrival of e-government, which signaled the acceptance of Internet connectivity as a tool that could be used to improve efficiency, cut costs, and change the way governments have traditionally interacted with citizens, constitutes an important shift in public administration.

E-GOVERNANCE

E-governance has become an essential part of any firm in globalisation process. Increasing demands of clearness in administration, rapid information transfer, more competent performance and improved public service has pushed organizations to choose electronic means for success in business. Organizations can give better performance through innovative use of information technology and e-governance. There are many advantages of e-governance and impact public management through, for example, improved access to services, decreased operational costs, enhanced knowledge management, and strengthened coordination of government agencies. E-government has been major developments of the web. It is well established that Internet supported digital communities, they present the national governments with a number of challenges and opportunities. The application of ICT and e-governance has huge potential for intermediate organizations in developing countries. The main goal of e-governance is to support and simplify governance for all parties' government, citizens and businesses. E-governance uses electronic medium to support and motivate good governance. Therefore the purpose of e-governance are analogous to the objectives of good governance. Good governance can be seen as an application of economic, political, and administrative authority to smoothly manage business activities of a country at, national and local level.

Concept of E-governance

E-governance is the good usage of information and communication technologies to transform and enhance the efficiency, effectiveness, transparency and accountability of informational and transactional exchanges with in government, between government agencies at National, State, Municipal & Local levels, citizen & businesses, and to authorise citizens through access and use of information. Fundamentally, E-governance, entails electronic governance which uses information and communication technologies at various levels of the government and the public sector to improve governance.

Theoretical studies demonstrated that E-Governance is the process of change of the relationship of government with its constituents the citizens, the businesses and between its own organs, through the use of tools of information and communication technology. Keohane and Nye asserted that "Governance implies the processes and institutions, both formal and informal that guide and restrain the collective activities of a group. Government is the subset that acts with authority and creates formal obligations. Governance need not necessarily be conducted exclusively by governments. Private firms, associations of firms, nongovernmental organizations (NGOs), and associations of NGOs all engage in it, often in association with governmental bodies, to create governance and sometimes without governmental authority." The objective of e governance is to embrace information and communication technologies and offer an opportunity to citizens, so they can get involve in decision making process. According to The UNESCO, E-governance is the public sector's use of information and communication technologies in order to enhance information and service delivery, motivating inhabitant involvement in the decision-making process and making government more accountable, transparent and effective.

E-governance involves new styles of management, novel ways to decide policy and investment, new ways of accessing education, and listening to citizens and new ways of organizing and delivering information and services. The purpose is to give better access, accountability and efficiency in the delivery of government information and services. E-Governance has capability to provide all government information and services on internet to the public and private sector. An e-governance initiatives and innovations will ensure a more democratic, transparent and accountable framework for the public and private apparatus to operate in. The governments of developing countries must establish a suitable environment for e-governance. E-governance is the method of service delivery and information dissemination to citizens using electronic means providing many benefits over the conventional system.

These include increased efficiency in various Governmental processes, transparency and anticorruption in all transactions, empowerment of citizens and encouragement of their participation in governance. Ray and Dash considered that e-governance should also include the aspects of internal working which cover use of information technology to increase competence and effectiveness of internal functions and internal communications and internetworking. Internal aspects cover the overall change of government hierarchy to adjust to the new requirements and expectations of efficient and improved services, simplification and rationalization in the business process to better serve the stake-holders in a transparent and cost-effective manner.

Evaluation of E-governance

With the technical development of internet technology in the nineties, there was global shifts towards increased deployment of IT by governments. The technology as well as e-governance initiatives emerged a long way since that time. World Wide Web offered good opportunities to global population to exploit their new mode of access in wide ranging ways. People have great expectation to get information and services online from governments and corporate organizations to further their civic, professional and personal lives, thus creating plentiful evidence that the new "e-citizenship" is taking hold. In India, the notion of e-governance during the seventies with a focus on development of in-house government applications in the areas of defence, economic monitoring, planning and the deployment of IT to manage data intensive functions related to elections, census, and tax administration. The National Informatics Center made great efforts to link all the district headquarters in the decade of eighties. Since the beginning of nineties, IT technologies were enhanced by information and communication technology to expand its use for wider sectorial applications with policy emphasis on reaching out to rural areas and taking in greater participations from NGOs and private sectors.

Conceptual Framework

The e-governance model can serve as a reference for governments to situation where a project fits in the overall development of an e-governance strategy. An e-governance strategy is essential to accomplish the corporate goals. Projects have structural value for development when entrenched in vision and supported by policies. Anderson had described the process of implementing e governance projects. He has perception of think big, start small, and scale fast.

Thinking big is vital to set the general vision and objectives of e-governance. Starting small is crucial to build immediate success and keep a positive driving force, both internally as well as externally. Scaling fast is only possible with a deep strategy that protects all necessary resources are available in time.

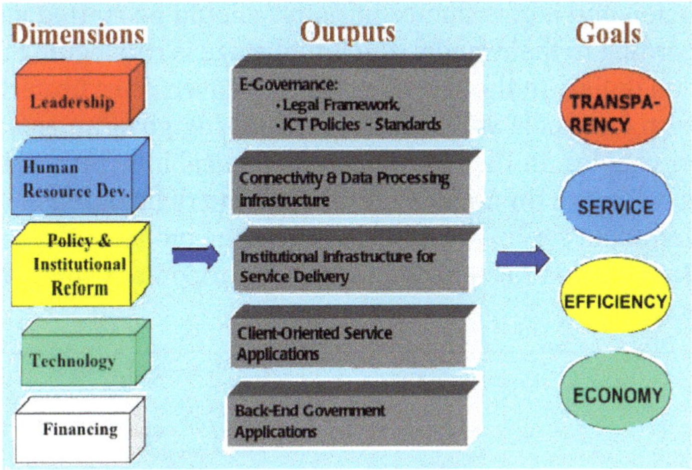

E-governance Implementation

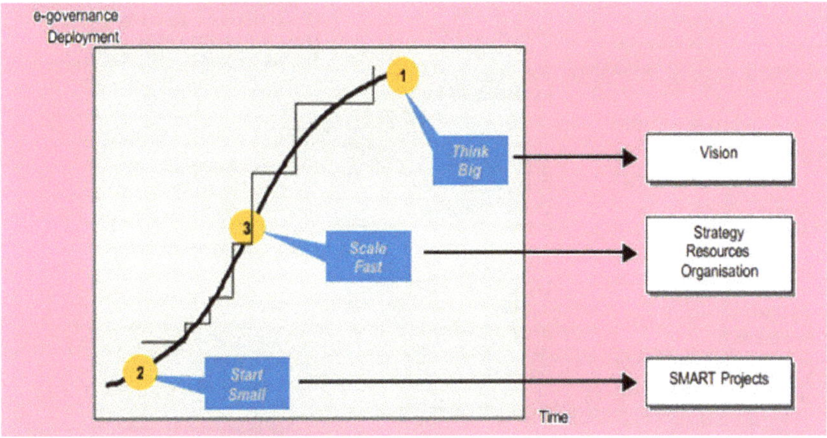

To understand deeply about the e-governance space, researcher developed four different frameworks and models. Gartner proposed a four-stage model for e-governance. In the first stage of "Presence", governments will go to the Internet and establish a least presence online. In the second stage of "Interaction", online presence will be reorganised and enhanced to include a searchable database of services and government staff will begin to interact with communication tools such as E-mail. In the third stage of "Transaction", governments will provide services online. At this stage, inhabitants will be able to benefit government services and governments can use E-authentication and payment services for providing services.

The Fourth stage of Gartner's model is called "Transformation" in which governments will begin to assimilate services across various levels and functions to provide integrated services from various departments. Gartner believes that pace layers can be used to develop a business application strategy that delivers a faster response and a better ROI, without sacrificing integration, integrity and/or governance.

Gartner's Model of E-governance

Another e-governance model is developed by Layne & Lee and they argued that e-governance is an evolutionary phenomenon and e-governance initiative should be started and implemented in an evolutionary way. According to their model, the initial stage is cataloguing in which governments will provide information online, in the second stage of e-governance projects, government moves to transaction. E-Governance tools will start revolutionizing governments by changing the way they interact with their peoples. In the third stage of "Vertical integration" theorists asserted that e-governance projects will move from mere automation and digitization of the existing process to transformation of government services. The last stage in the model of Layne and Lee is horizontal integration in which Information Technology tools will horizontally integrate services across different functions of government.

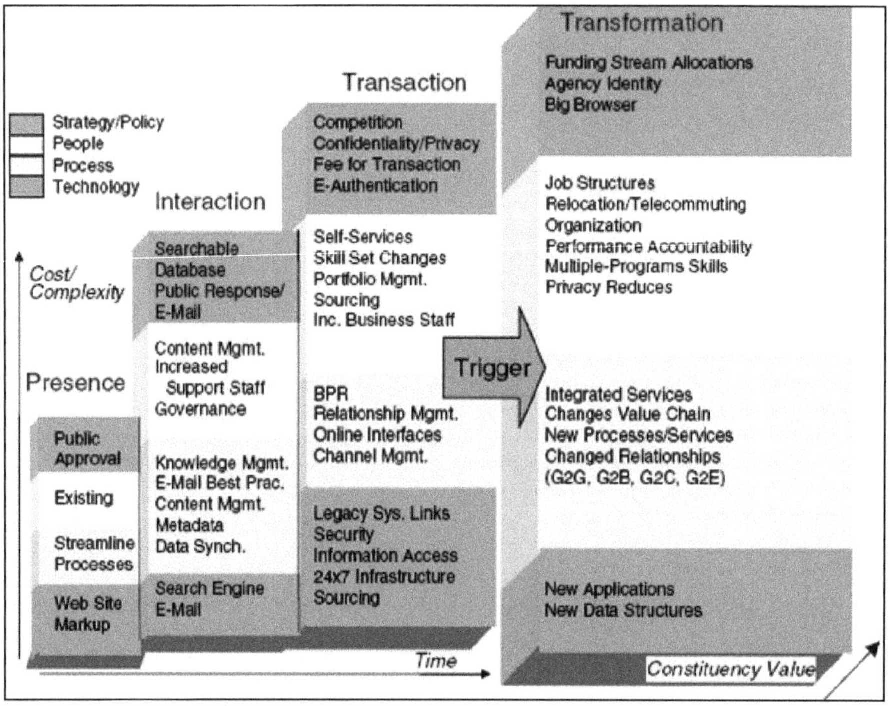

K. Layne, J. Lee Government Information

The United Nations Organisation provided a five-stage model of E-governance in 2003 after conducting survey. In this model, first two stages are similar to the Gartner's model. In the first stage of this model, there is limited, basic and static information through an official website or a portal. The second stage offer searchable databases and information related to laws and regulations. The third stage is recognized as "Interactive presence" in which government services will enter an interactive mode with electronic signature facilities and multimedia capability. In the Fourth "Transactional Presence" stage, government services will be offered as online transactions. Inhabitants will avail and pay for services using government portals. In the last stage of the UN's model, "Networked presence", Government agencies will be combined to offer integrated services from various departments. Another model suggested by Finger and Pecoud for e-governance based on three different policy levels which include local, national and global, three different sectors involved such as private sector, government and third sector, three different policy functions that are policy making, regulation and operations and three different degrees of making use of New Information and Communication Technologies.

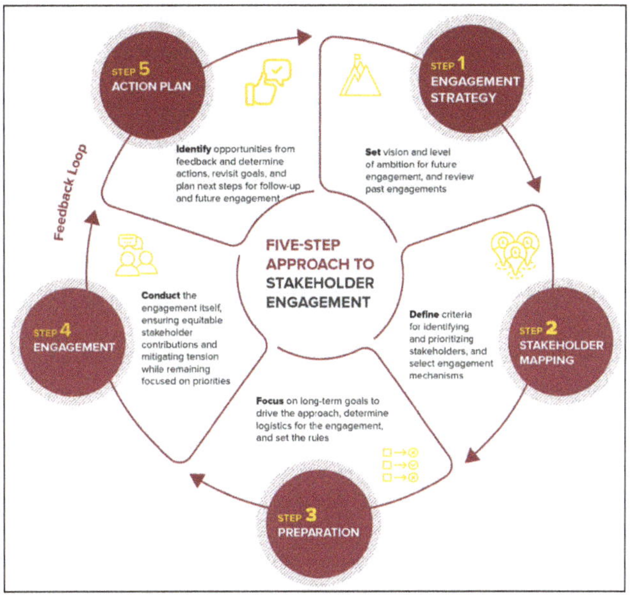

Types of Interactions in E-governance

1. G2G (Government to Government): When the exchange of information and services is within the periphery of the government, is termed as G2G interaction. This can be both horizontal, i.e. among various government entities and vertical, i.e. between national, state and local government entities and within different levels of the entity.
2. G2C (Government to Citizen): The interaction amidst the government and general public is G2C interaction. Here an interface is set up between government and citizens, which enables citizens to get access to wide variety of public services. The citizens has the freedom to share their views and grievances on government policies anytime, anywhere.
3. G2B (Government to Business): In this case, the e-governance helps the business class to interact with the government seamlessly. It aims at eliminating red-tapism, saving time, cost and establish transparency in the business environment, while interacting with government.
4. G2E (Government to Employees): The government of any country is the biggest employer and so it also deals with employees on a regular basis, as other employers do. ICT helps in making the interaction between government and employees fast and efficient, along with raising their level of satisfaction by providing perquisites and add-on benefits.

E-governance can only be possible if the government is ready for it. It is not a one day task, and so the government has to make plans and implement them before switching to it. Some of the measures include Investment in telecommunication infrastructure, budget resources, ensure security, monitor assessment, internet connectivity speed, promote awareness among public regarding the importance, support from all government departments and so forth.

E-governance has a great role to play, that improves and supports all tasks performed by the government department and agencies, because it simplifies the task on the one hand and increases the quality of work on the other.

TRANSFORMATIONAL GOVERNMENT

Transformational Government is the use of computer-based information and communications technologies (ICT) to change the way governments work. The term is commonly used to describe a government reform strategy which attempts to radically change the way people understand government, especially those working within government. For example, it is often associated with a 'whole-of-government' viewpoint, which tries to foster cross-department collaboration and provide 'one-stop-shop' convenience in the delivery of services to citizens.

The term Transformational Government is usually used aspirationally, as denoting the 'highest' level of what e-government can achieve:

1. Presence, where ICT, and usually websites, are used to provide information;
2. Interaction, where government interacts with citizens, and departments interact with each other, online especially by email;
3. Transaction, where such things as paying taxes or licenses are carried out online;
4. Transformation, which involves a reinvention of government functions and how they operate. In relation to developing countries, it is often associated with hopes of reducing corruption, and in relation to developed countries, with attempts to increase the involvement of the private and voluntary sectors in government activity.

During the last two decades, governments around the world have invested in ICT with the aim of increasing the quality and decreasing the cost of public services. But over that time, as even the least developed countries have moved to websites, e-services and e-Government strategies, it has become increasingly clear that e-Government has not delivered all the benefits that were hoped for it. One study found that 35% of e-government projects in developing countries resulted in total failures; and that 50% were partial failures.

In reaction to these poor outcomes, there has been a shift of perspective to 'Transformational Government', aiming beyond purely technical aspects of better enabling e-government processes towards addressing the cultural and organisational barriers which have hindered public service benefits realisation. Researchers have defined the rationale for Transformational Government as "the exploitation of e-government such that benefits can be realized".

In 2010 the Organization for the Advancement of Structured Information Standards (OASIS) published a report which identified a wide range of common pitfalls which have hampered many governments in achieving significant impacts through their technology investments. However, OASIS also noted that:

> "an increasing number [of governments] are now getting to grips with the much broader and complex set of cultural and organizational changes which are needed for ICT to deliver significant benefits to the public sector. This new approach is generally referred to as Transformational Government."

OASIS cites the UK and Australia as two of the leaders in this area:

> "Transformational Government. encompasses a new "virtual" business layer within government which allows an integrated, government-wide, citizen-focused service to

be presented to citizens across all channels, but at no extra cost and without having to restructure government to do so. Two very good examples of this new approach are South Australia's "Ask Just Once" portal and the UK Government's DirectGov portal, and the approach is explained in very good detail in the CS Transform's white paper entitled "Citizen Service Transformation – a manifesto for change in the delivery of public services".

Countries with Transformational Government Initiatives

Within the last decade, this new emphasis on a Transformational Government approach can be seen from a number of countries:

Country	Initiative(s)	Details
Canada	Government On-Line (GOL)	Report of the Auditor General of Canada: Chapter 1 Information Technology: Government On-Line 2003. "One of the key principles of Government On-Line is that programs and services will be transformed to reflect the needs and expectations of clients and citizens. From the government's perspective, the overall objective of the GOL initiative is full service transformation – to fundamentally change the way the government operates and to deliver better services to Canadians."
UK	gov.uk	Transformational Government: Enabled by Technology, 2005. "The future of public services has to use technology to give citizens choice, with personalised services designed around their needs not the needs of the provider".
USA	PIF, 18F, USDS	Presidential Innovation Fellows program where "teams of government experts and private-sector doers take a user-centric approach to issues at the intersection of people, processes, products, and policy to achieve lasting impact" launched in 2012. 18F a new digital government delivery service, was formed in early 2014 and United States Digital Service (USDS) was launched later in 2014.
Korea	Government 3.0	Announced in 2013 with "an ambitious plan to allow wider public access to government data to improve the transparency of state affairs.", this initiative includes: citizen-centered government innovation, core values of openness, sharing, communication, collaboration for all areas of governing, customized services to individual citizens, which will create jobs and support creative economy.

International Initiatives

The early pioneering work by some governments is now being picked up and championed by a range of global organizations which offer support to governments in moving to a Transformational Government approach. For example:

- The World Bank has set up an eTransform Initiative (ETI) with support from global IT partners such as Gemalto, IBM, L-1 Identity Solutions, Microsoft and Pfizer. "The eTransform Initiative is about tapping information technology, expertise and experiences", said Mohsen Khalil, Director of the World Bank Group's Global Information and Communication Technologies Department. "Government transformation is about change management facilitated by technology. This initiative will facilitate the exchange of lessons and experiences among various governments and industry players, to maximize impact and lower risks of ICT-enabled government transformation."
- A number of private sector organizations working in this area have published white papers which pull together global best practices on Government Transformation.

- OASIS launched (September 2010) a new Technical Committee tasked with producing a new global best practice standard for a Transformational Government Framework. The Framework is expressed as a number of "Pattern Languages", each providing a detailed set of guidance notes and conformance clauses on how to deliver the required changes in practice.

E-RULEMAKING

Electronic rulemaking (also known as eRulemaking and e-rulemaking) is the use of digital technologies by government agencies in the rulemaking and decision making processes of the United States. An interdisciplinary electronic rulemaking research community has formed as a result of National Science Foundation funding under the auspices of the Digital Government Program. Groups such as the Cornell E-Rulemaking Initiative (CeRI) have been focused on researching how technologies such as Web 2.0 can help foster greater public participation in the political process, specifically, in Federal Agencies' rulemaking.

In the United States, Electronic rulemaking (also known as eRulemaking and e-rulemaking) can be understood as a subset of a larger Federal eGovernment initiative. In the 1990s Federal Agencies that propose and enact regulations, such as the Department of Transportation (DOT) and Federal Communications Commission (FCC), began to modernize and create websites for publication of proposed regulations and online commenting from the public.

President George W. Bush made strides in increasing e-Government. Under President Bush, Congress passed the Honest Leadership and Open Government Act, which among other things, required agencies to accept comments electronically and make various information, including comments and rulemaking materials, publicly available online. Since 2008, President Barack Obama has greatly increased the number of Federal eGovernment initiatives.

2009 Initiatives and Reforms

In 2009, President Barack Obama directed government agencies to utilize new technologies such as Web 2.0 and other information technology to increase transparency and openness in government. Soon after, the Office of Management and Budget (OMB) issued a memorandum to the Federal Agencies reiterating three open government principles, "transparency, participation, and collaboration," identified by the President. OMB gave agencies four months to create an "open government plan," which would address each "cornerstone" of open government.

OMB gave details on how to address each cornerstone. For "transparency," the agencies were required to publish "high-value" data and other information in an "open" format, and "inform the public of significant actions and business of the agency." To address "participation," agencies were required to openly link to sites where the public could "actively participate," and to "include proposals for new feedback mechanisms, including innovative tools and practices that create new and easier methods for public engagement." Finally, to address "collaboration," agencies were required to "include proposals to use technology platforms to improve collaboration among people within and outside your agency," and use innovative methods to increase collaboration.

In addition to addressing the "cornerstones," agencies were required to identify a "flagship initiative." The flagship initiative had to be "at least one specific, new transparency, participation, or collaboration initiative that your agency is currently implementing."

Third Party E-rulemaking Initiatives

Cornell E-rulemaking Initiative

Cornell University has started a multidisciplinary collaboration known as the Cornell eRulemaking Initiative, or CeRI. Backed by a National Science Foundation grant, CeRI has begun researching and applying Web 2.0 technologies in a political setting. The group includes faculty and students from Computing and Information Science, Law, and the Scheinman Institute on Conflict Resolution. CeRI uses an interdisciplinary approach to discover and apply Web 2.0 and other technologies to "improve public understanding of, and participation in, rulemaking."

In 2009, CeRI launched the site RegulationRoom.org. The site, which is hosted by the Legal Information Institute, is an independent non-governmental online community that allows users to read, comment, and discuss proposed regulations from federal agencies. Professors and students at Cornell Law School summarize the relevant parts of the agency's proposed regulation, and post the information on the site. Once the proposed rule has been posted, users are able to comment, discuss, and critique the agency's proposal. At the close of a rule's comment period, Regulation Room moderators summarize the comments and submit this summary to the Agency as an official comment.

Although CeRI and Regulation Room are research projects unaffiliated with the federal government, In 2010, the DOT partnered with CeRI as part of the White House Open Government Initiative. The purpose of the partnership is to "discover the best ways of using Web 2.0 and social networking technologies to further rulemaking efforts." DOT has selected Regulation Room as its flagship initiative under the Open Government Directive. Similar open government initiatives have been launched at other federal agencies.

Since launching in 2009, RegulationRoom.org has hosted four "live" rules from the DOT. These rules included:

- DOT – Texting: The rule, which closed to commenting on January 10, 2010, dealt with the DOT's proposal to regulate texting by commercial motor vehicle operators. The rule received 48 comments on Regulation Room.
- DOT - Airline Passenger Rights: The rule, which closed on September 23, 2010, dealt with the DOT's proposed regulations for airline passenger rights. Regulation room received over 19,000 visitors and over 900 comments.
- DOT - Electronic Onboard Recorders: The rule, which closed on May 23, 2011, was a proposal to require commercial truck drivers with multiple operating violations to use electronic onboard recorders. The rule received over one-hundred comments.
- DOT – Air Travel Accessibility: The rule, which closed on January 9, 2012, was a proposal to require airlines to make their websites and airport kiosks accessible to travelers with disabilities.

E-PARTICIPATION

E-participation is the term referring to "ICT-supported participation in processes involved in government and governance". Processes may concern administration, service delivery, decision making and policy making. E-participation is hence closely related to e-government and e-governance participation. The need for the term has emerged as citizen interests have received less attention than those of the service providers in e-government development. It also emerged as the need to distinguish between the roles of citizen and customer has become more pressing.

A more detailed definition sees e-participation as "the use of information and communication technologies to broaden and deepen political participation by enabling citizens to connect with one another and with their elected representatives". This definition includes all stakeholders in democratic decision-making processes and not only citizen related top-down government initiatives. So e-participation can be seen as part of e-democracy, the use of ICT by governments in general used by elected officials, media, political parties and interest groups, civil society organizations, international governmental organizations, or citizens/voters within any of the political processes of states/regions, nations, and local and global communities.

The complexity of e-participation processes results from the large number of different participation areas, involved stakeholders, levels of engagement, and stages in policy making.

The term 'participation' means taking part in joint activities for the purpose of reaching a common goal. This encompasses both trivial situations in which participation mainly has a technical meaning, "doing things together". For example, a football team needs 11 players, and dancing often requires two or more people acting in a coordinated manner. But participation, even in trivial situations, also has a goal-oriented aspect which means decision making and control are involved. Participation in political science and theory of management refers to direct public participation in political, economical or management decisions. The two are not completely separated but belong on a spectrum of complexity and context. When participation becomes complicated, decision making becomes necessary. Hence, any participatory process is potentially important for the rule system governing the activities. In terms of points 2 and 3 above, this means that when service processes become complex, the implementation of them will not be in all details based on political decisions but also on what is found to be practical.

Instead of taking in and accepting knowledge as is disseminated by the media and government, by participating, one becomes an active citizen and further contributes to a democratic society. When such practical doings become implemented in government e-service systems, they will affect decision making, as many changes will later be hard to make simply because existing procedures are implemented in ICT systems and government agencies' procedures. There are many theories dealing with institutionalization, for example structuration theory, institutional theory, and actor-network theory. These theories all, in different ways, deal with how "ways of doing things" become established or rejected, and how those that become established increasingly affect the ways we "normally" do things.

Models and Tools

A number of tools and models have emerged as part of Web 2.0 that can be used or inspire the design of architecture for e-participation. In particular, "the emergence of online communities oriented toward the creation of useful products suggests that it may be possible to design socially mediating technology that support public-government collaborations".

Participation Tools

- Wikis,
- Online social networking,
- Blogs.

Mechanisms

- Electronic voting,
- Reputation systems,
- Internet petitions,
- Transparency tools (social translucence mechanisms).

Tracking and analysis

- Digital traces,
- Data mining,
- Data visualization,
- Simulations such as agent-based social simulation.

Crowdsourcing

To demonstrate e-participation at work, one can turn to one of its types - crowdsourcing. This is generally defined as the enlisting of a group of humans to solve problems via the World Wide Web. The idea is that this platform is able to collect human resources from the most unlikely and remotest places, contributing to the general store of intellectual capital. Crowdsourcing can be applied in different stages of the policy-making process and these could transpire on the information, consultation, and active participation levels. At the information level, there is a one-way relationship, wherein the participants receive information from the government. The consultation process entails a two-way interaction where citizens already provide their inputs, feedback, and reactions. Finally, active participation can refer to the deeper participatory involvement where citizens directly contribute in the formulation of policy content. This level of e-participation is increasingly being practiced through tools such as online petition, e-referendum, e-panels, citizen e-juries, and participatory GIS, among others.

European eParticipation Preparatory Action

eParticipation is the Preparatory Action lasts for three years (2006–2008). The EU is taking the lead in using online tools to improve the legislative process for its citizens. eParticipation which launched on January 1, 2007 will run as a series of linked projects which each contribute to a greater awareness and involvement by citizens in the legislation process from initial drafting to implementation at a regional and local level.

The individual projects will concentrate on ensuring that the legislative language and process is more transparent, understandable and accessible to citizens. In addition the projects emphasis on the communication of legislation will be used to enhance and grow citizens' involvement and contribution in the process of creating and implementing the legislation.

So far, 21 projects have been funded. The European Parliament, national parliaments and local and regional authorities are actively involved. State-of-the-art ICT tools are being tested to facilitate the writing of legal texts, including translation into different languages, and the drafting of amendments as well as making the texts easier for non-specialists to find and understand. New digital technologies are also being used to give citizens easier access to information and more opportunity to influence decisions that affect their lives. A report, which was published as a MOMENTUM white paper, highlights the major facts and figures of those projects while providing some initial policy recommendations for future use.

European eParticipation Actions

The European Commission has now launched a number of actions aiming at further advancing the work of supporting eParticipation.

Examples:

- FP7 : ICT Challenge 7 : Objective ICT-2009.7.3 ICT for Governance and Policy Modelling. The European Commission has launched some call in this area to finance researches. Currently the Integrated Program Future Policy Modelling (FUPOL) is the largest project in this domain.
- CIP ICT Policy Support Programme (or ICT PSP). The European project has open a call in the programme CIP (Competitiveness and Innovation Framework) on the Theme 3: ICT for government and governance.

E-SERVICES

E-services (electronic services) are services which use of information and communication technologies (ICTs). The three main components of e-services are- service provider, service receiver and the channels of service delivery (i.e., technology). For example, as concerned to public e-service, public agencies are the service provider and citizens as well as businesses are the service receiver. The channel of service delivery is the third requirement of e-service. Internet is the main channel of e-service delivery while other classic channels (e.g. telephone, call center, public kiosk, mobile phone, television) are also considered.

Since its inception in the late 1980s in Europe and formal introduction in 1993 by the US Government, the term 'E-Government' has now become one of the recognized research domains especially in the context of public policy and now has been rapidly gaining strategic importance in public sector modernization. E-service is one of the branches of this domain and its attention has also been creeping up among the practitioners and researchers.

E-service (or eservice) is a highly generic term, usually referring to 'The provision of services via the Internet (the prefix 'e' standing for 'electronic', as it does in many other usages), thus e-Service may also include e-Commerce, although it may also include non-commercial services (online), which is usually provided by the government.'

"E-Service constitutes the online services available on the Internet, whereby a valid transaction of buying and selling (procurement) is possible, as opposed to the traditional websites, whereby only descriptive information are available, and no online transaction is made possible."

Importance of E-service

Lu identifies a number of benefits for e-services, some of these are:

- Accessing a greater customer base;
- Broadening market reach;
- Lowering of entry barrier to new markets and cost of acquiring new customers;
- Alternative communication channel to customers;
- Increasing services to customers;
- Enhancing perceived company image;
- Gaining competitive advantages;
- Enhancing transparency;
- Potential for increasing Customer knowledge.

Importance and Advantages of E-shopping

- E-shops are open 24 hours a day.
- There is no need to travel to the malls or wait at the checkout counters.
- There is usually a wide selection of goods and services.
- It is easy to compare prices and quality by using the E-shopping tool.
- Price reduction and discounts are electronically conveyed.

E-service Domain

The term 'e-service' has many applications and can be found in many disciplines. The two dominant application areas of e-services are:

- E-business (or e-commerce): e-services mostly provided by businesses or [NGO|non-government organizations] (NGOs) (private sector).
- E-government: e-services provided by government to citizens or business (public sector is the supply side). The use and description of the e-service in this page will be limited to

the context of e-government only where of the e-service is usually associated with prefix "public": Public e-services. In some cases, we will have to describe aspects that are related to both fields like some conferences or journals which cover the concept of "e-Service" in both domains of e-government and e-business.

Architecture

Depending on the types of services, there are certain functionalities required in the certain layers of e-service architectural framework, these include but are not limited to – Data layer (data sources), processing layers (customer service systems, management systems, data warehouse systems, integrated customer content systems), exchange layer (Enterprise Application Integration– EAI), interaction layer (integrating e-services), and presentation layer (customer interface through which the web pages and e-services are linked).

E-service Quality

Measuring service quality and service excellence are important in a competitive organizational environment. The SERVQUAL- service quality model is one of the widely used tools for measuring quality of the service on various aspects. The five attributes of this model are: reliability, responsiveness, assurance, tangibles, and empathy. The following table summarizes some major of these:

SERVQUAL	Kaynama & Black	Zeithaml	Janda et al.	Alawattegama & Wattegama
Reliability	Content	Access	Access	Factual information
Responsiveness	Access	Ease of navigation	Security	Business information
Assurance	Navigation	Efficiency	Sensation	General information
Tangibles	Design	Flexibility	Information/content	Consumer- related information
Empathy	Response	Reliability		
	Background	Personalization		
	Personalization	Security/privacy		
		Responsiveness		
		Assurance/trust		
		Site aesthetics		
		Price knowledge		

The LIRNEasia study on benchmarking national telecom regulator websites focuses on content than on accessibility and ease of use, unlike the other studies mentioned here. Websites are increasingly important portals to government agencies, especially in the context of information society reforms. Stakeholders, including businesses, investors and even the general public, are interested in information produced by these agencies, and websites can help to increase their transparency and accountability. The quality of its website also demonstrates how advanced a regulatory agency is.

E-service Cost Factor

Some major cost factors are:

- Expense of setting up applications,
- Maintaining applications,
- Internet connection,
- Hardware/software,
- Security concerns,
- Legal issues,
- Training,
- Rapid technology changes.

Challenges to E-services in the Developing World

The future of e-service is bright but some challenges remain. There are some challenges in e-service, as Sheth and Sharma identify, are:

- Low penetration of ICT especially in the developing countries,
- Fraud on the internet space which is estimated around 2.8billion USD,
- Privacy due the emergence of various types of spyware and security holes,
- Intrusive characteristics of the service (e.g. mobile phones based) as customers may not like to be contacted with the service providers at any time and at any place.

The first challenge and primary obstacle to the e-service platform will be penetration of the internet. In some developing countries, the access to the internet is limited and speeds are also limited. In these cases firms and customers will continue to use traditional platforms. The second issue of concern is fraud on the internet. It is anticipated that the fraud on the e-commerce internet space costs $2.8 billion. Possibility of fraud will continue to reduce the utilization of the internet. The third issue is of privacy. Due to both spyware and security holes in operating systems, there is concern that the transactions that consumers undertake have privacy limitations. For example, by stealthily following online activities, firms can develop fairly accurate descriptions of customer profiles. Possibility of privacy violations will reduce the utilizations of the internet. The final issue is that e-service can also become intrusive as they reduce time and location barriers of other forms of contract. For example, firms can contact people through mobile devices at any time and at any place. Customers do not take like the intrusive behavior and may not use the e-service platform.

Major E-service Keywords

A considerable amount of research efforts already exists on the subject matter exploring different aspects of e-service and e-service delivery ; one worth noting effort is Rowley's study who did a review study on the e-service literature. The key finding of his study is that there is need to explore dimensions of e-service delivery not focusing only on service quality "In order to understand e-service experiences it is necessary to go beyond studies of e-service quality dimensions and to also take into account the inherent characteristics of e-service delivery and the factors that differentiate one service experience from another."

Acceptance

User acceptance of technology is defined according to Morris as "the demonstrable willingness within a user group to employ information technology for the tasks it is designed to support". This definition can be brought into the context of e-service where acceptance can be defined as the users' willingness to use e-service or the willingness to decide when and how to use the e-service.

Accessibility

Users' ability to access to the e-service is important theme in the previous literature. For example, Huang finds that most of the websites in general fail to serve users with disabilities. Recommendation to improve accessibility is evident in previous literature including Jaeger who suggests the following to improve e-services' accessibility like: design for accessibility from the outset of website development, Involve users with disabilities in the testing of the site Focus on the benefits of an accessible Web site to all users.

Administrative Literacy

According to Grönlund et al., for a simple e-service, the needs for knowledge and skills, content and procedures are considerably less. However, in complicated services there are needed to change some prevailed skills, such as replacing verbal skills with skill in searching for information online.

Benchmarking

This theme is concerned with establishing standards for measuring e-services or the best practices within the field. This theme also includes the international benchmarking of e-government services; much critic has been targeting these reports being incomprehensive and useless. According to Bannister "benchmarks are not a reliable tool for measuring real e-government progress. Furthermore, if they are poorly designed, they risk distorting government policies as countries may chase the benchmark rather than looking at real local and national needs."

Digital Divide

Digital divide is considered one of the main barriers to implementing e-services; some people do not have means to access the e-services and some others do not know how to use the technology (or the e-service). According to Helbig et al., "we suggest E-Government and the digital divide should be seen as complementary social phenomena (i.e., demand and supply). Moreover, a serious e-government digital divide is that services mostly used by social elites."

E-readiness

Most of the reports and the established criteria focus on assessing the services in terms of infrastructure and public policies ignoring the citizen participation or e-readiness. According to by Shalini, "the results of the research project reveal that a high index may be only indicating that a country is e-ready in terms of ICT infrastructure and info-structure, institutions, policies, and political commitment, but it is a very poor measure of the e-readiness of citizens. To summarize the findings, it can be said that Mauritius is ready but the Mauritians are not".

E-readiness, as the Economist Intelligence Unit defines, is the measure of a country's ability to leverage digital channels for communication, commerce and government in order to further economic and social development. Implied in this measure is the extent to which the usage of communications devices and Internet services creates efficiencies for business and citizens, and the extent to which this usage is leveraged in the development of information and communications technology (ICT) industries. In general terms, the definition of e-readiness is relative, for instance depending on a country in question's priorities and perspective.

Efficiency

As opposed to effectiveness, efficiency is focused on the internal competence within the government departments when delivering e-services. There is a complaint that researchers focus more on effectiveness. "There is an emerging trend seemingly moving away from the efficiency target and focusing on users and governance outcome. While the latter is worthwhile, efficiency must still remain a key priority for eGovernment given the budget constraints compounded in the future by the costs of an ageing population. Moreover, efficiency gains are those that can be most likely proven empirically through robust methodologies".

Security

Security is the most important challenge that faces the implementation of e-services because without a guarantee of privacy and security citizens will not be willing to take up e-government services. These security concerns, such as hacker attacks and the theft of credit card information, make governments hesitant to provide public online services. According to the GAO report of 2002 "security concerns present one of the toughest challenges to extending the reach of e-government.The rash of hacker attacks, Web page defacing, and credit card information being posted on electronic bulletin boards can make many federal agency officials—as well as the general public—reluctant to conduct sensitive government transactions involving personal or financial data over the Internet." By and Large, Security is one of the major challenges that faces the implementation and development of electronic services. people want to be assured that they are safe when they are conducting online services and that their information will remain secure and confidential.

Stakeholders

Axelsson et al. argue that the stakeholder concept-which was originally used in private firms-, can be used in public setting and in the context of e-government. According to them, several scholars have discussed the use of the stakeholder theory in public settings. The stakeholder theory suggests that need to focus on all the involved stakeholder s when designing the e-service; not only on the government and citizens.

Usability

Compared to Accessibility, There is sufficient literature that addresses the issue of usability; researchers have developed different models and methods to measure the usability and effectiveness of eGovernment websites. However, But still there is call to improve these measures and make it more compressive.

The word usability has cropped up a few times already in this unit. In the context of biometric identification, usability referred to the smoothness of enrollment and other tasks associated with setting up an identification system. A system that produced few false matches during enrollment of applicants was described as usable. Another meaning of usability is related to the ease of use of an interface. Although this meaning of the term is often used in the context of computer interfaces, there is no reason to confine it to computers.

Social, Cultural and Ethical Implications of E-services

The perceived effectiveness of e-service can be influenced by public's view of the social and cultural implications of e-technologies and e-service.

- Impacts on individuals' rights and privacy – As more and more companies and government agencies use technology to collect, store, and make accessible data on individuals, privacy concerns have grown. Some companies monitor their employees' computer usage patterns in order to assess individual or workgroup performance. Technological advancements are also making it much easier for businesses, government and other individuals to obtain a great deal of information about an individual without their knowledge. There is a growing concern that access to a wide range of information can be dangerous within politically corrupt government agencies.

- Impact on Jobs and Workplaces - In the early days of computers, management scientists anticipated that computers would replace human decision-makers. However, despite significant technological advances, this prediction is no longer a mainstream concern. At the current time, one of the concerns associated with computer usage in any organization (including governments) is the health risk – such as injuries related to working continuously on a computer keyboard. Government agencies are expected to work with regulatory groups in order to avoid these problems.

- Potential Impacts on Society – Despite some economic benefits of ICT to individuals, there is evidence that the computer literacy and access gap between the haves and have-nots may be increasing. Education and information access are more than ever the keys to economic prosperity, yet access by individuals in different countries is not equal - this social inequity has become known as the digital divide.

- Impact on Social Interaction – Advancements in ICT and e-Technology solutions have enabled many government functions to become automated and information to be made available online. This is a concern to those who place a high value on social interaction.

- Information Security - Technological advancements allow government agencies to collect, store and make data available online to individuals and organizations. Citizens and businesses expect to be allowed to access data in a flexible manner (at any time and from any location). Meeting these expectations comes at a price to government agencies where it concerns managing information – more specifically, ease of access; data integrity and accuracy; capacity planning to ensure the timely delivery of data to remote (possibly mobile) sites; and managing the security of corporate and public information.

References

- E-government, topic: britannica.com, Retrieved 2 June, 2019
- 'The failure of e-government in developing countries: a literature review'. The Electronic Journal on Information System in Developing Countries. Dada, D. (2006)
- E-governance, notes, Management, subject: civilserviceindia.com, Retrieved 3 July, 2019
- "Memorandum for the Heads of Executive Departments and Agencies: Open Government Directive". Office of Management and Budget. Retrieved 10 January 2012
- E-governance: businessjargons.com, Retrieved 4 August, 2019
- Scholl, H.J.; Glassey, O.; Janssen, M.F.W.H.A. (2016). Electronic Government and Electronic Participation: Joint Proceedings of Ongoing Research, phd Papers, Posters and Workshops of IFIP EGOV and epart 2016. Amsterdam: IOS Press. P. 218. ISBN 9781614996699
- Alasem, A. (2009). An Overview of e-Government Metadata Standards and Initiatives based on Dublin Core. Electronic Journal of e-Government, 7(1), 1 – 10
- Harper, Logan (June 10, 2013). "A Citizen's Guide to Open Government, E-Government, and Government 2.0". Retrieved June 4, 2017

7

Personnel and Financial Administration

The domain of public administration which is concerned with people at work and with their relationships within an organization is known as personnel administration. Financial administration refers to the management of financial tasks of an organization. It includes writing financial reports, controlling budget, etc. The topics elaborated in this chapter will help in gaining a better perspective about personnel and financial administration.

PERSONNEL ADMINISTRATION

People of a country are an important asset for it, so is the case with organisations. The successful functioning of an organisation depends on its manpower and quality of leadership. The manpower by itself does not contribute to the development of an. organisation, it has to be converted into human resources through systematic planning, adequate training and proper education. Without the growth of human resources called the human capital, goals and objectives of an organisation can never be achieved. Human capital can be defined as the sum total of knowledge, skills and aptitudes of the people in the society. Development of human resources poses a major challenge for the developing countries like India. Manpower planning is an important tool for developing human resources. Investments in manpower planning whether made by government or a, private organisation belong to the individual and do not depreciate. In fact they increase with the passage of time. Thus human resources are an important part of the total resources of an organisation. Though financial resources, physical resources (the work place, machinery etc.) and technological resources are also very important, it is the human resources which are most vital as they generate the other resources. Adequate utilisation of human resources would automatically lead to optimum utilisation of financial, physical and technological resources.

No organisation can achieve the desired goals without effective management of all its resources, but human capital is the most essential element of an organisation. As, personnel administration deals with the management of the human resources, the study of its concept, nature, scope and development assumes importance. These aspects will be highlighted in this unit.

Concept

The tasks of government are increasing everyday. Development and welfare orientations have led to the expansion of government and its administrative machinery. As the tasks, responsibilities and activities of organisations whether public or private multiply, the demands on personnel, at every level, in terms of efficient discharge of their duties also rise. Thus the task of personnel administration is to, assure a steady source of people who can contribute to the success of an organisation and meet the growing demands of development. To understand the concept of personnel administration, it is very essential to first understand the meaning and nature of the term.

Personnel administration is that part of administration which is concerned with people at work and with their relationships within an organisation. It refers to the entire spectrum of an organisation's interaction with its human resources from recruitment activity to retirement process. It involves personnel planning and forecasting, appraising human performance, selection and staffing, training and development and maintenance and improvement of performance and productivity. Personnel administration is closely related to an organisation's overall effectiveness. There is no standard definition of the term 'personnel administration'. Still there is a widespread unity among writers on its meaning, scope and purpose.

According to Flippo, personnel function is concerned with the procurement, development, compensation, integration and maintenance of the personnel of an organisation for the purpose of contributing toward the accomplishment of that organisation's major goals and objectives. Dale Yoder uses the term "manpower management" instead of "personnel management" and includes both labour relations and personnel administration within its ambit. According to him, "the term effectively describes the processes of planning and directing the application, development and utilisation of human resources in employment. Employers, employees, unions and public agencies all have important roles to play in these processes."

According to Thomas G. Spates, "personnel administration is a code of the ways of organising and treating individuals at work so that they will each get the greatest possible realisation of their Mrinsic abilities, thus attaining maximum qfficiency for themselves and their group and thereby giving to the enterprise of which they are a part, competitive advantage and optimum results." Michael Juciqk defines personnel administration as "the field of management which has to do with planning, organising, and controlling various operative functions of procuring, developing, maintaining and utilising a labour force such that the:

- Objectives for which the company is established are attained economically and effectively.
- Objectives of all levels of personnel are served to the highest possible degree.
- Objectives of the community are duly considered and served.

The Institute of Personnel Management in U.K. defines personnel management as "that part of the management function which is primarily concerned with the human relationships within the organisation. Its objective is the maintenance of those relationships on a basis which, by consideration of the well-being of the individual, enables all those engaged in the undertaking to make their maximum personnel to the effective working of that undertaking." The indian Institute of Personnel Management has also adopted this definition.

The above-mentioned definition was replaced in-1966 by a more elaborate definition. It reads, "Personnel management is that part of the management function which is concerned with people at work and with their relationships within an enterprise. Its aim is to bring together and develop into an effective organisation the men and women who make up an enterprise and, having regard to the well-being of an individual and of working groups to enable to make their best contribution to its, success.

In particular, personnel management is concerned with the development of policies governing:

- Manpower planning, recruitment, selection, placement and termination.
- Education and training, career development.
- Terms of employee, methods and standards of remuneration.
- Working conditions and employees' services.
- Formal and informal communication and consultation both through the representatives of employers and employees and at all levels throughout the organization.
- Negotiation and application of agreements on wages and working conditions, procedures for the avoidance and settlement of disputes.

Personnel management is also, concerned with the "human and social implications of change in internal organisation and methods of working and of economic and social changes in the community."

Thus we can say that personnel administration deals with the recruitment, placement, training, disciplinary measures, monetary and non-monetary incentives and retirement benefits of the human beings or the personnel within an organisation. It also deals with the nature of human relationships in an organisation, interaction between the human beings within an organisation and interaction of human beings with the organisation. Personnel administration includes all activities and functions. relating to policy formulation, planning, policy implementation, social change and modernisation, administrative reforms and public relations in an organisation. It aims at optimum utilisation of human resources in order to achieve maximum results with minimum wastage of funds and technology.

Personnel administration is variously known as 'personnel management', 'labour relations', 'manpower management', labour welfare management', etc. But the term 'personnel administration' connotes a wider meaning, it includes both personnel management and industrial relations. Many a times the terms labour relations and industrial relations are used interchangeably with personnel administration but it is always better to distinguish between them. The term 'labour relations' refers primarily to the relation between management and organised labour. It-clauses negotiations of contracts with unions. It deals with handling of differences with unions and business agents. Some organisations have a labour relations officer or director whose primary task is to advise and assist top management in their dealing with union representatives. This official may or may not to personnel administrator. In an unionised organisation, where there is no labour relations officer or director, the personnel administrator performs the task of labour relations officer.

Thus personnel administration aims at:

- Effective utilization of human resources.
- Desirable working relations among all members of the organisation.

- Maximum development.
- Meeting the organisations social and legal responsibilities.

According to Michael J. Jucius, personnel management should aim at:

- Attaining economically and effectively the organisation goals.
- Serving to the highest possible degree the individual goals.
- Preserving and advancing the general welfare of the community.

To obtain these objectives, personnel administration is concerned with planning, organising, directing, coordinating and controlling the cooperative efforts-of individuals within an organisation.

Nature of Personnel Administration

Personnel function is crucial in any administrative organisation. The organisation cannot afford to ignore it. Hence it becomes a basic responsibility of the management, be in the government or in semi or non-government organisations. The changes in the socio-economic environment has its effect on management. The management environment keeps changing due to the changes that occur in the total socio-economic environment. The political environment also affects the work environment in an organisation. Such changes get reflected in personnel administration. These changes can be:

- Changing mix of the personnel entering government service organisation.
- Changing values of personnel.
- Increasing expectations of the government from their employees.
- Increasing expectations of the people from the government at different levels.

Thus management is affected by the changes in the social, economic and political scenario. In fact it has to keep up with these changes. A higher number from schedule castes, tribes and other economically backward classes are joining the government service. A greater number of people with higher education, more women, more technically skilled workers are also joining the government service. This has really changed the ratios of working force.

With the proliferation of activities under 'development' and 'welfare' programmes, the employees are now expected to be more competent and efficient. People at large expect the administration to be efficient, effective and sympathetic. People's involvement in administrative activities is increasing. Due to the constant demands oh administration, the role of personnel administration is also changing. Personnel are required to perform 'line' and 'staff' functions. Activities directly related to the primary objective of an organisation are called as 'line' functions.

The 'staff' functions are those which facilitate and assist the performance of line work. They are in the nature of secondary activities and enhance the effectiveness of the line agencies. For example, assistance in processing and supplying the required number of personnel and training and development of personnel are essentially staff functions. An organisation cannot function without the assistance of line and staff personnel. At the same time, personnel function cannot be isolated from the rest of the administrative functions. Personnel functions include both line and staff activities in an organisation.

Personnel administration does not always function in a formal organisation. No organisation can solely run on the basis of formal rules and regulations, it comprises human beings who are structured in an authority and responsibility network in order to carry out the tasks and activities for the fulfilment of organisational objectives.

This formal structure is supplemented, supported or sometimes obstructed and on occasions taken over by the informal organisation. Informal organisation grows within the formal organisation. It is a natural phenomenon and is based on social and cultural relations among the personnel of formal groups. Political, economic and psychological factors also contribute to the growth of informal organisation. The functions of personnel administration are becoming more complicated day by day. The problems of personnel administration differ from one organisation to the other. Big organisations have more tasks to perform, they employ more people and serve varied objectives. The task of personnel administration in such organisations becomes more intricate. As personnel administration deals with human beings all the time, the crucial functions of motivation and morale of employees have to be performed by it. It has to meet the growing needs of the people as well as satisfy the increasing expectations of its employees.

Evolution and Development

While the evolution and development of personnel administration in U.K. and U.S.A. was largely voluntary, in India, the growth of personnel administration can be attributed to the efforts made by the government. Chile in the West, the pioneering work in the field of personnel management was motivated by the managerial preoccupation with the concept of welfare, in India, unsystematic recruitment practices, growing labour unrest, loss of production etc., initiated some interest in personnel management.

In U.K., personnel administration had its origin in the concept of welfare as propounded and practised by some of the enlightened entrepreneurs, who sought the establishment of modern personnel administration. The term personnel management actually originated in the U.S.A.

It was F.W. Taylor's scientific management which laid the foundation for the development of personnel administration. Taylor laid emphasis on scientific selection and systematic training and development of the individual worker. H.L. Gantt, a close associate of Taylor, in scientific management movements, foresaw the need for obtaining the willing cooperation of the worker. He maintained that it was not enough to tell the worker how to do a job, but it was also necessary to promote the ability and willingness to do a job. Mary Parker Follet also laid stress on training and development aspects of management. The pioneers of scientific management, apart from increasing efficiency, aimed at fighting fatigue and monotony among the workers.

Most important breakthrough for personnel administration was Elton Mayo's Hawthorne experiments and the human relations movement. These experiments paved the. way for using the disciplines of sociology, psychology, industrial psychology, social psychology etc., with a view to understanding employees and organisational behaviour and influencing them through a motivational approach. All this led to the gradual evolution and development of a theory and practice of personnel management.

There were also other events and influences which led to the growth of personnel management. Various revolutionary concepts like mass production, mass distribution and mass financing were evolved by industrial and business empires. The labour shortages during the world wars and various labour problems posed a challenge to management. With the Great Depression in 1929, big business suffered a severe setback. The State, the public and the trade unions, aimed at efficient professional management. Their demands were, elimination of waste and maximum utilisation of resources, particularly human resources.

All these developments in America emphasised the fact that management of people or personnel management is just as important as the management of production. Thus the entrepreneurial interest, apart from other events in the sphere of worker welfare provided the source of inspiration for the evolution of modem dynamic personnel administration.

The history of the evolution and growth of personnel management in our country is not very old. It was the Royal Commission on Labour which recommended in 1931 the appointments of Labour Officers to deal with the recruitment of labour to settle their grievances. The industrial disputes of 1920s forced the government and businessmen to think in terms of labour problems and promotion of personnel management. The recognition of trade unions in India gave a new perspective to the employer and employee relationship. Entrepreneurs like the Tatas, Calico Mills, British India Corporation etc. had appointed Welfare Officers as early as 1920. These Labour Welfare Officers performed the functions of employee grievances and promotion of industrial harmony.

In 1937 in Bengal, on the suggestion of the Government, the Indian Jute Mills Owners' Association appointed a Labour Officer to bring about a settlement of employee grievances with the mills and by 1939 five more Labour Officers were appointed. Other Employers' Associations like Indian Engineering Association, Indian Tea Association, the Engineering Association of India etc., also followed the example of Indian Jute Owners' Association in appointing labour officers. In 1941, the Government of India initiated the Tripartite Labour Conference with the representatives of Government, labour and employees in order to promote uniform labour legislation, determine a procedure to settle industrial disputes, and promote consultations on industrial matters affecting the country. Now they have become permanent and regular features of labour policy. In 1948, the Factories Act rules laid down the appointment, duties and qualifications of a new statutory officer in industry called the Welfare Officer.

The following years saw the emergence of yet another officer called the Personnel Officer. The Personnel Officer deals with labour welfare, industrial relations and personnel administration. Many companies in India now have specialised personnel departments and a full-time Personnel Officer in charge. Now the number of personnel is increasing at a very fast rate, expenditure on personnel is also correspondingly increasing. There has also been a trend in regard to the diversification in the personnel as more and more specialists, experts and technicians are being appointed in government departments, public and private organisations. Contemporary personnel does not just deal with welfare of employees but also aim at achieving profits for the organisation. The motive is to earn profits as well as benefits for the organisation and its employees.

Scope of Personnel Administration

Personnel administration is in all aspects of management of persons in organisation. The primary objective of personnel administration, as we have read earlier in the unit. is to ensure effective utilisation of human resources in pursuit of organisational goals. The personnel administration departments should design and establish an effective working relationship among all the members of an organisation by division of organisational tasks into jobs. defining clearly the responsibility and authority for each job and its relation with other jobs in the organisation. Personnel administration must try to enthuse among the employees feelings of commitment, involvement and loyalty to orgnisation. This is reflect among the employee and do away with frictional situation arising out of personal jealousies, rivalries and prejudices. Personnel administration also has to curb unfavourable practice like favouritism and nepotism in an organisation.

Personnel administration has to concentrate on various aspects of management like recruitment, training, promotion, conditions of service, employees welfare, employee and re- employee relations and processes of morale and motivation. It has to develop links with immediate, intermediate and external environment to make itself effective and efficient.

As the tasks of organisation increase, the responsibilities of personnel administration also increase accordingly. It is not possible to solve the problems with a one-time and one-stroke decision. Larger the system more are the complexities. Take for example, the Government of India, it is divided into ministries, departments, divisions, units etc. It is spread over the entire length and breadth of the country. Lakhs of people work in it, they operate at different hierarchical levels and carry out a large variety of functions. A number of services and their division into groups constitute the entire workforce of the Central government. Almost similar is the situation in each state. Personnel administration has to cater to all these aspects. It requires continuous managerial input.

Planning and providing for the regular supply of the needed manpower for different positions and in different numbers is an important task of the government. The process of recruitment and utilisation of each micro-unit of human resource calls for effective personnel administration, similarly, creating and maintaining desirable working relationships also call for a series of continuous efforts on the part of the personnel. Those responsible for personnel administration have to work for it constantly.

The achievement of these two objectives becomes easier if the organisation provides appropriate opportunities for individual development. These opportunities can be in the form of training. internal and external mobility, promotion, recognition and reward. They act as strong motivators and satisfiers. Besides, salary structuring of lakhs of employees is a wholesome task because each category has to be adequately and equitably compensated for the contribution it is expected to make towards organisation's objectives. This is also a work of personnel administration. The working force also has to be subjected to certain decipline in order to regulate proper performance of duty. Framing of conduct rules, laying down procedures of disciplinary action, enforcement of those rules and adoption of appropriate procedures are also a part of personnel administration.

Employer-employee relations, provision for Joint Consultative Machinery, establishment of public service tribunals for adjudication, adoption of welfare measures and payment of retirement benefits etc. to the employees are the added responsibilities of personnel administration. Trade unionism among government employees, has increased during the past few decades. Both employer and employee unions have come up. There is now a dire need for expert skills to foresee personnel needs and problems and to plan for their satisfaction and rectification. All this requires systematic personnel administration. Thus the scope of personnel administration is wide and varied, moreover it is continuously expanding with the changes in environment.

FINANCIAL ADMINISTRATION

Finance is the life blood of every organisation; Personnel and materials which are needed for the functioning of any office, industry, enterprise can be made available only if money is provided.

The efficiency of operating systems and maintenance systems depends upon the effectiveness of financial system as every administrative act may have financial implications. The significance of finance to public administration is quite obvious as is evident from the remark of Lloyd George: "Government is finance".

Financial administration, as an important aspect of public administration islas anc~ent as organised governments all over the world. In its rudimentary form, it was performing certain limited functions till medieval times. In the pre-modern times, it was conceived within the structure of legislative control over executive.

Socio-economic forces unleashed by industrial revolution have given a new meaning and a dynamic content to financial administration. In the changed context, it is expected to meet dynamic needs of planned development and social change.

The term Financial Administration consists of two words viz. 'Finance' and 'Administration'. The word 'administration' refers to organisation and management of collective human efforts in the pursuit of a conscious objective. The word 'Finance' refers to monetary (money) resource. Financial Administration refers to that set of activities which are related to making available money to the various branches of an office, or an organisation to enable it to carrying out its objectives. Whether it is the Department of Agriculture, Railways, Road Transport Corporation, Primary Health Centre, Municipality or Gram Panchayat, or for that matter, a family, its day-today activities would depend upon the availability of funds.

Now let us get to know some more accurate definitions of Financial Administration. According to L.D. White, "Fiscal Management includes those operations designed to make funds available to officials and to ensure their lawful and efficient use."

According to Jaze Gaston "Financial Administration is that part of government organisation which deals with the collection, preservation and distribution of public funds, with the coordination of public revenue and expenditure, with the management of credit operations on behalf of the State and with the general control of the financial affairs of public household.

Though this definition covers some important aspects of fiscal management, it fails to project a comprehensive scope of financial administration. Perhaps, after real king this limitation, G.S. Lall states that financial administration is concerned with all the aspects of financial management of the State. Since public administration is more and more concerned with public affairs and public interest, the frontiers of financial administration are expanding and therefore there is a need for a comprehensive definition of financial administration. As an attempt towards this direction, the following definition is presented.

"Financial Administration includes all the activities which generate, regulate and distribute monetary resources needed for the sustenance and growth of the members of a political community."

Distinction between Public Finance and Private Finance

Finance function appears to be a generic process which takes place in both public and private organisations. But, one should not conclude that the principles and norms which are applicable to private finance are equally applicable to public finance, for despite the challenge to the historic "separate but equal doctrine" from the integrationist movement of recent times, public organisations continue to possess certain distinct characteristics. Dissimilarities between public finance and private finance are quite sharp and clear. 'According to Sundaram, these dissimilarities can be outlined as follows:

Pubic Finance	Private Finance
1) Adjustment of income to expenditure	1) Adjustment of expenditure to income
2) Popular control	2) Corporate control
3) Elastic resources	3) Limited resources
4) Resource mobilisation through coercive power	4) No such power
5) Tendency towards deficit	5) Tendency towards balanced budgets
6) Direction of expenditure towards public service	6) Towards profit maximisation

Importance of Financial Administration

The importance of Financial Administration was not considered till after industrial revolution. The concept of minimum government as an offshoot of laissez faire doctrine, dictated observance of minimum taxation. When social life became more complex as a result of industrial revolution, the role of the government increased manifold. Further, the concept of welfare state has caused phenomenal increase in state activity. The governments have entered into new areas which were kept out of the purview of the State. In this changed context, financial administration has gained greater significance for exploring ways and means to generate resources to meet the ever-increasing public expenditure. The Great Depression had exposed the weaknesses of neutral economic stance of the governments. It enhanced the quest for stability in income and employment as well as for equality and social justice. Based on Keynesian perspective, the State has assumed an active and positive role for expanding national income and employment. It has also taken up the task of ensuring equity and of the government a non-profit i in influencing the socio-economic life of the people. Defence and administrative and Scope of Financial expenditure and its non-productive label and assumed a new significance as a lever administration for stimulating income and employment levels. Financial administration was entrusted with the responsibility of formulating effective policies to achieve these new objectives of the State. It was called upon to transform financial resources into public purposes and thus to improve the lot of the individual through distributive justice.

Influencing the socio-economic life of the people. Defence and administrative and Scope of Financial expenditure and its non-productive label and assumed a new significance as a lever administration for stimulating income and employment levels. Financial administration was entrusted with the responsibility of formulating effective policies to achieve these new objectives of the State. It was called upon to transform financial resources into public purposes and thus to improve the lot of the individual through distributive justice.

With the advent of democracy, as a popular social institution, the concept of 'parliamentary' control over public purse' has received universal acceptance. The principles of "no taxation without presentation", i.e. "no public expenditure without parliamentary sanction" have become the guiding canons of modern political communities. There appeared an urgent need to devise a simple and systematic financial procedure in order to make financial system intelligible to the common person. Financial administration became an instrument of 'modern governments for making "popular sovereignty" a social reality. The concept of planned development has enabled public administrators to play an active and dynamic role in the formulation and implementation of development schemes and projects. The time and cost of implementing these projects have become critically important. The accent of financial administration has shifted from one of controlling the disbursement of funds to one of management of various development projects and programmes. The rise of performance budgeting and other related budgetary innovations represent remarkable achievements of financial administration in meeting this challenge. From the early eighties onwards, resource crunch has become a very serious problem of modem governments. While there is a tremendous pressure on the modem governments to increase their expenditure outlays to meet the ever expanding ambitions and demands of the people the taxpayers are unable or unwilling to bear additional tax burdens. In this dilemma, a need has arisen for a careful prioritisation of public expenditure. Hence a study of financial administration and management which are a part of public administration has become important to seek out ways for eliminating unwanted expenditure and ensuring optimisation of output on a limited resource base. Zero Base budgeting is an attempt in this direction. To sum up, financial administration is playing a dominant role in modem times.

Nature of Financial Administration

There are two different views regarding the nature of financial administration. These are:

1. Traditional view
2. Modern view

Traditional View

Advocates of this view conceive financial administration as a sum total of activities undertaken in pursuit of generation, regulation and distribution of monetary resources needed for the sustenance and growth of public organisations. They emphasise upon that set of administrative functions in a public organisation which relate to an arrangement of flow of funds as well as to regulating mechanisms and processes which ensure proper and productive utilisation of these funds. When one looks at this view from systems perspective, it represents an integral sub-system of supportive system. A financial administrator shoulders responsibility for ensuring adequate financial backing for running public organisation in the most efficient manner. Higher job is to plan, programme, organise and direct all financial activities in public organisations so as to achieve efficient implementation of public policy. The participants of this system are considered as financial managers and they discharge managerial functions of financial nature. Further, this view reflects the stand taken by pure theorists of public finance like Seligrnan. The central thesis of pure theory of public finance is that public finance should deal with the problems of public income, public expenditure and public debt in an objective manner without any relation to a set of values and premises of the political party in power. Accordingly, theorists of financial administration subscribing to this view take a value-neutral stany. For instance, Jaze Gaston reflects this view when he says that financial administration is that part of government organisation which deals with the collection, preservation and distribution of public funds.

Modern View

The modern view considers financial administration as an integral part of the overall management process of public organisations rather than one of raising and disbursing public funds. It includes all the activities of all persons engaged in public administration, for quite obviously almost every public official takes decisions which are bound to have some direct or indirect consequences of financial nature. Further, it rejects the value-neutral stand of the traditional theory. It combines in itself three prominent theories of public finance, viz., the socio-political theory as expounded by Wagner, Edge worth and, the functional theory of Keynesian perspective and activating view of modern public finance theorists. According to this view financial administration has the following roles.

- Equalising Role: Under this role financial administration seeks to demolish the equalities of wealth. It seeks, through fiscal policies, to transfer income from the affluent to the poor.
- Functional Role: Under normal circumstances the economy cannot function on its own. Under this role, financial administration seeks to ensure, through taxation, public expenditure and public debt, and proper functioning of the economy. It evolves policy instruments to maintain high economic growth and full employment.
- Activating Role: Under this role financial administration involves the study of such steps that will facilitate a smooth and rapid flow of investment and its optimal allocation to increase the volume of national income.
- Stabbing Role: Under this role, the objective of financial administration is the stabilisation of price level and inflationary trends through fiscal as well as monetary policies.
- Participatory Role: According to this view, financial administration involves formulation and execution of policies for making the state a producer of both public and private goods with the objective of maximising social welfare of the community. It also seeks to promote economic development through direct and indirect participation of the State.

Thus, financial administration provides a framework of choices regarding ends and means which reflect the nature and character of the State and its ideological base as well as its values. For instance, financial administration of list countries differ from that in democratic countries. Thus, the essence of financial administration would differ under different socio-political systems depending upon particular mode of operation of socio-economic and political forces.

Scope of Financial Administration

In this topic where we have discussed the meaning of financial administration, Gaston Jaze's definition, quoted in that context, points out that the government organisation which deals with the following four aspects constitutes financial administration. These include:

1. The collection, presenting and distribution of public funds.
2. The coordination of public revenues and expenditure.
3. The management of credit operations on behalf of the State.
4. The general control of the financial affairs of the government.

In modern governments all the above aspects are dealt with by the Finance Department and its subordinate agencies. Though the Finance Department may be considered as central financial agency of modem governments, it cannot be equated with financial administration. Its role constitutes financial management rather than financial administration. As a financial manager it deals with the systems, tools and techniques contributing to economic decision making in government. These processes are, in fact, the integral part of financial administration. The scope of financial administration is much wider than what these processes suggest.

According to some authorities on public administration, the term financial administration refers to the financial processes and institutions involved in legislative financial control. In their view, the scope of financial administration encompasses the preparation of estimates, appropriation of funds, expenditure control, aciounting, audit, reporting, review and so on. In a democratic context, this view may gain wider acceptance as it ensures executive responsibility to legislature. But, the experience of modem democracies has shown that the legislative involvement in the determination of the desired volume, range and direction of programmes, the use of independent judgement relating to the financial resources required by administrative agencies is becoming nominal day by day. It is a known fact that the average member of the legislature is not adequately informed to ensure effective control over executive. Thus, the view appears to be of no significant validity. Further, legislative control of financial aspects of the government does not represent the scope of financial administration in its entirety.

Yet another view advocates a budget oriented outline for the scope of financial administration. According to them the scope of financial administration is limited to the preparation of budget, the enactment of budget and execution of budget. Though the budget is the core of financial administration, certain operations which precede budget preparation are equally important. There is a pertinent need to include planning process as an integral part of financial administration. In the ultimate analysis, there is a need to adopt an integrated approach so that all the above views are incorporated into the scope of public administration.

As an outcome of such an approach, the following aspects emerge as the core areas of financial administration:

1. Financial planning,
2. Budgeting,
3. Resource mobilisation,
4. Investment decisions,
5. Expenditure control,
6. Accounting, Reporting and Auditing.

Financial Planning: In a restrictive sense one may consider budgeting as planning since its basic concern is to facilitate the formulation and adoption of policies and programmes with a view to achieving the goals of government. But planning, in a broad sense; includes the concerns in terms of whole range of government policy and it demands a time frame and a perception of the inter relationships among policies. It looks at a policy in the framework of long-term economic consequences. There is and objectives a need to coordinate planning and budgeting. The kept of planning-programming. Budgeting System (PPBS) represents an attempt in this direction. Financial Administration, under this phase, should consider the sources and forms of finance, forecasting expenditure needs, desirable fund flow patterns and so on.

Budgeting: This area is the core of financial administration. It includes examination and formulation of such important aspects as fiscal policy, equity and social justice. It also deals with principles and practices associated with refinement of budgetary system and its operative processes.

Resource Mobilisation: Imposition of taxes, collection of rates and taxes etc. are associated with resource mobilisation effort. Due to the ever increasing commitments of government, budgetary deficits have become regular feature of government finance. In this context deficit financing assumes greater importance. But deficit financing, if used in an unrestrained manner, may prove to be a dangerous problem for a nation's ecology for it can cause galloping inflation. Another challenge faced by administration is tax evasion and growth of parallel economy. Finally public debt constitutes yet another element of state resources. The proceeds of debt mobilisation effort should be used only for capital financing. Thus, modem financial administrator has to be fully conversant with all the dimensions of resource mobilisation efforts.

Investment decisions: Financial and socio-economic appraisal of capital expenditure constitutes what has come to be known as project appraisal. Since massive investments have been made in the public sector a thorough knowledge of the concepts, techniques and methodology of project appraisal is indispensable for a financial administrator.

Expenditure control: Finances of the modem governments are becoming quite inelastic. Almost every government is suffering from resource crunch. Further, the society cannot be taxed beyond a certain point without doing a great damage to the economy as a whole. Thus, there is an imperative need for careful utilisation of resources. Executive control is a process aimed at achieving this ideal. Legislative control is aimed at the protection of the individual tax payers interest as well as public interest. There is also the need to ensure the accountability of the executive to the legislature.

Accounting, Reporting and Auditing: These aspects are designed to aid both the executive control and legislative control. In India, the Comptroller and Auditor General (C & AG) and the Indian Audit and Accounts Department over which the C & AG presides ensure that the accounting and audit functions are performed in accordance with the provisions of the Constitution.

Components of Financial Administration

Theorists of public finance have identified three elements of public finance. They are:

- Public Revenue.
- Public Expenditure.
- Public Debt.

Since financial administration concerns itself with public finance and deals with the principles and practices pertinent to the proper and efficient administration of the state finances, the thinkers of financial administration have included the administrative aspects in the scope of financial' administration.

Some other thinkers, taking clue from Luther Gulick, have tried to project POSDCORCs view wherein:

- P - Stands for Financial Planning.
- o - Stands for Financial Organisation such as Finance Ministry.
- S - Stands for financial Personnel.
- D - Stands for Direction such as Financial advise.
- CO - Stands for Coordination of Income and Expenditure.
- R - Stands for Financial Reporting such as accounting.
- C - Stands for control which includes executive control, audit control and legislative control.

The above exposition does not reveal the exact picture related to the elements of financial administration. An organisational system consists of the following basic elements:

- The People.
- Work and structure.
- Systems and procedure.

People represent human resources of the organisation. Work and structure represent efforts and processes concerning definition of tasks and roles, and organisation of reporting relationships. Systems and procedures represent framework to facilitate interactions between the people and the work.

These interactions result in organisational output. It is possible to identify the following elements of financial administration:

a) Human Element:
   - Tax payers,
   - Fee Remitters Suppliers (Funds and materials),
   - Employees (Public Officials),
   - Entrepreneurs (Politicians),
   - Customers and Common person.

b) Work and Structures and Objectives:
   - The Legislature and its financial committees,
   - The Cabinet,
   - The Finance Department,
   - The Administrative Departments,
   - The Executive Departments,
   - The Audit Department.

c) Systems and Procedures:
   - Planning Systems,
   - Budgeting systems and procedure controlling systems such as accounting and auditing.

Human element consists of participants whose involvement is determined by contribution-inducement equilibrium. This consideration implies that people, for instance, wish to contribute their money (tax etc.) and support the government as long as there is a feeling on their part that they are suitably rewarded for their sacrifice and support. No public organisation can easily overlook this consideration. Work and structure refer to the organisation processes viz. divisional processes and integration processes by means of which organisation subdivisions are created with a provision for mutual interaction. Systems and procedures are the devices which link the people to the work and structure. These three components interact with each other to produce organisational outcomes.

No discussion on administration's components would be complete unless there is a reference to the environment which affects content, character and capabilities of the components. Financial administration is enveloped by two environments. Everyone is aware of super system known as socio-economic and political environment in which the financial administration operates.

There is an intermediary sub-system comprising the goals pursued by financial administration, the norms, values, beliefs and behaviour as reflected in the culture of financial administration and the nature of technology employed by financial administration.

Permissions

All chapters in this book are published with permission under the Creative Commons Attribution Share Alike License or equivalent. Every chapter published in this book has been scrutinized by our experts. Their significance has been extensively debated. The topics covered herein carry significant information for a comprehensive understanding. They may even be implemented as practical applications or may be referred to as a beginning point for further studies.

We would like to thank the editorial team for lending their expertise to make the book truly unique. They have played a crucial role in the development of this book. Without their invaluable contributions this book wouldn't have been possible. They have made vital efforts to compile up to date information on the varied aspects of this subject to make this book a valuable addition to the collection of many professionals and students.

This book was conceptualized with the vision of imparting up-to-date and integrated information in this field. To ensure the same, a matchless editorial board was set up. Every individual on the board went through rigorous rounds of assessment to prove their worth. After which they invested a large part of their time researching and compiling the most relevant data for our readers.

The editorial board has been involved in producing this book since its inception. They have spent rigorous hours researching and exploring the diverse topics which have resulted in the successful publishing of this book. They have passed on their knowledge of decades through this book. To expedite this challenging task, the publisher supported the team at every step. A small team of assistant editors was also appointed to further simplify the editing procedure and attain best results for the readers.

Apart from the editorial board, the designing team has also invested a significant amount of their time in understanding the subject and creating the most relevant covers. They scrutinized every image to scout for the most suitable representation of the subject and create an appropriate cover for the book.

The publishing team has been an ardent support to the editorial, designing and production team. Their endless efforts to recruit the best for this project, has resulted in the accomplishment of this book. They are a veteran in the field of academics and their pool of knowledge is as vast as their experience in printing. Their expertise and guidance has proved useful at every step. Their uncompromising quality standards have made this book an exceptional effort. Their encouragement from time to time has been an inspiration for everyone.

The publisher and the editorial board hope that this book will prove to be a valuable piece of knowledge for students, practitioners and scholars across the globe.

Index

R

S

T

W

CPSIA information can be obtained
at www.ICGtesting.com
Printed in the USA
LVHW060826120122
708212LV00006B/300

9 781647 260781